# Israel in Egypt
## Egypt's Place
## Among the Ancient Monarchies

### By Edward L. Clark

ISBN: 978-1-63923-955-9

All Rights reserved. No part of this book maybe reproduced without written permission from the publishers, except by a reviewer who may quote brief passages in a review to be printed in a newspaper or magazine.

Printed: March 2023

Published and Distributed By:
Lushena Books
607 Country Club Drive, Unit E
Bensenville, IL 60106
www.lushenabks.com

ISBN: 978-1-63923-955-9

# PREFACE.

WE see upon the walls of tombs and temple-palaces many illustrations of the ancient civilization of Egypt. There we meet that singular people face to face. One desire, however, remains unsatisfied. We wish they would speak to us. The faces of those who move in the processions of men and gods are without expression. In funeral rites, and in sports, we see only pantomime. Then we inquire of the characters which accompany the groups of figures, and fill the long rolls of papyrus. One by one they yield up their secrets. After centuries of silence, the priests, and kings, and people, talk with us. They describe, with wonderful clearness, the very thoughts of those who conquered or taught the sacred mysteries, or worked under the taskmasters in the valley of the Nile long ago.

By the light of this literature, we are better prepared to speak with confidence concerning the dynasties of ancient kings. The condition of the sciences, and the origin of the Hyksos, with many other inquiries, are no longer entirely hidden from our sight. But such discussions are not the only fruit of the interpretation of hieroglyphics, or sacred writing. These characters have, as it were, embalmed the precious thoughts of most distant ages. They have kept for us those sentiments which escape all effort of description, but which distinguish nations one from the other as truly as persons are distinguished by the features of their countenance. By them we can truly say that we not only know something *of* the ancient Egyptians, but also we *know them*. Many have not leisure to investigate original sources of information, which are principally the monuments themselves, the great folios of the French Commission, and of Lepsius, with the works of Sir J. Gardner Wilkinson, and Lenormant's "Ancient History of the East;" and, above all, the Scriptures of the Old Testament. For lovers of Egypt, such monographs as F. De Lanoye's "Egypt Three Thousand Three Hundred Years Ago" will prove most useful guides. It may be that, in addition to these, general views of Egyptian civilization will contribute something to our familiarity with this people. Such views have become possible only the past few years. They help us understand the springs of feeling which developed the industry, the ambition, the philosophy, and the religion of Egypt.

If any one may be tempted to spend an hour in the ancient kingdom with these impressions of life, let him remember that he is to journey with the spirit of an observer, not a philosopher. He will find those names of people and places, whether ancient or modern, which are most familiar. He will meet certain subjects many times. He will not be surprised if he finds a view completed by a city or subject not literally within the knowledge of an Israelite of the olden time. He will miss the pictures of cities which can be restored only by the imagination. He will be amused to see many things spoken of as facts concerning which there is still some doubt. It is to be expected that he may not agree with all the conclusions he finds. He will not forget that there is much room for difference of opinion. But the views, after all, are conscientious, and the writer is satisfied that those who have studied the subject with the greatest patience will be the ones who will have most charity.

Frequent references, under the general name of Assyria, have been made to the monarchies of the Euphrates, which were well known to intelligent men twenty-two centuries ago. These could not be forgotten without losing sight of influences which were continually at work shaping the history of the covenant people. Nor should we overlook the deeper interest of that prophet who believed, in all its folly, there was much good in Egypt: "Israel shall be the third with Egypt, and with Assyria in the midst of the land! When

the Lord of Hosts shall bless, saying, Blessed be Egypt, my people, and Assyria, the work of my hands, and Israel, mine inheritance."

It might be well to refer to authorities for the confirmation of statements if these pages were designed to introduce or sustain any theories. But in a collection of impressions they would only burden the attention of the reader, and are therefore omitted.

One word more. Modern Egypt has received nothing from the ancient kingdom except her broken monuments. We need not know anything of the people who now live to-day beside the Nile, in order to become acquainted with the subjects of the Pharoahs. Let us then leave entirely behind us the mosques, the citadel, and courts of modern Cairo, and go out to dwell under the pyramids, and restore the glories and griefs of old Memphis, which have before been only shadows on the distant horizon.

# CONTENTS.

WHY WE SHOULD GO DOWN INTO EGYPT............Page 9

ENTERING IN........................................... 14

    Through the Desert—Its Stations—What Goshen is—What Goshen is to Egypt—The Great Highway—The First City, Heliopolis.

THE TEMPLES........................................... 30

    Structure—Ornaments—Use—Chapels—Resemblance to Tabernacle.

HOME LIFE............................................. 50

    Plan of House—The Feast—Amusements—Position of Women.

THE RIVER............................................. 76

    The Nile Valley is Egypt—Abundance of the River—The Inundation—The Nile Worshiped—Seasons Regulated—Fish—Fowl—The Great Highway.

AT WORK.............................................. 110

    Castes—The King—Priests—Soldiers—Farmers—Mechanics—Shepherds and Brickmakers.

RELIGION............................................. 138

    Religion claims the first Place—Whence it Came—The Gods—Sacred Animals—Sacrifices, Resemblance to the Institutions of Moses—Reason in Them—A Fête Day.

## Contents.

LAND OF THE DEAD .................................. Page 184

    The Future always in Mind—Book of Manifestation to Light—Embalming—Funeral—Tombs of the Poor—Tombs of the Kings—Pyramids—Sphinx—Extent of Tombs.

STORY OF EGYPT ..................................... 232

    Annals Unreliable—Menes—Whence the Race came—Early Civilization—The First King—Thebes Appears—The Middle Ages—The Shepherds—The Restoration—Tothmes III.—His Successors—Rameses II.—The Decline—Assyria in Egypt.

THE EXODUS ......................................... 316

    Israel in Egypt—A Personal God—Love to God—Unity of God—The Present Life—Israel Must Leave the Land—Moses—The Going Out.

AN EGYPTIAN GENTLEMAN ON A JOURNEY.

# List of Illustrations.

| | |
|---|---|
| Triumph of Joseph | Frontispiece. |
| Modern Egypt and the Pyramids | Page 8 |
| Holy Family from Kaulbach | 11 |
| Chariot restored from Wilkinson | 14 |
| Palm Trees | 16 |
| Fly of Egypt | 18 |
| Quail | 18 |
| Locust | 19 |
| Fowl Dressed for salting in Jars | 20 |
| Wooden Dove found with a Mummy | 20 |
| Hunter bringing Gazelle from the Desert | 23 |
| Light-armed Soldiers | 23 |
| Wooden House | 25 |
| An Egyptian Prince | 26 |
| Basin and Ewer | 27 |
| Watchmen with Lantern | 28 |
| Island of Philae | 30 |
| Sphinx with a Man's Head | 32 |
| Dromos, or Street of Sphinxes, in ruins | 32 |
| Outline of Edfoo, half buried in soil | 34 |
| Ramessium, with Broken Statue of Rameses | 35 |
| Angle of Court, showing Screens of Stone, and Tower, with entrance between | 36 |
| Central Columns of the Great Hall at Karnak | 37 |
| Dedication of a Pylon | 39 |
| Queens bearing the Lotus Flowers and the Systrum, an Instrument sacred to Isis. The Systrum has metal disks, which move on wires when shaken | 40 |
| View south from the Temple Roof at Philae | 41 |
| Chapel | 42 |
| Hypethrael Chapel at Philae | 43 |
| Ark of Hebrews, with Cherubim | 44 |
| Ark of Nilus | 45 |
| Luxor in ruins. A Temple of Thebes | 45 |

## List of Illustrations.

| | |
|---|---|
| Ground Plan of Tabernacle..........................Page | 46 |
| High Priest................................................ | 48 |
| Group of Women at the Feast............................ | 50 |
| Chair with woven Seat.................................... | 53 |
| The Visitor entertained by the Host...................... | 54 |
| Broken Doll with form of Typhon........................ | 56 |
| Doll........................................................ | 56 |
| Wooden Crocodile........................................ | 56 |
| Toy Stone Polisher........................................ | 56 |
| Vase in Wooden Frame.................................. | 57 |
| Mirror with Head of Typhon............................. | 60 |
| Box for holding Black Stain for Eyebrows................ | 60 |
| Inlaid Vase................................................ | 62 |
| Musical Instruments...................................... | 62 |
| Censer..................................................... | 63 |
| Vase with Ibex Heads.................................... | 65 |
| Clay Jar with Name of Rameses.......................... | 67 |
| Bronze Image of Osiris with Crook and Flagellum......... | 67 |
| Folding Stool.............................................. | 68 |
| Games of balancing...................................... | 70 |
| Reveler on his way Home................................ | 71 |
| King and Queen playing Draughts........................ | 71 |
| Caricature of above...................................... | 71 |
| Isis......................................................... | 74 |
| Nile Scene................................................ | 76 |
| Lotus Flower.............................................. | 81 |
| Asouan below Cataracts.................................. | 83 |
| Silsilis Quarry Temple.................................... | 84 |
| Modern Shadoof for Raising Water...................... | 86 |
| Ancient Shadoof.......................................... | 86 |
| Spring Landscape from the Tomb Pictures............... | 87 |
| Sakkiah for Lifting Water................................ | 89 |
| Gentleman Fishing in his Canal.......................... | 92 |
| Taking Water Fowl in a Flat Net among the Papyrus Plants. | 94 |
| Fowling, and Spearing Fish, in Boats.................... | 95 |
| Nile Barges............................................... | 96 |
| Boat of a Nobleman...................................... | 99 |
| Royal Boat................................................ | 100 |
| Granary surrounded with Walls.......................... | 104 |
| View of the Jordan from the Hills of Judah............... | 108 |

## List of Illustrations. xiii

| | |
|---|---|
| Royal Harper | Page 110 |
| Temple Musicians | 115 |
| Panel Painters | 119 |
| Drum, Triangle, Systrum, Bells | 120 |
| Stone House | 123 |
| Monkeys gathering Fruit | 124 |
| Assyrian Seal on Roller with Metal Handle | 125 |
| Basket made of Gold and Silver Thread | 126 |
| Sacrificial Table | 126 |
| Entrance to the Sanctuary of Sinai, near the Ancient Egyptian Mines | 131 |
| Scribes writing the Account of the Steward | 132 |
| Shaping Bricks and carrying Clay | 134 |
| Bricks dropped from the Mould, breaking the Ground, bending under the "Tale" | 135 |
| Royal Chair | 136 |
| Restored Temple (from the Egyptian Commission) | 138 |
| Vulture with Wings grasping the Ostrich Feather | 140 |
| Winged Sun | 140 |
| Rude Ark with Cherubim | 140 |
| Assyrian Winged Sun | 141 |
| Assyrian Winged Bull | 141 |
| Name of Pharaoh | 145 |
| Sphinx with Head of Ram, most common at Thebes | 146 |
| Assyrian Zodiac | 148 |
| Astarte of Assyria | 149 |
| Isis | 149 |
| Genii from the Walls of Nineveh | 151 |
| Isis and Nephthys | 152 |
| Theban Ark | 155 |
| Apis with Sun between his Horns | 159 |
| Name of Apis | 159 |
| The King presents Lotus Flowers | 161 |
| Beetle sewn on the Mummy Bandages | 162 |
| Ark of Chons under a Canopy, resting on a Pedestal, with Sacred Trees and Cups on the Altar | 163 |
| Wreath and Basilisk | 164 |
| Bracelets | 164 |
| Figure of Isis | 164 |
| Figure of Anubis | 164 |

xiv         *List of Illustrations.*

| | |
|---|---|
| Table of Show-Bread used in Tabernacle............Page | 165 |
| Altar of Incense........................................ | 165 |
| Divining Cup, interior engraved......................... | 167 |
| Exterior of same........................................ | 167 |
| Troop of Soldiers....................................... | 171 |
| Coat of Mail made of Metal Scales....................... | 172 |
| Chariot................................................. | 173 |
| Axes and Knives......................................... | 173 |
| Bel, with Thunderbolts.................................. | 175 |
| Outer Gateway of the Temple............................. | 184 |
| Assyrian Altar.......................................... | 186 |
| Judgment Scene.......................................... | 194 |
| A Son offers Onions to his Departed Parents............. | 196 |
| Tombs of the Mamelukes.................................. | 199 |
| Face of the Sarcophagus................................. | 200 |
| Jars of the Four Genii of Amenti........................ | 201 |
| Wooden Sarcophagus, Mummy completed, Inner Case, bandaged... | 202 |
| Signet Rings............................................ | 202 |
| Preparing the Mummy Case, bringing the Bandages, polishing the Plaster Covering............................. | 203 |
| Ear-rings............................................... | 204 |
| Anubis watching the Dead................................ | 206 |
| Funeral Procession...................................... | 207 |
| Funeral Boat on the Sacred Lake......................... | 209 |
| Negro Doll.............................................. | 213 |
| Sarcophagus............................................. | 214 |
| Door with Bolts......................................... | 216 |
| Chamber of Tomb......................................... | 218 |
| Clay Image of Mummy..................................... | 220 |
| Lamp from Tombs......................................... | 220 |
| The Pyramids in the Inundation.......................... | 222 |
| Temple of Belus at Babylon.............................. | 223 |
| Ruin of Temple.......................................... | 224 |
| Sphinx and Pyramid...................................... | 226 |
| Greek Lamps............................................. | 230 |
| Temple of Ipsamboul..................................... | 232 |
| Nisroch, the Osiris of Nineveh.......................... | 236 |
| Border for Assyrian Paintings and Garments.............. | 237 |
| Court of Assyrian Palace after Rawlinson................ | 238 |

## List of Illustrations. xv

| | |
|---|---|
| Goats treading Seed into the Mud | Page 240 |
| Chariot with Outrunners drawing up before the Gate of a House | 241 |
| Street Barbers | 242 |
| Gentleman with Staff and Lotus Bud | 243 |
| Holy Women of the Temple | 244 |
| Bed with Pillow and Steps | 250 |
| Couch | 250 |
| Banners with Names of Kings | 252 |
| Rock-cut Tomb | 254 |
| Baal, the Sun God | 257 |
| Front of Assyrian Palace | 258 |
| Prisoners brought by Officers before the Assyrian King. The Fan-bearers stand behind the Throne | 260 |
| Lion over Prostrate Man | 263 |
| Assyrian Ship | 264 |
| Bear, from Assyrian Cylinders | 266 |
| Assyrian Standard | 268 |
| The Attack, from Walls of Nineveh | 271 |
| Colossi of Western Thebes | 272 |
| A Foreign Queen from Nineveh | 273 |
| Assyrian King, from Slab of Palace | 275 |
| Egyptian Battle Axes | 278 |
| Antioch | 279 |
| The Overshadowing Arms | 281 |
| Army Standards, (see page 171) | 282 |
| Threshing Wheat | 286 |
| Brick with Name of Rameses II | 288 |
| Modern Gateway of Egypt | 291 |
| Long Boat | 293 |
| Roman Galley | 298 |
| Heavy-armed Spearman | 300 |
| Swords | 300 |
| War Ship in Battle | 302 |
| Heavy-armed Assyrians | 303 |
| King of Judah | 305 |
| Jewish High Altar | 305 |
| Assyrian Horses with Trappings | 306 |
| Assyrian King | 307 |
| The Foot of the King on the Neck of his Enemy | 308 |

## List of Illustrations.

| | |
|---|---|
| Systrum | Page 309 |
| Jerusalem | 310 |
| Musical Instruments from Greece | 311 |
| Persian holding the One-horned Goat, Emblem of Greece | 312 |
| Broken Statues before the Gate of Luxor | 313 |
| Good Deity of the Assyrian King | 314 |
| Plain of Sinai | 316 |
| Egyptian Box | 317 |
| The Pastures of Bashan | 319 |
| Spicery Box | 323 |
| Stool | 324 |
| Locks and Keys | 324 |
| Bronze Apis | 326 |
| An Egyptian Brick-field | 329 |
| High Priest of Israel | 332 |
| Vine | 333 |
| Tabernacle and Laver | 336 |
| Altar of Burnt-offering | 336 |
| Holy of Holies | 338 |
| Kneading Troughs | 341 |
| Slinger | 343 |
| Reaping the Harvest | 343 |
| Winnowing the Grain | 344 |
| Hoes | 344 |
| Defiles of Edom | 347 |
| Plains of Jericho and the Dead Sea | 348 |

# WHY WE GO DOWN INTO EGYPT

THE highlands of Bethel are growing brown in the "famine." Where shall the flocks and herds of Abram find pasture? The troubled patriarch calls his nephew, Lot, and his steward, Eliezer. They talk of fields which do not depend upon the early and the latter rain, but are kept green through all the seasons by a bountiful river. Then they hasten among the servants. The tents are taken down. The children are packed, with mats and jars of water, in baskets swung from the saddles of the camels. The sheep are called in. All are saying, "Come, let us go down into Egypt."

Many years pass away. The Ishmaelites are carrying down from Dothan a slave-boy. He looks anxiously to the hills, but no help comes. His dreams about sheaves of wheat bowing to him have brought him into trouble. But as he plods sadly along, he remembers one comfort. His great-grandfather, Abram, went along that same way, and God brought Abram back again to his home at Hebron.

Not far behind Joseph are the hungry brethren. The staff of bread was broken in Hebron, but they find their sheaf in Egypt! Then comes old yet happy Jacob, with wagons, to dwell near Joseph, in Goshen.

Four hundred years after this a Midianite shepherd takes his wife and children to go down from Sinai into Egypt. He has a single ass. In his hand is a staff. He has no servants and flocks; but no earthly possession can add to the interest with which we follow in the footsteps of this man Moses, whom the God of Abram and Isaac and Jacob has sent to honor his name before Pharaoh.

Once more a company of Israelites passes this way. There are officers in rich armor, chosen soldiers, and chariots full of presents. They do not ask for corn, but will bring back Pharaoh's daughter, to be the wife of Solomon, and queen of Israel. What a change since the days of Moses!

Then we see princes like Jeroboam, prophets like Jeremiah, scribes like Baruch, and high priests like Onias, either fugitives or captives, going down from the Holy Land to the house of bondage. A temple is built, lamps are lighted, and psalms are sung in honor of God among the fields of Zoar.

But we forget them all when, a little later, another group comes this way. It is like the company of Moses. There is a mother and child upon an ass, and a strong man beside them. An angel had

warned them of danger in the night. That door of refuge was open which had sheltered so many before. The angel pointed it out to Joseph. He woke the mother of "the young child" Jesus, and said, "Let us go down into Egypt."

We may see the same things which surrounded the childhood of Jesus, of Moses, and of Joseph. The rude but faithful drawings on the tombs prove that the every-day life of this people was unchanged from the time of Abram and Sarah to the days of Joseph and Mary. These drawings will lead us through Goshen and Egypt. They will show us temples and homes—how they worked in shops and cared for fields, how they fought, how they were buried, and what they believed of another life. Let us walk in this wonderful land. We will use familiar names and avoid hard questions. We will not reason with the priests or dispute with the wise men. But, while we journey, we will try to be at home where so many of God's people have been before us. In that noble company we may learn that there are treasures better than the wealth of mines and harvest fields, a higher wisdom than earthly teachers can give us, a more excellent power than that which armies may gain and temple walls record. "Godlikeness is profitable unto all things." The children of the covenant have such a promise. But how hard it is to obtain this "recompense of the reward" and "endure, as seeing Him who is invisible," we can only learn when, like him of whom this was said, we behold "the treasures of Egypt." "Come, let us go down into Egypt."

ENTERING INTO EGYPT.

# EGYPT.

## ENTERING INTO EGYPT.

Through the Desert—Its Stations—What Goshen is—What Goshen is to Egypt—The Great Highway—The First City, Heliopolis.

### I.

WE have left Gaza, the capital of Philistia, fifty miles behind. The hills are melting into a plain which stretches far away to the west. The sea is on our right. The blue sky on our left is marked with a line of purple mountains. At our feet is a gray and dry water-course, the "river of Egypt," the boundary between the land of Israel and the land of Pharaoh.

A half hour more and we climb the western bank through pebbles and sand. Here is a poor city, with mud walls, small houses, and men who seem quite weary of life. We push on into the silent desert, over drifting sand, or rough flint stones, or reaches of stunted thorn-bushes. Seventy-six hours of toiling westward have the patient camels before them, and then—Goshen!

Sometimes groups of palms wave their branches to us over the rolling plain. The camels push eagerly on, and plunge their noses deep into

the shallow, muddy, bitter springs. More often there seems to be a lake, with hills and trees about it, like Gennesaret, suddenly rising in the south and as quickly melting away. Its sparkling waves and green shores are a plaything of the sun and sand.

Now and then a huge pillar moves across our path. We think of the guiding pillar of Israel. But these pillars often bury the traveler they overtake, and are signs of danger and death. Scarcely less terrible are the storms which suddenly darken the sky and rush down upon us. With cries of fear and prayers, we throw ourselves on the ground. The camels groan as they lie down with their backs to the wind. There is perfect stillness. Then the murmur of the wind rises into a hoarse, deep sound, and bursts upon us. The air is hot and lifeless. If the storm lingers we shall die. But it is gone as quickly as it came. The sun again appears upon the "waste and howling wilderness."

At noon the sun is fearful. Every thing seems to quiver with heat. The skies are a furnace, the light is glaring; not a breath of the sea refreshes us. A bush would give a grateful shadow, but not even this is to be seen. The poor beasts drop their heads. The songs of the drivers are still. All things lie helpless. Surely "nothing is hid from the heat thereof." How impossible seem the cool heights of snowy Hermon, the shadow of the great rock of Edom, and the cool depths of shade under the rich vineyards of Eshcol!

The nights always bring relief. Then the soft sea-breeze ventures back again. The dew refreshes the scanty thorn-bushes. Troops of stars come out in marvelous clearness, like globes of light. The camels lie in a circle, crushing their dry supper of peas. Our servants, children of the desert-loving Ishmael, kindle a fire of thorns, and, in undertones, tell stories of Solomon and his evil spirits. Then they loosen the rolls of mats, and in the sweet, pure air we lie down to sleep; such sleep as we never know in cities. The deserts are the resting-places of the world.

## II.

As Solomon built Tadmor, so the Pharaohs have built many a city along the paths of the desert. The bitter springs, which hide under the roots of a few palms, are first deepened. Under his patient care man then begins to realize that even deserts may rejoice and blossom as the rose. Gardens and groves appear. The fields bear rich harvests. Other springs are found, and a city is built. There, in times of peace, the soldiers are quartered. At Avaris, which thus came to life, two hundred thousand soldiers wait the call to battle. These cities also protect the shepherds, who lead their flocks in search of pasturage far beyond the green plains of Egypt.

In the days of the wanderings the children of Israel must have built many such cities, when the cloud rested long and the years of waiting seemed endless. They tell us there are no trials beneath which there are not comforts if we will search for them, no deserts without hidden springs.

## III.

At last a green point of land rises in the west. Then other points are seen far off on either side, like lines of hills which come out into the sea. We turn more southward. The city of Pelusium, which Ezekiel calls the "Strength of Egypt," is hidden among the trees on our right. Tephanes is not far away. We see the lofty walls of the palace spoken of by Jeremiah. Here we find the fly of Egypt, which Isaiah speaks of, the terrible plague in the days of Moses.

Two days we thus journey from point to point of the land. We now drink the water of the wells, which, like shining stakes, hold fast the fringe of the green curtain of Egypt as it stretches into the desert. Abundance of quail fly out from the grass within easy reach, as they did for the fathers, two cubits from the ground. Their flesh is sweet and nourishing.

On the third day we

## Entering into Egypt. 19

fairly enter this land of Goshen. It is rich with all manner of vegetation. Far and near the larger canals glitter like a net-work of silver. The smaller streams are hidden with vines and blossoming shrubs and stately trees. Most of the country is given up to pastures, where the sleek herds feed knee-deep in grass. But there are also fields of grain, and delicate shoots of millet and lupines. Nor are there wanting groves of fruit trees. Among these rise the forests of date palms, which supply the people with food, clothing, plows, fires, ropes, roofs, and houses.

The villages are built on mounds to escape the overflowing waters. Rude as the houses are, they are so inviting a trellis for the vines that little of their mud walls or thatched roof can be seen. About the houses are gardens enclosed with hedges of prickly pear. Here the scarlet blossom of the pomegranates and the yellow orange trees share the sunshine with broad-leaved fig and the pale-leaved olive trees. Here the garlic and onions and great melons flourish. There is one great enemy in the fields, hardly less troublesome than the flies which torment the cattle in the meadows. The grasshopper, or locust, is a burden, coming often in clouds and turning gardens to deserts.

Even this trial has its happy side. The people roast and grind and make bread of the locust. But more eating is done by the locusts than the people.

Near the villages we notice long reaches of marsh land overgrown with reeds. These are the homes of the water-fowl.  Immense numbers of geese and ducks are flying back and forth.  Beside them are booths where the fowl are plucked and hung up, salted, and put away in jars for future use.  Evidently this is the great business of Goshen.

Besides the quails and ducks, vast numbers of doves are raised in lofty towers for offerings in the temples. These doves glean in the fields through the day, but when the evening sun touches the meadows they rise up in clouds and fly to their windows. Their helplessness and love of home, not less than their beauty, made them to be, to the Egyptian, a symbol of the soul after death.

In the tombs is often buried a wooden dove, and many an Israelite has said on these fields, when he crept, weary and sad, to his hut in the evening, thinking perhaps of the land beyond the desert, or life beyond death, "O that I had the wings of a dove, that I might fly away and be at rest!"

## IV.

Goshen is a frontier land. It is therefore exposed to all the dangers of sudden invasion. The mountains, which shut in the rest of Egypt, are here lost in the Desert. Besides, Goshen is almost the only frontier. For this reason no merchant or worker of precious things considers the land safe. No great men, who could have palaces on the Nile, would build here. It was, therefore, just the place in which shepherds—"who are an abomination"—could live apart from the Egyptians. So long as the herds of Pharaoh were well cared for, and abundance of fowl was sent up to the soldiers and priests, they would be likely to be let alone. To be left by themselves was all they wished.

The mild air, the abundant harvests, and the simple life, were all fitted to the growth of a family into a nation. Besides this, every caravan and army from the Land of Promise passed this way. Once it would seem that Ephraim went up into the land given to Abram. No doubt many knew the way there, and the hope of "returning" was kept continually in mind.

As Goshen was the threshold of Egypt, it was alike a place of coming and of departure. Here the vine, Israel, was most easily brought, here it could take deepest root, and from this place it could best be carried into the goodly land promised to the fathers.

## V.

We are now some eighty hours from Gaza, traveling about five hours in the early morning and as long in the afternoon. A broad canal, with boats upon it, is seen coming in from the east. Upon its banks is a crowded highway. This is the great entrance to Egypt. The way of the exodus lay along this canal. The Israelites followed its stream all the way to the Red Sea at Migdol. Thus they had at first abundance of water.

Here the road from the Holy Land and from Goshen joins the caravan route from Sinai and India. The former must enter Egypt by journeying south past the great branches of the Nile. The latter must go north of the mountains which shut in the eastern side of the valley. What a crowded way! Here are camels bearing in open baskets apes and peacocks from India, emeralds from the desert mines, incense and precious woods from Arabia, cedar timbers from Lebanon, copper, lead, and iron from the Red Sea, and gold dust from the mines of Sinai. Long trains of Egyptian merchants are on their way abroad with bales of fine linen, carpets, and glass-ware. Among them are the chariots and horses of the sportsmen returning from the chase in the Desert. One servant carries the game, still alive, and holds the dogs, not yet satisfied with their sport; another clears the way, with loud cries, for his master's chariot. The harness glitters with gold and the rich colors of the stamped leather. A quiver hangs by one side of the chariot and a case of javelins by the other. The master

## Entering into Egypt.

wears a quilted coat as if in battle. The driver has a whip, which is as useless as the bow of his master. Nothing can be more proud than the horse, except the master himself. Pride is ever the best whip!

Fleets of asses pass noiselessly by, covered with the green treasures of the gardens. Troops of soldiers march to the sound of trumpets and drums. The spearmen carry shields and have a dagger or knife in their right hands. They are from Phœnician or Syrian garrisons. Here, too, are slaves or criminals chained together, on their way to the terrible mines of Sinai. A few herdsmen carry lambs in baskets suspended by a pole from their shoulders. They meekly put their right

hand to their left knee in sign of respect. Not many shepherds, however, will venture to take up the way during the busy afternoon. The scanty girdle shows the poverty of their station. They are held in great contempt.

The poorer women have short, tight skirts of cotton, with faded borders. Their head-dresses hang with plaits of hair on their back below their shoulders. Singular result of pride: it makes thick head-dresses cool, and scanty garments warm. The men, more sensible, have their heads shaved.

There is a loud shout. It is half song, half chorus. We quickly overtake long lines of men harnessed to stout ropes. They are drawing a sled laden with stone. One man, standing on the stone, strikes his hands that all may draw together. The rest spend the greater part of their breath in shouting, and what little of strength remains in a long pull.

In such a confused crowd we come into Egypt. How strangely busy it must have seemed to the quiet patriarchs fresh from the sheepwalks of Judea!

## VI.

It is now late in the afternoon. The sun looks like burnished gold through the dusty air. The people quicken their steps. From the broad plain is heard the song of the herdsmen driving home their cattle, or the reapers binding their last sheaves. The brick walls and towers grow more frequent. Far in advance a vast mountain-like mass of stone rises above the groves. Before it glitters, on a slender shaft of stone, a flame of light. It is the point of the obelisk which stands before the temple, to mark our journey's end. It is "Beth-shemesh"—"House of the Sun."

We still had hopes that the land might rise before us, and, after all, the ascent might be like the going *up* to Jerusalem. But, lo! the Egyptians are right, when names of foreign places are shown in their picture language by mountains, and the sign for their own country, "the world," as they call it, is a circle inclosing two canals.

Houses have become more frequent. They are usually brilliantly painted. From their flat roofs are hung the awnings. The upper part is open to the breeze. Beneath this, in the second story, the shutters keep out the glare of noon. The entrance by the lower story is imposing. The pillars are in imitation of the stalk and bud of the lotus or papyrus plant, and in keeping with the groves by which they are always surrounded.

How delighted are we to find that the lintel of the

doors have not so often the owner's name upon them as some sign or sentence of prayer or thanksgiving to God, just like the houses of Jerusalem.

Many streets now appear on either side. They are straight, broad, and planted with shade-trees. Each tree has a mound of earth about it to retain the water. Servants are continually going about with water-skins from tree to tree. The houses are usually inclosed in walls of brick, and, for the most part, are built of the same material. Blue and red flags are flying gayly from the roof.

There are an unusual number of young men in the streets. They are distinguished by a single lock of hair hanging over the left shoulder, and broad necklaces, after the manner of princes.  The royal family alone can wear the asp over the forehead. Heliopolis is the resort of students from all Egypt. Its priests are famous for their learning. Both Joseph and Moses studied here. The chariot of Joseph was doubtless most often seen before the door of Potipherah, until Asenath shared the palace with him. Here played also his boys, Ephraim and Manasseh.

It is impossible to say where the country ends and Heliopolis begins. There are no city walls. Any stranger may come and go at will, though he cannot escape the watchful eye of the city guard.

## Entering into Egypt. 27

What a relief we feel in entering the quiet door of one of these houses only those can know who have plunged suddenly from desert-life into a city crowd. It is like gliding into the quiet harbor of Tiberius when the ship has been tossed and driven by the storms of Galilee. An Egyptian seems never happy out of doors, unless he is hurrying to and fro about his business. But once within the house he seeks seclusion and repose.

Immediately upon entering a servant brings a basin and ewer, to wash our feet. Another offers us a long white robe, while he carries ours away to be dusted. A third puts a garland of flowers on our neck, and hands us a lotus, then leads us to the host, who gracefully welcomes us to Egypt.

A few dishes of boiled papyrus roots, honey, and bread are placed before us. Dinner was served at noon. A light supper is thought most healthful.

Scarcely have we finished before the sun drops down below the horizon, and at once it is dark. The houses are but poorly supplied with lamps. A wick floating in oil glimmers on the tables, and a few torches are held by the servants. We are soon glad to escape from the gloom and the smoke. A servant precedes us with rolls of thick cloth. We follow after, and are taken to our bed on the roof of the house, where the North wind blows softly up the Nile, bringing to us the fragrance of a hundred gardens.

What are our first impressions? Every one, from the poorest to the richest, seems quite satisfied with himself and his country. The people of Edom and the desert are restless of eye and hand. The Hebrew seems ever weighed with serious thought, as if he were meditating something for the future more grand or happy than the past has given to him. But the Egyptian appears satisfied that the rest of the world has brought him already its best gifts, and that there can be no better world before him than his own Egypt. But still more surprising is the evidence, in the quiet of the streets day and night, of the respect every one feels for law. No one carries arms except the soldiers or the great men, who serve the King. In Jerusalem frequent conflicts take place in the streets. The walls do not protect the city from sudden attacks of lawless men, who come up

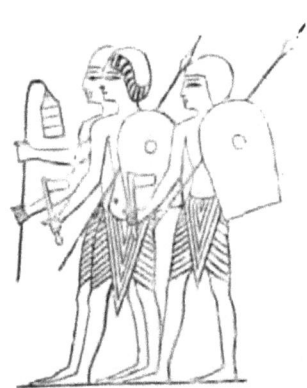

like lions from the swelling of the Jordan. Every man must guard his own house—have stout door and strong bars. Even in King Solomon's day encounters took place between strangers and the people of Israel. But here no walls are necessary. The people, whether native or strangers, go about unarmed and undisturbed. The houses are scarcely protected by locks and bars. Were it not for the light of the watchman, as he goes about the streets, one might suppose that the city needed no care. Happy the people where the entering in is peace.

# THE

# TEMPLES OF EGYPT.

## TEMPLES.

Structure—Ornaments—Use—Chapels—Resemblance to Tabernacle

THE Egyptians worship their gods, like other nations, in "high places." But these high places are not the mountains which guard the Nile valley. Beautiful for situation as these sites would be, they have neither springs, streams, ponds, or groves, which are necessary to the worship carried on in these temples. Nor are these "high places" platforms rising from the plain, like the foundations of Chaldean temples. The Pharaohs prefer to build immense towers, or gateways, from the plain itself, and to mark by these the groups of buildings which are the homes of the gods. The tower of an Egyptian temple is often over two hundred feet in height, throwing a great shadow upon the busy streets and quiet gardens of the people.

Let us enter the temple enclosure. First of all we are admitted by a gate in a lofty brick wall. On either hand are groves of palms and olives. Two large lakes, alive with sacred water-fowl and blossoming with lotus flowers, glisten through the well-trimmed trunks of the trees. Broad stone steps surround these tanks. The priests use the water for bathing.

Before us is a street so wide that a procession with forty men side by side can march in it. This street is lined with images, cut in stone, having the head of a man joined with the crouching body of a lion. The mildness of the countenance suggests a reserve of force. The alertness of the body suggests to an approaching worshiper how powerful such a creature must be when human intelligence directs the strength of the noblest of animals. These images are seventeen feet long, and the pedestals on which they are placed are thirty feet apart. They all face toward the street, as if waiting only a word of command to avenge any insult to the god of the temple. Some of these ways, leading to a single temple, these dromos of sphinxes, contain six-

teen hundred images, and are miles in length. They are peculiarly Egyptian, and are liable therefore to be the first to be broken and defaced by

## Temples. 33

enemies. But adversity cannot quite destroy a greatness which has dignity and patience for its foundations.

Beyond the double row of sphinxes rise the two obelisks. These are stones of finest granite, brought from Syene, five hundred miles away. They are about eight feet wide at the base, sloping slightly inward till they reach eighty or ninety, or even one hundred and twenty feet, a single polished stone! In the Egyptian language they are called " Ubenra," " sunbeam," or " Petobhra," " finger of the sun." Whether by their shadow they are designed to point out the hours of the day, or are monumental pillars, like those Jacob raised at Bethel, or mere ornaments, like the Jachin and Boaz of King Solomon, we know not. We cannot fail to admire the perfect beauty of the figures cut upon them to record the name, titles, and services of past kings; and the skill with which such masses of stone are carried, without injury, from one part of Egypt to another. We are told of these particular obelisks at Heliopolis—and doubtless so good a story is told of all—that the prince who raised them, in the days before Joseph, was commanded to bind his son to the summit, that he might spare no pains to secure at the same time the safety of the obelisk and the life of his own child.

Behind the obelisks are the broad and lofty towers, two hundred and twenty-five feet wide. Between them is the entrance to the great court. These towers have within them stairways and chambers, in five or six stories. They are at the same time granaries, guard-houses, and the resting-places of the astronomers. The lines of the sides, as they rise, slope inward, to give an appearance of great strength. It is just here we feel most of all that, while the Egyptians are not forgetful of beauty, their first thought is of eternity. The massive retaining stones on which the platform of Solomon rests do not tell the

story of faith in the nation's future so plainly as these enormous twin mountains of stone. The temple of Israel could not be built without great walls. But the walls of Pharaoh are built for pure love of building. They serve little use but to honor the gods.

We now pass within the gate into the court. This court is four hundred feet long. Half that length is the breadth. Opposite is a portico. In front of this are standing figures, thirty feet high, of the god Osiris, supported by flat pillars. The figures cross their hands upon their breasts, carrying their shepherd's crook in the left hand and their whip in the right. If the story of the walls be true, the whip is needed more than the guiding.

It is by this second entrance that the gigantic figures of the king are usually placed. Here is one in ruins. It lies upon its face, flat as Dagon at Ashdod. The shoulders are twenty-two feet broad. It was cut from a single stone of hardest granite, and weighed fourteen thousand three hundred times as

## Temples. 35

much as the king himself. How was it carried one hundred and sixty miles to its present resting-place?

On either hand, this court has a colonnade. The walls are without windows, and the columns which hold the roof are half closed by screens. The capitals of the columns are the blossoming in stone of papyrus plants. Within the colonnade unbroken shadows invite the priests to exercise.

We walk across the court; the towers are behind us, the colonnade is on either side, and before us rises the portico. (See sketch-plan, p. 34.)

The screens shut in all save a central way. This vista of shadows and painted columns is closed by an inner door. Beyond this no one save the priests can enter. But the chambers which fill either side of the portico, and the busy sound of preparation with the smoke of incense which comes out from the half-parted folds of the curtains, the sound of music and the chant, convince us that those are right

who say that swarms of priests live in luxury within. We hear of richly-embroidered curtains and thick carpets; of stone inlaid with ivory, or sheathed with beaten gold; of walls made by bright colors warm and cheerful to the eye; of ceilings painted blue, with golden stars; of loaded tables of offerings; of sacrifices of all manner of fowl and the choicest of the herds, which are eaten freely here. We learn, too, that when the holiest of holy places is reached, for which all the solemn grandeur of the approaches is designed to prepare the high-priest; when the embroidered curtain is drawn aside from the apartment of red granite, which few have ever seen, whose walls are too sacred for any building to lean upon; that here, even in Heliopolis, the city of scholars, is found only a hawk in a gilded cage and the calf Mnevis!

In some temples, a vast hall roofed with stone takes the place of the portico. At Karnak—a temple of Thebes—there is no effort to support this roof by clever devices, but the ceiling is carried by one hundred and thirty-four columns, eleven feet in diameter and twenty-seven feet apart, carved and colored from base to capital. These break and soften the light into such distances that there seems a world of glory within the walls. The management of light adds still more to the solemnity and grandeur. It does not come from either end of the hall, but the central row of columns, eighty feet high, rises clear above the others a story by themselves. The lintel stones are forty feet in length, and beneath them the light falls into the lower forest of massive masonry. In the brilliant sun of Egypt these shafts, clustering among the shadows, seem too grand to  be the work of human hands. When the banners with their mysterious symbols are flying from the staffs on the gateways of all the temples; when along the dromos of sphinxes, kings, warriors, and priests join the great procession; when the clamor of cymbals and drums resounds with the clangor of trumpets through the city, who can wonder if the hearts of the enslaved Israelites were secretly enticed, and "their mouth kissed their hand" in token of reverence to the gods of Egypt.

## II.

Every part of the temple—not only the platforms of the sphinxes, the obelisks, gateways, court, portico, apartments of the priests and holy places, but also the corridors, aisles, stairways, and walls, are carved and colored. No people knew so well how to treat masses of stone. The face of the wall is the outer surface of the figures, but the figures appear raised by cutting away the stone around them. They do not care for a correct imitation of the human figure. They always put a full eye upon a profile. Different parts of the body seem put together from recent agreement, not a life-time of association. But for a likeness of the men they represent, for action and meaning, they are above reproach. Inscriptions, figures, and colors all harmonize. When a moulding exists only in color; when a king is drawn ten times as large as the prisoners at his feet; when winged globes hover in all the intensity of red and blue and white over the entrance; when the stone, even of granite obelisks, is covered with stucco and painted black and yellow, one feels no surprise. There is something in the arrangement of color, in the quantity, in the variety of lines on the capitals, and the change of direction in the parts of the temple, which pleases the eye by change without disturbing the harmony.

The subject of these ornaments is varied. Here we have the king of Lower Egypt offering a gateway to the god Amun. Between the figures is the picture and writing which tells the story. Both king and god carry the cross, which is the sign of life. From the royal robe depends in front the name of his ancestors, at the bottom of which are the serpents, and behind is doubtless the tail of the leopard skin worn in sacrifice. The god extends his sceptre in sign of favor.

Often the king is represented swinging his sword over a handful of little enemies, while in the accompanying writing the god says, "Slay, slay!" Over a library hall is the sign, "Dispensary of the mind." A picture represents Thoth—God of Letters—writing the king's name on the leaves of the tree of history with such inscriptions as this: "It is my will that your structure be stable as the sky." "I grant you long life to govern Egypt." "Knowledge is the food of the mind." One god has a single eye, with the motto, "Source of light is single." Sof—" Lady of Letters," " Source of Learning"—watches the young king. The ceiling is covered with astronomical figures.

More often there are gigantic pictures of war. The king charges full speed over prostrate, supplicating enemies. There are sieges with battering-rams, towers undermined, walls falling, ditches filled with the dead, captives slain, and nations humbled at the feet of Pharaoh. Then there are triumphal processions, feasts, and sacrifices.

Nor are the queens without some part in the temple service. They present lotus flowers to the gods and shake the sacred rings on the sistrum. The

wings and head of the holy Ibis form the headdress, above rise the horns of the cow encircling the moon— both emblems of Isis. Their garments are of finest linen, and their necklaces are of woven gold thread, set with precious stones.

The gods of the Egyptians are thus associated on the walls with the kings. The wayfaring man cannot fail to read a lesson as he runs to his morning tasks. The temples are his books. He learns to fear and serve the gods as he hopes to escape the anger of the king, and learns to obey the king as he hopes to find favor of the gods.

### III.

The temple is most of all useful in its impression of grandeur. To accomplish this it breaks in upon a straight line with successive buildings, and grows

## Temples. 41

by numerous additions utterly irregular in plan, and the receding doorways and courts are made smaller to increase the apparent distance and immensity. The lines always slope away from the eye, in order that

they may impress you more and more with their greatness as you study them. The Egyptians spare no pains to prove themselves masters of the building art, that those who first only wonder at the temples may come at last to fear and honor the men who built them.

Then these buildings are especially fitted to that form of worship which consists for the greater part in processions.

Here also are the schools so famous in all nations. The quiet and repose of the cloisters is as profound as if they were a desert.

Here, too, is often the palace of the king.

The temple not infrequently has been found to be

a safe fortress. From its lofty towers the country is in full view. If the Ethiopian comes down from the south, or the Tahe-nu comes in boats from the north, or over the hills appear the hated Shepherd kings, the alarm from the temple calls the people within the shelter of the courts, when they are fed from abundant granaries until the armies can be gathered to drive off the invader.

## IV.

One peculiar feature of these temples is the number of smaller chapels about them. Sometimes these stand upon the roof. Here is a roofless chapel of Isis, whose face looks down from the capital. There

is but one room within. Over the door is the usual figure of the good deity with the wings, under whose shadow the worshiper finds refuge.

# Temples. 43

Some of these little buildings are cut from a single stone. One of them, though it weighs twelve hundred tons, and has been carried nine hundred miles, lies unused because the workmen sighed at the journey's end. They will not insult the gods by offering what is given with regret.

Another of these roofless chapels stands by the water-side. To such a chapel as this came the daughter of Pharaoh to worship the rising sun and bathe in the sacred river. But when she sees the

little ark of reeds, she remembers how the priests had told her that Isis, the goddess, was saved on that river by such a little ark. They bring the basket. Moses wakens and cries when the cover is opened. But the smile of the princess must have been like the bow to Noah when the sun came up again on Ararat and the ark rested.

The most frequent use of these chapels is for observance of mysteries. They are often built to record the safety of the king in war or hunting, the gift of a child, a great victory, or a year of plenty. They greatly add to the beauty and extent of the main temple. If we include the chapels among the buildings of Karnak, this temple alone covers nearly as much ground as was occupied in David's day by the entire city of Jerusalem.

## V.

The Egyptian temple reminds us in many ways of the tabernacle and the building of Solomon. God gave the plan of the tabernacle. But this is in itself no reason why there should not have been a resemblance. So God gave the plan for the ark, with its

cherubim, and its staffs, and its priests clothed in linen. But in Egypt, where nothing of building or ceremony changes from century to century, there was a similar ark with cherubim overshadowing the seat of the great god, Anubis, (see page 44.) The Israelites had often seen this ark crowned with the peculiar flowers of Upper and Lower Egypt, and worshiped by priests kneeling. The ark of the god Nilus they had also seen, surmounted by trees, and carried by priests clothed, like the Levites, in fine linen.

If we recall the plan of the Egyptian temple from this sketch of one in ruins, we shall see that the

great gateways were unfitted to the moving tabernacle, and were therefore omitted. They were imitated by Solomon. The Egyptian court had the same general proportions with the tabernacle court. The holy place of Egypt, with its pillars, was like the porch of Moses, save that Moses added a central pillar which carried the ridge-pole, a change made necessary by the snows and rains of the new land. It seems that the curtain of the tabernacle roof ran over and beyond the side wall, making, with it, a narrow chamber. Did this give shelter to the priests, like the corresponding chambers by the towers of Egypt? Similar rooms, we know, were built around the inner temple of Solomon. Then, the holy place, which none but the priest could enter; the holiest of all, with its perpetual

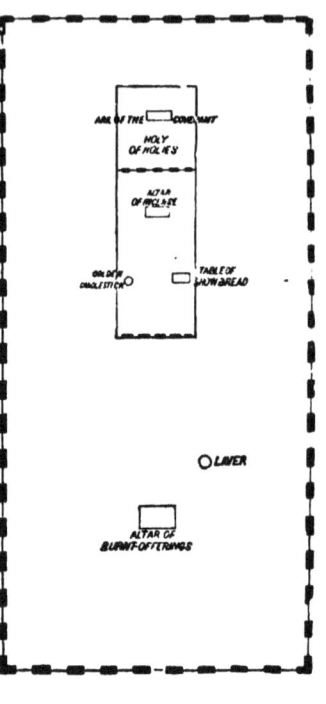

darkness; the altar without for victims, and within for incense; the laver, or pool, for washing, and the table for bread, were both Egyptian and Israelitish.

The massiveness and mystery of Solomon's towers, bathed in light, in striking contrast with the darkness of the adytum and the groves round about, which was called "the leafy covert of the lion of Judah," were but successors to those of Egypt.

When Solomon supported the roof of his towers with cedar pillars and distributed the ten lavers between the spaces, he built in a rhythm of form which the eye was trained to enjoy before his people had broken away from the idolatry of Egypt. The low wall, with three courses of stone and its row of cedar beams, in the court of Solomon, recalls both the curtains of linen in the tabernacle and the screens of stone in the temple courts of On. It was thought by Solomon that, in this approach to an audience with God through successive courts, as in the desert tent, God was honored; and it is interesting to recognise the same feeling in a temple near Memphis, which is the oldest in Egypt. These courts are built one beyond the other, with beautifully-polished alabaster stones, simple piers without capitals, plain architraves, and courts without statues or tablets. We may well be reminded of the winged cherubim on the curtains by the emblems of Hor-hat, good genius of Egypt, whose globe, with serpents and wings, often inlaid with glass, sets forth the union of brightness, wisdom, and swiftness.

Truly there was more difference in the use made of these temples than there is any resemblance in plan; but we need not in remembering the one forget the other. God permitted Israel to remember the Egyptians just so far as the Egyptians remembered him. In whatever view the temples rise before us, we cannot but admire the devotion of those who have reared them. Their immense size, and the pains shown in all the detail of building and furnishing, bear witness to a zeal for the honor of Him who gave them life and power. There may be much confusion in the symbols of gods and goddesses on temple walls, and there may be much idolatry in the reverence paid to the images of stone within; but there was nothing selfish or poor in the labor they lavished upon them. The name of God could not have quite perished from their hearts when it received such labor from their hands.

We can hear the High Priest of Israel—even when the breastplate of twelve precious stones kept in mind the peculiar blessing promised to his people; when mitre and garments of embroidered linen, fringed with pomegranates and bells, told him that he was to bless only those whom God had blessed—when he came forth from the holy place, saying, with outstretched arms of blessing, to those who were yet coming in and going out from these temples of the Nile: "The Egyptians shall know the Lord in that day, and shall do sacrifice... whom the Lord of hosts shall bless, saying, Blessed be Egypt, my people!"

# HOME LIFE.

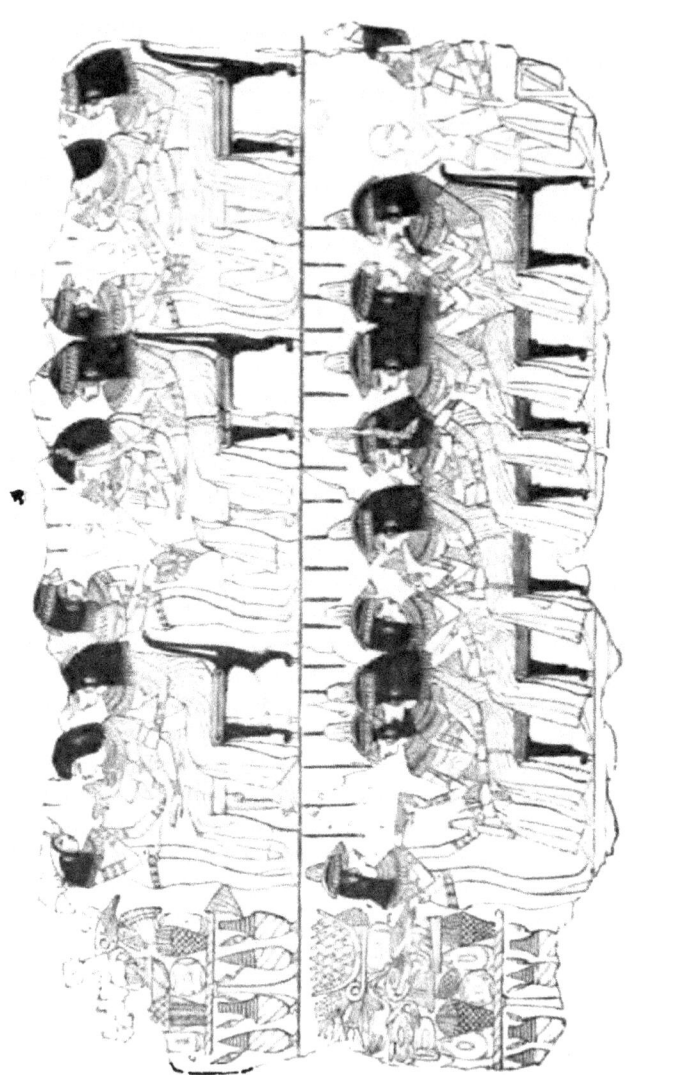

## HOME LIFE.

#### Plan of House—The Feast—Amusements—Position of Women

IF the Egyptians were to be judged by their temples alone, they would be considered the most formal of nations. In the temples, the entire building, every motion of the processions, every form of sacrifice, every song and service, is regulated by law. But in their houses the utmost liberty prevails. The house may have one or three stories. It may be built of bricks, with a single room, sheltered by a roof of split palm trees and interlacing boughs, or it may gather a score of rooms, all built of stone, about a noble court. The priests leave every one to care for his own comfort as he pleases. There is no fear of offending the king or gods by any new manner of building or ornamenting the house. This gives to the city streets an animated and varied appearance.

They are accustomed to speak of these homes as "inns." "The tombs," they say, "are our dwelling-places." But this does not interfere with their actual life. If they expected to live forever, they would not take greater care to surround themselves with comforts, and even luxuries. This they do the more easily because the necessities of life are by no means expensive. The climate is never severe, and food and water are abundant. What men spend at Jerusalem in making the house dry and themselves warm through the winter rains, in building cisterns to hold the water for summer, and buying supplies of meat and grain, would, in Egypt, furnish and adorn a house richly. As the buildings do not suffer decay in the climate of Egypt they are encouraged to make them expensive. What is once done lasts through several generations. In Israel every man builds anew, but in Egypt the son only enlarges the house he receives from his ancestors.

## I.

The royal scribe with whom we are to dine, like most public servants, does not mean to serve for honor alone. The front of his house has brick walls covered with plaster and painted. Before it are trees with earthen cases to guard them from chariot wheels and the browsing goats. Over the lintel of the door are the symbols, "A good house" and "The good are welcome." On the right is painted the banner of the king, to show that he has duties at court. On the left is the name of the owner, with the pen and tablet, the instruments of his profession. Two smaller doors, at equal distance from the center, are used by servants and clients. Ascending three steps we knock. The door opens inward, and is divided right and left. We enter a porch which stands on the north side of a court-yard. An old man takes our staff. Every Egyptian gentleman carries a staff of acacia wood. This is usually inlaid, and has its owner's name on it. It is carved to represent some bird, or serpent, or animal. The bolt slides behind us. The porter turns the key, puts it in his girdle, and leads the way to another porch, whose columns are built up half way from the ground with wooden screens brightly painted. The

## Home Life. 53

cool air comes in over these screens. The sun is kept off by the roof—for it is now noon—and a busy servant sprinkles water from a leather bottle over the marble pavement. Another servant hands us a chair having a seat woven with strips of leather. The back is well braced with wooden supports, and the feet are carved into leopard claws. The bronze nails have very rough heads in an amusing attempt to imitate poorer chairs, which are fastened with wooden pins. It is easy for the great to appear humble. One slave washes our feet, wipes them with a linen napkin, and replaces our sandals. Another anoints our head with sweet Syrian oils. A third takes from a light wooden stand a garland of flowers for the neck, places one large lotus bud over our forehead, and, taking pity on our hands, which of all things are most in the way when not in use, gives us a bouquet to hold. Meanwhile the porter has returned with a white outer garment of fine wool. He throws this over our shoulder. We pass across the court, through an inner door, and the servant announces our name to the host.

This is the reception-room. Its sandal-wood doors are carved into running vines. The linen curtains, which hang from the ceiling on two sides of the room, are embroidered in gold and blue to represent a chase. The antelope is struck with a javelin, and the dogs are leaping eagerly forward. On the two remaining sides are columns which represent the stem and buds of a lotus. These columns run east and west, in order to give space for the cool north wind. The center of the ceiling is also open, having a board inclined to the north, carved into the foliage of the palm. This drives the air down through the room.

Here sits the host and his wife, on a single broad chair. The polite host lifts his left hand, and the wife

her right, in token of welcome. He wears a short tunic with large sleeves, and a large embroidered skirt. She wears a long dress without sleeves. Both have immense head-dresses of false hair, necklaces, rings and bracelets in profusion. They express their unbounded pleasure in seeing us, and then drop into silence, as if trying to remember why they are so happy. Meanwhile we thank the slave who gave us a lotus to converse about, and regret that we cannot have the change of weather to speak of, as we might were we in our own land.

Another guest appears. By his sweeping gait, his

## Home Life. 55

long full apron, the emerald scarabeus hung from his neck, and his important manner, we are sure he, too, is a scribe. The robe he wears is gathered at the neck by a strap which is half hidden by the necklace. The host invites us to amuse ourselves as we please. He evidently desires us to appreciate his house. , The inner curtain is drawn aside.

Here is a little paradise. Rows of palm trees weave their broad leaves over the paths. Trailing jessamine and blossoming henna cluster so thickly that they hide the side walls. Thickets of shrubs, and small ponds full of tame fish, and canals with graceful bridges, are arranged in studied disorder on either side the palms. The ibis, flamingo, and graceful gazelle wander up and down, and taste the water, or sleep in the shade. Here is evidently the plan of a temple court, but realized in all the freedom of nature. Beyond this is an open gateway.

Here, again, we enter a court, but there are now only beds of flowers, lotus plants growing in the pools, and papyrus stems shooting up beside the canals. The walls are broken on three sides into many inviting rooms, with a colonnade running in front of them. On our right and left are two stories. Before us, in the tower, is a third tier of rooms. From this to the great tower by which we entered, and dropping away on the side on which the sun appears, are striped awnings. In one angle of the walls, within a net so fine that at a little distance none is seen, are birds brought from India, with brilliant plumage and harsh voices. In the other is a little summer house, open only on one side. Within are the hoes, and jars, and seed baskets of the gardener, and on the floor lies a

headless doll. The inlaid figure represents the evil

genius in the form of a pig. The whole body is marked with little teeth, and evidently has beguiled many hungry moments. A second doll shows the same marks of attention. Both of them are so very ugly as to

be quite interesting. This, then, is the play-room of the children. The Egyptians, who are reputed to be so solemn, are not so unlike those of other countries. A clatter of wood astonishes us. It is followed by a merry shout of laughter. An attack is made by three children. One thrusts a crocodile at us. A string
pulls the lower jaw up and down in a famished way.
We are making our defense, when, under cover of the attack, a little girl quietly snatches away her footless doll. The third child carries the model of a stone polisher, which moves with a string. It is held in the left hand and made to run up and down the board. Like all such

men in real life, the lifting is difficult, the falling down is easy; and we noticed, too, that not much work is done when the hand of the master is taken away!

## Home Life. 57

Our escort now leads us about the court. On the lower floor on the west is a room full of robes for guests, and the different sandals of the host. Some sandals are highly embroidered for the palace; some are made of papyrus plant for the temple; some are of thick leather for the street, and one is made of the finest kid, with a fawn embroidered in gold on the broad band which passes over the ankle. The linen tunics, which are fringed about the bottom and tied in knots to prevent raveling, are called *calasiris*.

Another room seems devoted to books, as the shelves have rolls of papyrus. These books, however, are out of the children's reach.

Beyond this is a wine room. Siphons hang on the walls with which to draw the wine from the larger to the smaller jars. The great vases are pointed at the bottom and stand in wooden rests, open in the center; the smaller and more graceful jars are in light wooden frames. These are mostly made of clay and painted in bands. No two of them are alike. Their openings are stopped with fragrant leaves.

A fourth room has hunting scenes painted upon it. Lions are represented slaughtered by the king as he rides at full speed in his chariot; the antelopes, however, are the modest prey of the scribe himself. Within this room are bows and arrows, spears, javelins, and armor. In the center, in its painted case, stands conspicuous the fan of ostrich plumes, which the host carries in the sacred procession.

Upon the east side of the court we look first into the treasure-room. There strong boxes contain rings of gold, stamped with the king's name; bags of gold dust; coils of gold thread; fine rings, twisted and braided; necklaces, ear-rings, and precious stones.

Beyond this, on the same side, are the wooden figures of the ancestors of the scribe, with their names and titles painted upon them. Here, also, in a costly wooden case, is the mummy of his son, waiting until the family tomb is finished. The folding doors of the case are left half open, that the fine painting and gilding of the coffin may be seen within. This mummy does not disturb the pleasure of the household. Indeed, it is said that these bodies are sometimes drawn out on a sled to stand in the place at the table which they occupied when living.

Beyond, taking the space of two rooms on the opposite side, is the dining-room, now filled with servants. We pass by and ascend a broad stairway within the tower which closes the north end of the court. A gallery on the three sides of the court gives access to this upper story of apartments. A window of fine bars lets the light from the court into each room. Another and smaller opening in the outer wall is closed with shutters. This at morning and evening gives a view of other gardens or houses in the neighborhood, the broad plain full of harvests, and the shining river beyond.

Here is situated the guest-room. A broad couch, with three steps by which to ascend to it, a rest for the head in the shape of a new moon, three chairs, and a low, square chest of cedar wood, compose the furniture. The lotus flower is the pattern for all the chairs and bed. The floor is covered with a carpet having a border of blue, bright with stars: Within this are broad stripes of white, black, and red. The rest of the carpet

## Home Life.        59

is a blue-gray color, with the representation of a pond in the center, full of lilies. The walls are painted to represent the hunting of fowl in the marshes. The ceiling is ingeniously ornamented in blue background with many devices of straight and curved lines, all gracefully setting forth the movements of the stars.

Just beyond is the room of the host. It is fourteen feet deep, but twice that in width. Its carpet is made of wool woven on linen threads, but as there is much space the border has a running pattern of vines inclosing four circles on each side, which represent the twelve stages of life. In the first a child lies beside a heavenly pilot in the sacred boat. The next is marked with two stars. He now directs the boat; then all alone he urges it on. The fourth star finds the stream more difficult. At the eighth he has called back the heavenly guide. At the twelfth he glides safely into the presence of Osiris, the great god. For the center of this carpet there is the figure of a boy with his hand upon his mouth, as a sign of simplicity. The walls represent gardens of flowers and fruits. The gardener waters his trees. The vine-keeper presses his clusters. The herdsmen drive in their flocks. The hunters bring in the wild cattle to be tamed. The shutters are sycamore wood, painted to imitate cedar. The ceiling has the same bright colors with gilding on purple, and lines marvelously tangled, and, still more strangely, getting straight again, as they go winding in and out in a most bewildering way. How much easier it is to astonish than to please.

Upon the broad and high chest, which is full of drawers, appear the many boxes and articles of toilet.

A mirror of polished bronze has the head of Typhon upon its handle, which must have made any face seen above it handsome by contrast. Such mirrors were 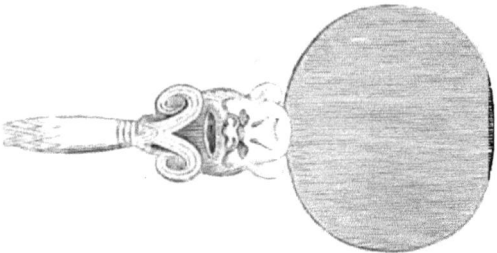 given at the door of the tabernacle for the laver of Moses. There are boxes with sliding covers for pins, ointments, curling-sticks, brushes. Among them appear the alabaster boxes of kohl, or black ointment, which is placed under the eyes to give them a deeper luster, and collyrium for the eyebrows. The figure of Anubis, the guide in the dark regions, stands by these as if for a support. There are also wicker baskets, full of bottles containing medicine and cordials; and vases made of scales like the fish, joined with soft metal, the edges of which are covered with gilded arrows. It must require hardly less ingenuity to use than it did to  make all these trifles which lie about us. The bed is ebony, inlaid with ivory. There is a heap of splendid embroidered coverings and ornamented cushions upon it. All the furniture in this room carries in detail the shape of the head, wings, legs or feet of the ibis, which is the favorite bird of the Egyptians.

We are now summoned by the host to the dining-hall. The guests are assembling. There are many different tables about which the company is seated. The master of the house asks the blessing of Osiris upon the food. He then excuses himself, and we follow him. Beyond the court upon which the dining-room opens is still another. This court is smaller than those we have already seen, that the rooms may be larger. It contains vegetables, and has an awning over it. Here is the vast store-room for grain, the stones upon which it is pounded, and the scales for weighing it. On the right, in the kitchen, are fish and game, ready for the table. The fires of charcoal are lighted. The slaves stand by ready for the meat. Beyond them we see, through an open door, the bakers, with round and square rolls of dark and white bread sprinkled with fragrant seeds, mixing fresh bread with the feet, or blowing the fires, or suspending the confectionery on trays, out of reach of mice and little fingers. Still beyond are numerous ducks and desert fowl roasting over small fires, and vegetables from the kitchen garden, close at hand, being washed and prepared. The door on the left is thrown open and three men lead in an ox. The host prays if any harm threatens his guests that it may descend upon this head. It is for this ceremony he left the dining-room. He must repeat these words over the meat his company are to eat. Two servants with cords throw down the ox, and a third draws a sharp knife across the throat from ear to ear. The head cook catches the blood in a vase. Blood makes a black pudding, which is one of the favorite dishes in Egypt. Moses forbade its use.

We turn and hasten with the host back to the company. Servants with plaited hair looped up behind their ears or hanging over their backs, wearing long tight gowns, are moving noiselessly to and fro.

Acinon flowers, and bright stychnus, and pale xeranthemum, are carried to the dining-room in baskets.

## II.

The feast has fairly commenced. The servants have washed the hands of all the company, renewed the lotus flowers, and are now serving the wine. The men drink from goblets, the women from shallow vases, some of which, being filled, appear full of fish. It is an act of civility to discuss wines. "Mareotis" is thought most delicate, because the soil of Lower Egypt is stony and loose for the roots of the vines. "Teniotic" wine is pale white, of agreeable flavor, and fragrant, but, like honey, must be diluted before drinking. The host raises his special cup of gold, inlaid with dark lines and ornamented with the heads of the bull Mnevis. It suggests to us his education at Heliopolis.  He pledges the guests in the name of the king with Anthylla wine. This, out of compliment to him, all declare surpasses every wine beside.

Cabbages cut in small pieces are now distributed to stimulate the appetite.

Meanwhile the musicians appear. They sit upon the ground by the

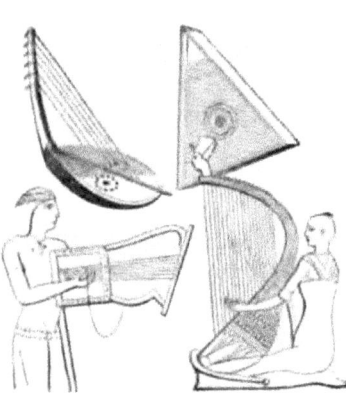

## Home Life. 63

door. Six of them mark time by clapping the hands. One has a harp of great beauty, surmounted by the head of the king—a privilege granted to the musicians of the scribes. There are also lyres, struck with a small piece of wood; guitars, flutes, single and double, and small drums.

While we listen, we do not fail to observe the dining-room itself. There is the same generous display of columns and painted panels which we have seen before; but the walls are here alive with warlike figures. In every scene the scribe appears. In one place he takes account of booty; in another he records the names and rank of the prisoners; in still another he counts the hands of the slain. He evidently thinks his pen more important than the swords which gained the victory, and reckoning of results the principal event of the battle. Between the panels are the statues of the gods and the ancestors of the host in gilded bronze and painted stone.

There are also distributed about the room dwarf trees and tall flowers in red earthen pots, and stands full of fragrant roses and violets. To increase the sweetness of the room a slave swings a censer with Arabian frank- incense, and, opening the cover, leaves the vessel upon a side table to be admired. The monotony of regular spaces, such as the temples delight in, is here utterly disregarded.

Neither doors nor windows are exactly in the center of the side walls, nor do they stand opposite one another. No two of the capitals of the columns, which are twelve feet from the floor, are alike. The banners which fly from the towers are also different in form and color. The outer walls themselves are usually seven feet thick, to shut out the heat, but this also varies in different parts of the room, as one may see by the depth of the window-sills. The screens, which rise half the height of the columns nearer the court, are cut into imitations of every variety of plants. The line of the cornice is broken by an edge of spear heads, shields, fans, or towers, as the artist fancied at the moment. The floor is of polished stones of many shades, with inscriptions of praise to the king and warriors. Even the vases and spoons are of different materials and patterns, bronze, ivory, wood, or even stone. They are cut into the shape of all things that fly, or walk, or creep.

The dress of the guests differs but little. There are a few folds, more or less; sleeves broader or narrower; a band round the forehead of silk or gold; stripes of fawn color or red, and sandals according to fancy. The young men are seated by themselves. They rise when elder men enter the room. The embroidered fold, hanging from the head-dress over the left ear, and sandals which turn up at the toes, are the marks of youth. All, however, as Moses commanded the Israelites, wear a fringe on the border of their garments. The Egyptians, unlike other nations, shave. In processions, or on great occasions, a small beard of plaited hair, two inches long, is strapped to the chin. The king only has a long, square beard, turned out at the bottom. But the

## Home Life. 65

gods, and souls after death, wear beards similar to that which on earth distinguishes the king.

The ornaments defy description. There are emerald images of the sacred beetle, rubies blossoming like cacti, gods of gold set in lapis lazuli, hoops of porcelain and gold, worn about the ankles, arms, and fingers; jewels hanging from the neck and ears, and sparkling in the hair, and all manner of splendor which, but for the fashion, would be sad burdens. Joseph's necklace was a badge of honor. But even the tall Ethiopian slaves, bought at Thebes, and the singers at the door, have similar trinkets in ivory or blue porcelain. The poor man who begs at the gate, and sits on his heels in sign of respect, and the man who holds the staff and takes the head of the ox which serves the tables, will wear rings though he goes hungry.

The musicians are now dismissed with a cup of zythus or barley beer, flavored with lupins. They will, however, be sure to find in the kitchen another liquor, made of the palm, which after fermentation is exceedingly strong.

The vegetables appear in rich dishes. A round dish, whose handles represent an ibex with emerald eyes, contains boiled papyrus roots; another, made like a goose pluming her wings, has watermelons or lotus; a  third, with a fox climbing up the sides, contains onions. There are also gourds in porcelain dishes made at On, and the famous leeks in crystal dishes, which flash and change their color in different lights. Then come twenty kinds of fish, boiled and fried, with their heads and fins removed. Next we see geese and beef served on platters; wild goats and kids, ibex and gazelle from the deserts; with ducks and teal from the meadow. Doora bread and wine is continually passed. The profusion of these dishes is supposed to display the hospitality of the occasion and the resources of the host.

Soups are also brought in, made of lentils as red as in Esau's day. A most inviting "mess of pottage" it is. Every one in turn dips his bread into it, as one dish serves for all to use who gather about the separate tables.

Then appears the fruit. The grapes are usually served in flat wicker baskets, covered with palm leaves; but almonds brought from Syria, and walnuts from Lebanon, are brought in thin boxes of wood. Sycamore figs and dates, either fresh or preserved, appear in metal vases glittering with gold and gems. The honey, however, the best of which still comes from the land of Jacob, is the favorite dish, and is worthily carried in glass-ware, whose edges of purple and stripes of brown and blue run round the vase without mingling, brilliant and clear, from side to side. The honey made from Egyptian flowers is of poorer quality.

The host has reserved, as usual, the choicest wine till the last. Striking his hands together, he calls the slave who waits upon him, and presently a rude earthen vase appears bearing the name of the

Pharaoh of the Exodus. From this he fills a small cup for each in turn. Its great age and value seem its only commendation, yet that is value enough. It receives unbounded praise.

Now the image of Osiris, about two feet long, in whose form the dead appear, is brought in and passed from table to table. Everywhere the words are repeated, "See what you will soon become. Love one another, and avoid those evils which make that life seem too long, which in reality is never long enough."

Once more the servants wipe the tables with napkins, and wash our hands, sprinkling over them powder of lupins for soap. Then they bring in the confectionery, of which all are exceedingly fond. Some of it is carried in baskets of fragrant wood brought from beyond Syria; some in vases of purple amethyst, with two Asiatic captives for handles, and some of it on green leaves.

The lamps with floating wicks are now lighted, and, like far-off constellations, hang from the ceiling. This marks the end of the feast, and the tables are taken away.

## III.

The entertainment, however, is not ended. The children are brought in. The smallest is smothered in robes, and tucked away in a basket, with a porcelain charm round its neck. The charm represents the figure of "Truth," or Justice, and is supposed to keep off an envious eye. And certainly there would seem need enough to guard it from envy, for every one pronounces it the fairest thing in Egypt. The hostess, already convinced they are right, assents and is satisfied.

The wonders about town are discussed: what leaves are the most fragrant as stoppers for bottles of wine; how the superintendent of royal buildings came to be Governor of Southern Ethiopia; how a certain fan-bearer of Pharaoh still keeps on a sled the chest with folding doors in which his grandfather was dragged about town, and how impossible that any fashion should supplant the dignified cart, drawn by oxen, in which men ride in these days; how another nobleman lost his favorite dwarf; how miserable those countries must be where no one is safe without weapons, and how the embroidered leather parted from the seat of a snake-headed chair, and threw the favorite cup-bearer down under the

## Home Life. 69

table. Such conversation, with the delicate compliment of exchanging flowers, beguiles the time till the musicians, with the jesters and dancers, again appear.

At first we listen to the airs of the country, the "maneros" of the feasts, the "epithalmia" of the wedding procession, and the rude thrashing song of the husbandmen. Then the "Linus" of the grape gatherers is called for. Livelier airs follow, and singing. With the lyre of many strings, which Hermes, the god, invented, and the harp, with its score of strings, is heard a fan covered with bells shaken with the hand, clappers of hollow metal heads struck together, double pipes and flutes.

As the music grows more gay we are surprised that even the gravest guests, priests and old men, grow animated and beat the measures. Then the dancing commences. Keeping time to tinkling bells and castanets, the women balance now on one foot then on the other, by the graceful motions and striking attitudes calling forth the most lavish applause. The measure grows more rapid, the movement swift; the panting dancers become excited and whirl swiftly about, then suddenly sweep out of the room, while others take their places.

The buffoons leap into the center of the room. Their towering head-dresses and black faces, the long scarf hung from their elbows, and the absurd postures, win shouts of laughter. Their dress is a scanty bull's hide with its tail hanging behind. Their object is to make sport of every thing. They walk as if they wore the thin robes of the female dancers, which restrain the feet; then suddenly roll across the floor like wheels; they turn each other over, ride upon each other's backs, stand upon their heads, and twist their faces into every oddity of expression, keeping time with the music.

These are succeeded by the trained slaves, who wrestle, leap on each other, touch the ground by

leaning backward, and a hundred things which are considered very amusing only because they are difficult. A female servant holds the prize before them. A necklace rewards the best performer.

So exceedingly fond are the Egyptians of sport, that when the hard day's work is over, and they are released from the staff of the taskmaster, they wield their own staffs and beat one another with "single stick;" race, wrestle, and play with hoops and knives and balls. It is even said that at times the king joins their games in disguise, though many deny this. At least, in feasts of Isis, he has put on the mask of a dog, and, attended by the queen in the figure of a cat for a fan-bearer, has made the temple courts resound with laughter. Sports seem to be necessary to every Egyptian gathering. Entire evenings are devoted to dancing, and listening to the pipes and lyres of blind musicians.

The light and cheerful temper of the people delights in finding sport even in sacred things. Those

## Home Life.

accidents which, for some unknown reason, give us pleasure in proportion to the trouble they give others, are the favorite subjects of the wall paintings. Two boats in a funeral procession run against each other. The bottom of the boat receives a medley of arms, 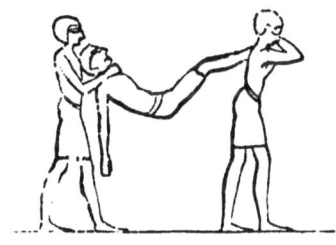 legs, sacred images and altars, while the rowers plunge overboard, or shelter their heads from the showers of cakes and fruits which come down from the falling stands. The result of too late nights and too much beer is a favorite subject. A sentimental young man, pensively gazing at a woman with chariot-wheel ear-rings, 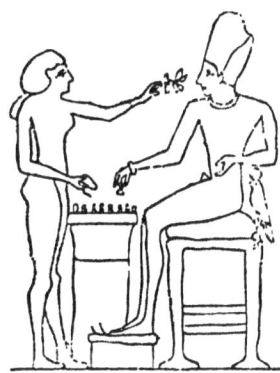 leans against a column. His graceful posture wins attention from more than one. The pillar gives way, and roast ducks soups, fish, and flowers, cover the unhappy guest as he strikes out wildly on the floor to regain his feet. In a coronation scene, the skins of the Ethiopian escort hang so near the ground that

they are stepped upon. The king and queen do not escape caricature at their games of draughts. These and a thousand similar subjects abundantly prove the cheerful temper of this merry people, and the gay spirit which animates their feasts.

## IV.

The foundation of all the joys of home life in Egypt is the respect shown to women. The Egyptian has but one wife. She is associated with him in all his honors and sports, as well as the management of the household. At every feast, and finally in the tomb, husband and wife share a single seat, and have their arms lovingly placed upon each other's shoulders.

It is even claimed that by marriage contract the wife has rights superior to her husband, that daughters are obliged rather than sons to support their parents, because they are better able to provide, and that the will of the mother is supreme in the family. However this may be, there have been many queens upon the throne. Great Scemiophia reigned nobly at Thebes. Nemt Amon was sister, if not colleague, of Tothmes III., and shared the glory of his monuments with him. Their names are side by side at Karnak, as if in government no distinction was known between them.

As Isis is worshiped more than Osiris, and in honor is at least his equal, women in Egypt claim the same privileges with men. Not that women attempt what belongs by disposition and fitness to

## Home Life. 73

the pursuits of men, but count themselves in their own sphere as worthy of the same respect and praise with those who serve in public stations.

The two figures of the gods of "Home" and "Religion" are always associated, and usually the goddess of Love stands between. In this way the Egyptians confess that there is no serving in house or temple which can long endure unless it has its springs in an ardent affection. The mother therefore seeks to gain the love of her children by her kindness and sympathy, just as the gods claim her reverence because they are not so far removed as to forget the wants and trials of her daily labors. As the king in his grandest monuments is represented with his wife and family beside him, so every man in social life associates the children with all his honors and sports. Nothing is more common than to see the little people at play with their parents. The mother joins in the favorite game of ball. The balls are made of leather and stuffed with bran. The father teaches his boys to play chess. The chess-men have human heads, or, as the fashion was in Rameses' day, they are made round, an inch and a half high, with balls for heads. Drawing lots, games of chance, hoops, riding upon each other's backs, swinging bags of sand, are all familiar sports. We often see the upper robe laid aside, and a strap over the shoulder is made to support the girdle and the dress, while both parents join in the sport. Yet at the same time the utmost respect is required of the children. As in Israel, so in Egypt many faults are overlooked; but a want of reverence and consideration for years is a sin which cannot be forgiven. This duty of respect the priests the more insist upon, since only those who are taught to obey at home are able to obey in civil affairs, and only those who are disciplined by their parents can enforce discipline in the army or in foreign provinces. Beside this, the young are accustomed to regard their parents as their teachers. Thus every child grows up to revere and love his home. He wishes for no better place in which to enjoy life.

In bidding our host farewell, the hostess receives an equal share of thanks, of compliments, and congratulations. She is conscious of that merit which Solomon ascribes to the virtuous woman. If the wool and flax of curtains and garments are woven well; if the fruit of the vineyards is well ripened; if her children rise up to call her blessed, and her husband praises her, and trusts her with all the house, it is because she has made herself to be respected and loved. So long as these homes endure, and these sources of power and happiness are ordered aright, Egypt will rule in the gates of her enemies. The goddess of home will be the power behind the throne of Osiris.

# THE

# RIVER OF EGYPT.

## THE RIVER OF EGYPT.

The Nile Valley is Egypt—Abundance of the River—The Inundation—The Nile Worshiped—Seasons regulated—Fish—Fowl—The Great Highway.

### I.

THE rolling hills on the western shore of the Red Sea rise rapidly to the height of eight hundred feet. Their barren slopes are broken into ravines. After journeying beyond these full a hundred miles westward, over plains of yellow sand and sharp ridges of rock, a broad valley opens at our feet. It reaches south and north, and thus breaks across the desert of Africa from the far-off mountains to the sea. Winding from side to side of this depression is a noble river, bordered with green fields. These fields are Egypt—a country not far from six hundred miles in length, varying in breadth from ten miles to a mere chasm, with scarcely room for the river. Yet this country, under a glowing sky, with its fresh waters and rich banks, is said to have fed seven millions of people, who lived in twenty thousand cities.

In earlier times the river found its way by a channel still farther west, beyond the low hills which now guard it from the Desert of Sahara. The banks are fifteen thousand yards from shore to shore, and the dry water-course is still to be seen, full of well-worn pebbles. The plains are strewn with trunks of trees turned to stone. A little oasis here and there bears witness to a gleam of olden richness, but for hundreds of miles the burning desert shows what Egypt would be were it not for the river which the people call Nile, "blue," or Hapi-mau, "abyss of waters."

## II.

In all its course through Egypt the Nile does not receive the tribute of a single stream or spring of water. No clouds ever bring up the rain to fill its channels. The canals, and lakes, and hot sun, are continually drawing upon it for their supplies. Yet though there have been seasons when it wanted in fulness, and there was a famine in the land, it never quite failed. When Syria and Phœnicia have almost perished in severe droughts, and even the water-courses of Edom have become dry for want of the early and latter rain, the vineyards of Moeris were flourishing, and the willows of Thebes abundant, and the fields of Memphis were white with rich harvests. Even where the Nile flows by the pyramids in a broad stream many hundred miles from Philae, its current moves three miles an hour, and at its lowest state is six feet deep. Certainly a river which keeps so vast a garden well watered through centuries of time, and between thirsty deserts, deserves peculiar mention. The country is indeed "Mazor," "shut in," as the Hebrews say. But it can never suffer from its narrow boundaries so long as this kindly river supplies its wants.

## III.

The great wonder of the Nile is its yearly overflow. This is watched with intense interest. The height of the rising river will decide how plentiful the harvests will be.

Just when all Syrian streams are shrinking in the last days of a hot June sun, the gathering Nile begins to fill its banks. This they call "manifestation." It scarcely varies its coming by a week. The officers of Pharaoh proclaim through the land how high each day the waters ascend the stone steps in the measuring chamber on its banks at Memphis.

In August the grand festival of Nilra is held in honor of the river. Then an image of the Nile god and a gilded ox is carried from city to city with processions of singing men and women. Every household has a similar image of clay, or precious stones, or plate of gold or silver, which it casts into the current with chants and the offering of incense and prayers for still higher waters. It is said that a noble maiden was once offered at this season as a sacrifice to the river. The north wind now freshens, and by staying the current it lifts the surface of the Nile nearer the flood-gates on the top of the banks. At last these gates are opened. All over the land men gather hurriedly the last cattle in the fields, and the remaining stacks of wheat, carrying them for safety to the villages, which are built on mounds. Every form of boat and raft is in full use. The sailors are reaping their harvest of gain. The people swim from dyke to dyke. Troops of foot soldiers or cavalry are placed on guard along the banks. Woe be to any man who is caught tearing up his unthrifty neighbor's wheat, or putting his hand to the stone land-marks, or opening without authority new channels through the mounds. He will be transported to some oasis, or branded and condemned to work in the mines.

Before September is gone the river has risen twenty-five feet, and has a red color. Its tide sweeps by Lycopolis full forty miles an hour. It has now reached its greatest strength.

In October the red color of the water disappears, and it becomes green, then blue, and has again retired into its banks.

It is believed by some that the great Mediterranean Sea sends its clouds before the north wind far away into the country, where they descend from the slopes of the mountain into the river, bearing with them the soil on which they fall. But the people cannot be persuaded that this abundance is any thing beside the gift of the gods sent direct from the unseen world. Whoever has learned of Moses, when he sees the flow of rivers of water about the roots of these trees, whose leaf never withers, or watches the Nile as it glides along the edge of the singing villages, or waits beside it to catch the praise of joyful threshing-floors, cannot fail to see in it all that Being who sent the rivers through Paradise.

## IV.

It is not strange that where many gods are worshiped the Nile should be honored among them. The mystery alone of its inundation claims reverence. Then "Ta Res," the southern region, has never given up the secret of the Nile springs. The farther inland the armies of Pharaoh have gone, the larger the river became. They found lakes of great extent, blue with the sacred double lotus flower,

and papyrus plants, spreading the golden rays of their flowers twenty feet above the water, giant tamarind trees, tangled vines, and strange fruit. White giraffes, troops of elephants, dark red storks and snowy pelicans were seen in vast numbers. It was like the gates of Paradise. But of the origin of the river they discovered nothing. To this people whatever is mysterious is an object of worship.

In the movement of the river is the story of Osiris. When it is lowest, they mourn four days for this god. The land, like Osiris when forsaken, they say, is dead. The cow, sacred to his wife Isis, is clothed in black. The priestesses mourn. Then, as the water rises, the cry is heard from white-robed priestesses in the temples, "Osiris is found." Straightway an image like the new moon is carried up the river to the temples which stand at the southern entrance of Egypt.

When the full tides flow in over the land they say Osiris has found Isis, and a festival of peculiar magnificence is held at Philae when the movement of the river is first seen.

They have still another reason for their worship in their gratitude for the richness which the stream brings with it. When the inundation reaches its full height, a soft dark earth, oily to the touch, without odor, stiff as potter's clay, is quietly dropped upon the fields. In this all things grow rich and strong. Through successive ages by this means the soil has been building up the entire land. However deep the king digs for new canals, or the people for wells, the same dark soil is found. Then the bed of the river continually rises, as well as the banks, and the yearly overflow is more easily carried away from the banks to the lower plains beyond. As the people increase, the wider do the green fields of Egypt become, till they touch the hills on every side. If Nilus were not a god, he would not do all this so wisely, say the priests.

The power of the river is yet another reason given for its worship. "See," they say, "where the Nile spreads out broadly and quietly at Philae, preparing for its fearful struggle with the old red granite barriers of Syene. How he rushes down upon them, breaks their bands asunder, and flows on his mission of mercy majestic as a god." And the plunge of the water, down the eighty feet of cataracts into the lower river where the ships wait with furled sails, is indeed wonderful to see.

Again at Silsilis, where the Nile breaks the sandstone cliffs, there is a strife worthy of the river.

But above all the priests praise the conflict of the river with desert sands and desert winds. The line of green is driven in during the low Nile on the river. But the tide of life is pushed victoriously back again when the energies of the Nile are roused in the inundation. All the year the strife goes on, and the Nile saves the land.

For these reasons they worship the statues of this god Nilus, and paint them blue and crown them with water-lilies. Sometimes he is represented sitting under the rocks; sometimes pouring water from a jar which he holds with both hands. Flutes are his favorite music, for their soft wail is like the rippling of the quiet waters, and their lower notes like the sound of the far-off cataracts. At the full waters the clash of cymbals and shouts of joy set forth the struggle of a conquering god.

Every city has a temple and priest of Nilus, with feasts in his honor. If a human body is found in the stream in any part of Egypt, the priest of the Nile must embalm it, and the nearest city must pay the expense of a costly funeral. The waterfowl, the fish, the river plants, and even the crocodiles, are, in different places, sacred to Nilus. At Nileopolis his name stands first in the assembly of the deities, and seven hundred thousand people are said to assemble at his festivals.

At Silsilis, where the quarries come down to the

river, the streets cut through the banks are often eighty feet high, reaching back half a mile into the hills. They have tablets and temples at every step,

## The River of Egypt.    85

where Nilus receives divine honors, and sacrifices, and prayers, that he may guard the stones which are here committed to his care, save them from shipwreck, and permit them unbroken to reach their journey's end.

Upon the throne of the king is represented the figure of Nilus binding reeds and grain. The security and power of the kingdom is thus acknowledged as the gift of the river.

How great, then, the dismay of the Egyptians to find the red Nile suddenly a source not of blessing, but of death, when touched by the rod of Moses! Along every garden and field, by every path, in temples and houses, in canals and streams, in jars of stone and wood, were the red waters, bringing suffering and death. The chief god seemed smitten. The sacred fish died. The wells gave no relief. The entire country mourned. Egypt alone could thus have been plagued, and Egypt could have suffered in no other way so sadly and strangely.

## V.

As the climate remains the same in Egypt through the year, the river alone divides the seasons and marks the changes of labor among the husbandmen.

The year opens with the month of Thoth, "the dogstar." This is the season when vegetation droops. The black plains are burned into dust, and cracked under the fierce sun. The sky is brilliant as burnished brass. The air is the breath of a furnace. The cattle which come up from the river, are all lean and weak. The desert seems taking possession of the fields. From the banks

is heard the monotonous song of men who, panting in the sun, with only a strip of cloth about their loins, are lifting, in dripping palm-leaf baskets, the precious water. The sweep, which carries the basket by a rope, is suspended over a horizontal pole, and thus, resting on piers of mud, groans at every swing. If the banks are steep, four rows of men stand above, and yet a little way from each other, each lifting the same water. The result of all their painful labor, and much sweat of the brow, is a few drops, which disappear quickly

## The River of Egypt. 87

in the field. A man follows this silver thread, and turns into the little squares just so much of it as may keep the trees and crops alive. Thus Egypt is a land "watered by the foot." With all his care the husbandman might despair and give way to the mocking, yellow sands, did he not see on the walls the pictures of similar toil and troubles which the flowers and grain have outlived.

It is a glad day when the rising waters drive away the lower tiers of baskets. Soon the next are useless. The third rank find no need for their work. The river at length runs out far and near over the banks. This is the season of "waters." The Nile valley is a lake with the mounds built to support the cities appearing like islands just above its surface.

After the departing waters, as the river drops back, comes the season of "vegetation." The seed or bread "is cast upon the waters." It is "sown beside all waters"—canal, lake, river, and reservoir. Thither they lead the feet of the willing ox and goats to trample in the grain, and ere many days, at least by the middle of November, a flush of green overspreads the fields. The lighter crops already have appeared. The water-melons follow.

Then the much-prized leeks, onions, and garlic rejoice the people.

The trees must now be pruned, that they may

recover from that violence through the scent of the abundant water. The higher ground, already dry, must be broken by hoes and plows. Fields which are too wet must be drained by syphons. The pigs root up the reeds, which start into life after the inundation.

Various are the crops put into the ground. Each may choose as he likes. If he has clayey soil on the edge of the desert, he sets out his vines, builds his arbors and wine-presses, where the ripening grapes will be trodden by the feet or crushed in cloths. He buys jars with pointed ends to be thrust into the sand, and his resin to give that flavor which people learned to enjoy in earlier days, when skins instead of jars were used. If the soil is moist, he rejoices in the bloom of the doora and sesamun vines, the juicy thrift of beans and lettuce, castor plants, cnicon, and cyprus, bearing seeds like coriander, suitable for oil. The first ripening lentils are dedicated to Osiris, for the seed, like him, soon dies, and the shoots quickly reappear, slender and weak as his child, the god Harpocrates.

From November to March three crops are often taken from the same field.

A large share of labor is given to groves of trees. Palms bearing dates are planted most in Lower Egypt, and acacias in Upper Egypt. Sycamore trees bear figs every-where. Orange and lemon trees, with peach trees from the Euphrates, and many rare fruits, hang their foliage over the walls. Papyrus reeds overhang the brooks full fifteen feet. Their filmy bark is beaten into thin layers eighteen inches in circumference, and pressed together, to make the papyrus for the scribes. Isaiah speaks of these, now most abundant, as doomed to perish.

From November to March flowers and harvests flourish every-where, but not without peculiar care. The endless chain of clay jars creaks and groans

like a thousand hand-sweeps, and the patient, blinded oxen lift the splashing water over the shaky wheel.

The canals, too, require care. Their embankments are repaired, their channels deepened, and new connections made with the river, or the inner lakes. The Government has charge of the work, and often transports entire villages, which die from exposure to the sun and hard labor. One large canal brought the overflow of the Nile to lake Moeris, " Mou Res," or "the southern water." This lake is four hundred and fifty miles in circumference, with a depth of two hundred and fifty feet. It has two pyramids rising fifty feet above its surface, with colossal sitting figures upon their summits. These lakes not only relieve the too abundant waters from the river banks, but also provide a vast reservoir for the fields when the Nile is low. They also change full three hundred square miles of the Lybian desert into a rich province.

Another canal connects the Red Sea with the eastern branch of the Nile at Bubastis. It creates by its waters, in the dreary desert, gardens and flourishing cities. It also brings the ships of India to the quays of Memphis. Among the men who built this canal was the great Rameses.

Another canal is three hundred and fifty miles long. Another is a hundred and fifty feet wide and fifty deep, carrying the water a little distance from the river banks for a hundred miles. Then there are innumerable streams which flow by every harvest-field and garden-bed; by every winnowing-floor where the grain is trodden by the unmuzzled oxen and tossed by wooden shovels; where the acanthus and momosa trees are grown for the carpenter, or the grapes ripened; where the cattle are gathered in sheds or the flocks fed in the pastures. All these channels must be put in order when the river goes down. In this way Nilus determines the labor of the farmers.

## The River of Egypt.

## VI.

When the Israelites were weary of the desert quails and manna, they remembered the fish they did eat abundantly in the land of Egypt. In all their poverty they had found the Nile generous. An unfailing abundance of fish, and of every variety, were ready to be taken by hook, or net, or spear. The canals of Goshen are still alive with them, and, except a few, like the phagrus or eel, which is supposed to be unhealthful, and kept from the people by being declared sacred, the Israelites could take them at pleasure. This they must have depended upon, since the severe tasks of brick-making left little leisure to cultivate grain. If they had scanty supplies from their patches of field, during the inundation they must have been reduced to the condition of the poorest of the Egyptians. These soon consume their meager supplies, and then the fish left at their doors by the receding water are their only support till their little harvests ripen again.

The fishermen are a separate class. Their boats are at all times upon the river, drifting with the current as the net, leaded at one side, and floated at the other with wood, drops slowly down the stream. At times the net is fastened to the bank while they drag the quivering fish ashore. Often the net is large enough to employ several boats. Some fishermen prefer, as Isaiah speaks of them, to angle along the brooks or canals, or spread their nets beside ponds, or stretch them across sluices where the stream runs swiftly.

Others raise fish in lakes, feeding them daily until they become so tame as to come at the call of their keepers. Fish are thus especially cared for in temple inclosures, that the tables of the priests may be supplied, and the sacred cats and ibises fed.

The favorite sport among the richer classes is to take fish from their own canals. The quiet excite-

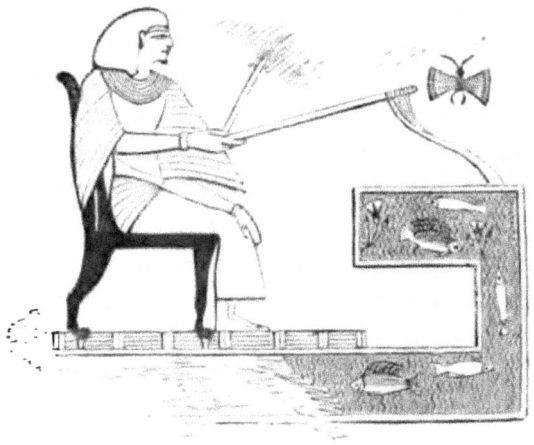

ment of seeing the prey come and go among the lotus flowers, the pleasant reflection that this is having an occupation, and the hope that something will disturb his double line, gives the Egyptian gentleman whole days of comfort. He has no idea of needless exposure to fatigue or want of dignity, and, therefore, when he fishes, has his chair and carpet made ready, and full head-dress carefully prepared.

If the Egyptian has a mind to more stirring sport, he takes his daughter and servant with him, and pushes his punt through the papyrus plants. Often his quick double spear strikes two fishes at once. His daughter, who has more interest in adorning herself with lotus flowers than in using a cruel weapon, clings to him, lest in his ardor he should become food for fishes when seeking fishes for food. His servant carries the prey in one hand and a spear in the other. The broad carps lie quietly sunning themselves by the reeds.

The richer class have often small ponds set apart for angling. In these the water-plants grow wild, and water-fowl build their nests. But it is far more common to stock with fish those water-tanks which supply every garden.

Every city has its markets where fresh and salted fish are sold. The tax from this alone is considerable, and the right to use the net in the royal lakes furnishes an immense revenue. The queen often claims this as her peculiar right, and thus supplies herself with jewels.

Yet much as this industry is valued, there has never been a fish-god in Egypt, as there is in Nineveh or Philistia. The reason may be that the Egyptians dread every thing which might remind them of the sea, while the empire of the Euphrates, coming up from the gulf, gratefully serves Dagon.

## VII.

The fowl of the Nile are not less numerous than the fish. All variety of waders, with geese and ducks, abound among the shallow pools. Some of these are tamed and driven in flocks, but most of them are wild, and may be taken by any who have the skill. The common flat net has grain sprinkled on it, and its sides turn together upon the center when the rope is drawn. One watches the flock from the hiding-place in the reeds; and when the prey has gathered, the men, at a signal, pull the rope and entangle the birds. The geese are then carried to the city hung from either end of long poles.

Others kill the birds with a hard-wood stick, and send a cat or ichneumon to bring in the dead and wounded game. A son often accompanies the hunter, and imitates him in every thing but obtaining the birds. The daughters are busy in looking after themselves

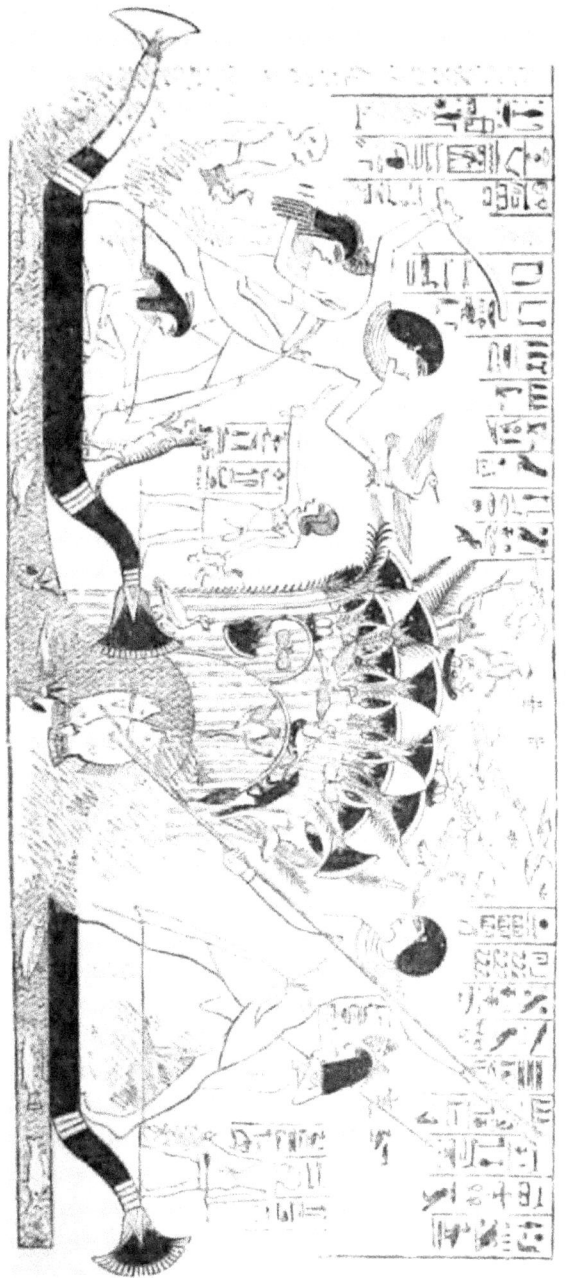

as the boat moves unsteadily through the water. All the air is alive with half-fledged, ambitious nestlings and bright insects. The tall water-plants bend with the weight of nests. All this the sportsman will have painted in long lines of characters upon his walls. He is sure to excite the admiration of his guests, since he has admired similar pictures in their houses.

## VIII.

The river of Egypt performs its best work as a highway. The north winds prevail most of the year, and quietly push the ships against the current. The return voyage is accomplished by the use of oars, or by floating with the stream. As the cities lie along the banks of the river, or on the great canals, every thing is floated to their doors, and transportation is inexpensive.

In the first glow of the morning, when the palm-trees begin to be lighted with the coming day, the

sailors make the banks noisy with their songs. The pegs, which hold the boats by ropes, are

## The River of Egypt. 97

loosed. The cords which bind on the cabin are tightened, that the cattle and hay within may not suffer from the wind. The rudders are set free. The careless boy is warmed with a stick for the day's work, and the dog, who knows what the stick means, is by no means sorry to have the boy who beats him understand its discomfort. These heavy boats are laid up under the shelter of mats during the greater part of the year.

Groups of sailors are offering incense to the Nile, in hope of a prosperous voyage. Others draw down from the higher banks boats made of hide stretched over a light frame, and drive the cattle before them across the stream. Here is a boat which is slowly drifting down the river. It has a light stone dragging behind, and a bundle of reeds in front to catch the force of the water, and so keep the bows of the boat always downward. This is laden with stone.

Beyond this is a long file of sailors, in too much haste to wait for the wind, towing a boat against the stream. Each man encourages the rest to work by doing more than his own part in shouting. The captain meanwhile gets furious over some slower boat which lies in his way. Bright and lively-colored sails drop idly from the yards of travelers' boats, while the crew wash the decks, and build a little fire at the bows for the morning meal. The mast is made of Syrian fir, and rests on two beams at the bottom of the vessel. One bracing-beam runs the length of the boat, and the other across. The deck and sides are built of acacia.

Little floats of the husbandmen are paddled

gayly about, like leaves on the stream. They are hollow bundles of reeds, such as Isis used, and are therefore never harmed by the crocodiles. They are made tight with pitch, like the ark of the child Moses. These boats will be carried from the shore by the men they have carried across the river.

Flat rafts, made of empty jars, are pushed with poles or urged by an oar moving over a wooden pin. These are dropping down the river with the grain heaps upon them. They will be broken up and sold at the journey's end. More substantial barges have their papyrus sails folded and laid upon the cabin. Beyond is the funeral-boat, with its tall cabin painted in imitation of blossoming plants, having the eye of Osiris upon the bows. The priests are almost hidden in flowers. The brightly-dressed oarsmen and somber mourning-women are making the shores resound with sharp cries and plaintive songs for the dead. Then the innumerable ferry-boats add to the din. Why those who serve the people should be such tyrants it is hard to say, but the most important men in Egypt, who despise their fellows thoroughly, are these same petty ferrymen. The timid throng are urged with words and blows, which they return with interest on the unwilling donkeys. Troops of slaves are unloading the merchandise at the quays, filling grain-sacks, or weighing money "full weight," as in Joseph's day, with rings of brass and seals of clay. Lines of camels stalk across the dykes like giants in the morning sun.

But through all this confusion glides the state barge of a nobleman. The sail is made of white

## The River of Egypt. 99

flax. The deep border of blue has a rope sewed upon it for strength. One man at the stern swings the yard to meet the wind as the boat turns to the east or west. The pilot on the bows watches for shoals. These bars of mud the boat itself more easily finds, as a harsh sound is heard under its flat bottom, and every thing moves suddenly onward and downward. The captain, in the center, gives a cry. The sheet flies loose. The three rudder-men

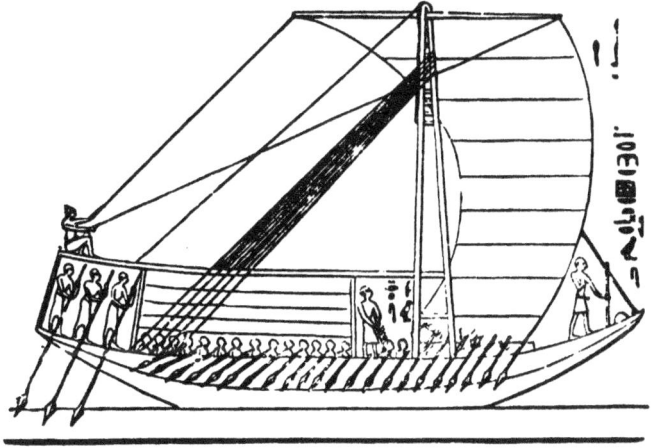

lift their paddles. The forty oarsmen back the ship off the shoal. The most vigilant pilot cannot know just where to find the ever-shifting channel, nor can he see through the dark brown water. Some boats have sails which fold like blinds, and carry a painted cabin thirty feet long. Indeed, there is no end to the varieties of vessels which vex the surface of the great river.

The trains of animals along the shore are scarcely ever seen moving north or south. They only go east and west to wait upon the great traffic of this noble highway of the Nile.

At noon the river faints under the intense heat. No sound is heard even from the insects in the trees. The birds, too, are silent. But when the sun drops down the western sky, the whole country seems to start into life. From every small canal push out the pleasure-boats of the nobles to enjoy the north wind, while here and there through the fringe of trees are seen the less adventurous men under canopies, towed along their canals by a line of servants to inspect the day's work.

Every one is ambitious to display his wealth by the beauty of his boat. Only those, however, who belong to the royal family may carry the king's feathers, and necklace, and sphinx, at the prow, or

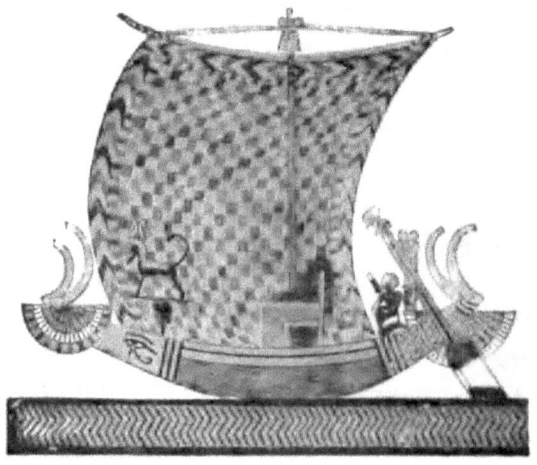

place the crowned asp upon his gilded rudders. Silken sails, ropes of gold, and inlaid cabin, are not uncommon. Some of these boats which wait upon

## The River of Egypt. 101

the king exceed two hundred feet from rudder to prow; and one troop barge at Thebes is double that length, and is said to carry seven thousand soldiers.

The exceeding beauty of the river shores is the admiration of strangers. The fragrant papyrus plants, thick as a man's arm, their summits crowned with flowers and feathery leaves, are not more useful to art than delightful to the eye. The thick foliage and white blossoms of shade trees, which half hide the portals of the temples, and the running vines which hang over their walls, take away their gloom without depriving them of their dignity. All about them are the ivy vines, sacred to Isis, and the peach-tree, sacred to Athor. Farther from the shore are broad reaches of purple lentils, yellow-blooming cotton-poppy, and white barley, with lilies, and crocuses, and the groves of palms between. At the foot of the distant gray hills, on the less valuable land, graze the herds, watched by dwarfs, and still beyond are the flocks, sheared twice a year. Here and there, through the ravines, is seen a caravan laden with wood from the oases, or sportsmen bringing home the hyenas. A reward is paid for these animals, because they are destructive to the fields.

Still closer by the shore the boys are driving away the birds with slings from the summer fruits, bringing the grapes to market in wicker baskets, or taking the hives of bees to the rafts, that they may find up or down the river the few honey-bearing flowers. The women are coming to the stream, graceful as Ruth or Rebecca, with jars upon their heads, chattering along the way like the swallows, which dart in and out their nests in the banks beside them. Sounds of lyres and flutes are heard in the summer-houses among the thickets, whose cool retreats the sun scarcely invades. A song answers from the lodge of reeds in the garden of cucumbers. The trumpet of the encampment announces that the day is almost ended. The cattle which drag the sled laden with stone are hurried at their task. The geese rise screaming from the pools, and draw their long ranks through the air. The too abundant wasps, and hornets, and wild bees, pass swiftly by. The dogs bay at the belated travelers. The creaking of the water-buckets dies away, and the sweeps stand ghostlike against the sky. The children no longer call to each other at play. The great portals of the temples grow somber. The distant hills are full of shadows. The crickets at length are still in the corn. The stars come out. The pelican and cormorant have dropped to sleep. The senegal doves and blue pigeons "fly like clouds to their windows." The lotus flower shuts its blossom, true to its god, the sun, and refuses to open till he appears again. Along the shore is seen the flicker of fires with groups of boatmen about them. These, in turn, disappear, and in all the crowded valley only the river itself moves on, breaking through the granite walls of Philae, the sandstone cliffs of Silsilis, past the limestone hills near Memphis. Everywhere, in palace, hut, or field, never weary in welldoing, it is at work refreshing the land after the burden and heat of the day.

The glory of the Nile is in her cities. We go sailing past Memphis and the long lines of pyramids which come up in the southern sky. Then we reach Heracleopolis, the seat of a royal family, just where the valley opens by Beni Hassan to the province of Fayoom. Vast grottoes here excite our wonder. From them Tothmes III. built a temple to the cat goddess Pasht. The quarry walls are full of pictures of stone-moving. Still beyond we come to alabaster quarries on the east. The city of Licopolis rises on the west. Then we reach the city of Chen, named perhaps for Ham, first of patriarchs and oldest of Egyptian divinities. The city of This now appears. Its many temples have figures of Rameses viewing the shields of his predecessors, which are ranged in two rows. The hills are full of the graves of those who are brought to their rest near the holy shrine of Osiris. Here is a broad cliff, broken into shadows by bold cornices and tablets, with reliefs of famous battles and triumphs where Hor-em-het, successor of Amumph IV., is seen riding down his enemies. Then he comes back from Ethiopia in triumph, borne on a platform by the strong shoulders of his guards, a lion standing by his side. So lofty is the cliff that the eagles seem like spots on the sky, hovering over their nests upon its face, or swinging in circles watching for prey.

Beyond this cliff the people are hunting the crocodile, saying that Typho, the god of evil, escaped in the form of this horrid monster. A strong hook, covered with bait, tempts him, or he appears on the sandbank to lay his eggs. He is killed with spears. Yet a little above this we find the crocodile worshiped. Tamed crocodiles are kept as emblems of the power and beneficence of the Nile, and hundreds of caves are filled with the bodies of old and young, carefully mummied by the priests.

Far on we journey, passing on either side the same busy scenes. Scarcely ever are we out of sight of temple towers, or beyond the din of city traffic. On every group of fields are the oven-shaped granaries, where the fruits of plentiful years are gathered. A procession with leathern sacks of grain is ever coming and going. The entrance always lies through a gateway not unlike a temple,

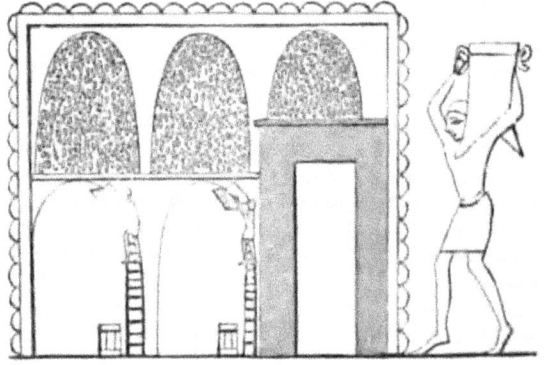

as if even here they would keep in grateful acknowledgment the service of the river god. The top of the granary is reached by a ladder. A trap-door receives the grain and serves as a ventilator. The grain will be removed from the bottom.

But all our wonder is lost in astonishment as our ship glides by the projecting angle of the Lybian range, and a great plain, the only plain of Upper Egypt, opens on either side for three miles. It is filled, from the eastern to the western hills, with the glory of great Thebes. This is the city of No Ammon, against which the prophets declared God's vengeance. Winged gateways, galleries of columns, and towers with the royal pennon flying, line the eastern bank for twelve thousand feet. This part of Thebes is occupied by the temple of Luxor, from which two broad avenues of sphinxes, wearing the ram's head, lead to the east. One ends at the funeral lake, and the other six thousand feet away, under the lifted gateway of Karnak.

At Karnak the impression of wonder is beyond all description. Here are statues of Rameses and Tothmes, forty feet high, obelisks over a hundred feet; forests of colonnades, vast roofing stones lifted eighty feet above the pavement; halls over three hundred feet long, full of figures in relief, portraits of kings, battle scenes and acts of worship; beside splendid thrones and noble apartments, hung with thick cloths. Yet this is a single temple in a city of temples. The grand hall bears the name of Tirhakah, a king too well known to Hezekiah. The light comes in upon its glories through the roof, which at the center is lifted on columns higher than their fellows. Here audience is given to embassadors. Here scribes take down the words which will afterward be graven on rose-tinted obelisks, or massive walls, that they may live forever.

Beyond the granite quays on the west bank the ways are alive with chariots, mule carriages, and palanquins, soldiers and workmen. For many miles of streets, whichever way we go, we mingle with the crowd, which finds something to admire: either colleges or palaces, sitting statues sixty feet high, or long, shady colonnades, warehouses or shops, painting or sculpture on the walls, vast grounds made smooth for games or review of the troops, bands of music, and bright processions of priests. But when we go beyond the western lake to the hills where the ground is dedicated to Athor, we find only the homes of the dead. The commerce which calls together the Greek from the Hellespont, the rich merchant from Phœnicia, the humble Ben Eben from Goshen, the son of Asshur from the Euphrates; which gathers spices, ores, goodly garments, and rare fruits from distant countries, through thirsty deserts, which even lays tribute on most distant India, finds no relief from the fate which overtakes all the living. The priests leave the halls of the Ramessid, Petumenah, Assasif, and all his attendants; the merchant his shop, the prince his ten nomes, the beggar his shady corner, and, among the ample galleries of these hills, is laid away by his fellows. Here he comes, careless of the brilliant gateways cut two inches deep with sacred writing, forgetful of gardens inclosed within spacious marble and porphyry colonnades. The best can keep only a grave.

Above Thebes we see the castle where tolls are collected by the governor of Hermonthis. Then, beyond, is Latopolis, where the fish Lato, and the goddess Neith, are worshiped.

From Edfoy to Asovan, sixty miles, there is scarcely room for a garden between river and mountain. Abydos and Tentyros are on the edge of the desert. Sharp cliffs and somber hills take the place of green banks.

At last Philae is reached, where rests Osiris, whose name must not be mentioned, the meekhearted "Lord of Lords." The quiet face of Isis

## The River of Egypt. 107

looks down from the columns as if waiting for her husband, "the unnamed and unnamable."

Still far on in the inner land the cliffs are hewn into the colossal form of Rameses. His battles and triumphs, his warriors and sons, with all their mighty acts, are cut on these pages of the rock. Within the mountain stand erect the figures of Ammon, the Supreme, and Phra, with arms on their breasts, as if holding up the everlasting hills. This was the work of Hag-an, afterward Rameses III. He thus cherished in exile the memory of his father. And when the Nahazos, the usurper, no longer kept him from his throne, he left this refuge of kings for his palace at Thebes. We have then passed beyond the bounds of Egypt.

These are but faintest shadows of the glow of life which brightens the Nile. The bright genius of this people seems to reflect its inspiration. The quiet flow of its waters is like the serious temper of the nation. The power of the river when a barrier is thrown before it is like the wrath of the Pharaohs, which has so often broken through the nations. The abundance of the stream is like the wisdom which goes forth from the mysterious depths of the colleges, quietly calling into life the innumerable forms of belief in a future life and the unseen land in the great fields of the world. If one thoughtfully travels upon this highway he will feel that no other river can be compared with it, unless in his love for his country an Israelite may think it resembles the Jordan. There are the same barren low ranges of hills running by its side. There are the same rich plains through which they find their winding paths to the sea. There is the same annual overflow. Both rivers have their cataracts. Both rivers glory in rich vegetation. But the Promised Land could

do very well without the bustling, noisy Jordan, on which no boat can find its way through its little journey. But the Nile boasts its many forms of usefulness in its long course to the sea. Whether these have been seen by captive kings, embassadors, or adventurers, this testimony has been given, that whatever Egypt is, or whatever light of wisdom she has displayed when the rest of the world was in darkness; whatever she has done for the development of the world, her splendor, and wealth, and power, her very soil, depends upon the bounty of the river. The river made and the river is still the life of Egypt.

# THE

# EGYPTIANS AT WORK.

## THE EGYPTIAN AT WORK.

Castes—The King—Priests—Soldiers—Farmers—Mechanics—Shepherds, and Brickmakers.

### I.

Every man in Egypt has his distinct place in society. This place, or caste, is determined by his occupation. The occupation of every man is just that which his fathers had before him.

In the higher ranks some change of place is possible. A priest may become an officer in the army. A scribe may become a judge. This, however, takes place without any interference with his rank in society. A priest would no more be permitted to become a farmer than a weaver of fine linen could become a courtier.

In the inferior classes of society there is a fixed place for every man. The seed basket, or boat, descends from father to son. The weaver leaves the loom to his children, and they put it in the hands of their children. The same house, and the same occupation, shut in the infancy and the old age of the Egyptian workman. His ancestors and his descendants follow one pursuit. At regular intervals every man appears before the magistrate and testifies to his means of subsistence. If he is untruthful, he is liable to be put to death.

By these severe rules undivided attention is secured

for each trade. Every man feels that his only hope of prosperity is in the excellence of his work. It is no wonder that the Egyptians are famous for all handicraft.

The ruling classes, by the same laws, hold the government securely in their hands. The king and his nobles do not fear any interference in their affairs from an industrious people. The nation seems to labor for the support of a few favored men. The bee is the emblem of the king, because Egypt is a social hive of obedient and hard-working people.

## II.

The representative of the great sun god, Ra, is the king. His name, Phrah, or Pha-ra-oh, continually reminds the people that he is a child of the deity who is the source of all life and joy. On every temple wall the king is seen, pouring out oil and wine, ordering the sacrifices, judging his rulers, and teaching his wise men, in the name of Ra. The gods alone give him the throne. The gods carry him away at death. The gods watch with deepest interest his children. To be able to touch the knees of the king, to sit and not prostrate one's self before him, and to wear one's sandals in the king's presence, are the greatest of honors. It is an approach to the gods themselves.

The king is the leader of the army. He is most terrible in battle. To him all the praise of conquest belongs. No one thinks of the poor brave man that gives his life for his master, but whole walls are covered with stories of the king's valor, or wisdom, or mercy. His generals and admirals may be cursed, but the king himself can do no wrong. "It is thou, O good warrior, who art the lord of armies. It is thou, O king of the great heart, who art foremost in the strife, doing battle for thy soldiers."

All young princes are carefully trained by the priests in the wisdom of the Egyptians. They learn how to measure ground, to calculate the movements of stars, to write the sacred language, and read from papyrus rolls the stories of past generations. They know the order and the meaning of the temple ritual, the offices of the gods, and the mysteries of the future life. During his father's life-time the prince who will receive the throne wears a lock of hair over the left ear, as a sign of his childhood. He carries a fan beside his father, attends to the royal granaries, or leads the cavalry and archers to battle. Only the children of priests or soldiers can attend a son of the king. The best food, most carefully prescribed, in order to prevent excess in eating, is set before him. His public duties and prayers begin at daybreak. He attends his father to the temple, and listens to the priests as they mingle the praise of the deities with the honors due the king for wisdom, self-command, justice, truthfulness, and, most of all, for generosity in building noble halls and temples. Then the prince hears the record of sins which have sometimes made the judges deny, even to kings, the right of honorable burial. He returns home to put these lessons in practice, giving audience to embassadors, settling difficult cases of law, reviewing the soldiers, or directing the industries of the country.

At the death of the king there is mourning for seventy days throughout the land. The temple gates are closed. No sacrifice is offered at the altars. Festivals are suspended. Wine and all delicacies are untouched. No hired mourners go about the streets, but the ways are full of processions, throwing dust on their heads, rending their garments, and chanting the sincere grief of this affectionate people. It is not till these days of mourning are ended, and the king rests in his tomb, that the cities resume their accustomed life of gayety.

## III.

The nobility of Egypt consists of priest and soldiers. From these ranks are chosen the councillors of state, the leaders of armies and navies, the governors of provinces, and the embassadors. In social life they may intermarry; but in their pursuits they are entirely separate.

The priests have charge of the temple service. They alone stand before the holy place clad in leopard skins, to offer resin to the rising sun, myrrh at noon, and kuphi in the evening. Their attendants and musicians, with harps, flutes, and guitars, are seated upon the ground. The king himself is, in some offices, a high priest, and often ministers before the altars. The queen is also seen leading the sacred dance, or conducting the chorus of the priestesses.

## The Egyptian at Work.

The learning of this wise people is carefully cherished by the priests. Whatever facts are known of the movement of the stars, their signs, eclipses, and relation to each other, is recorded in the temple

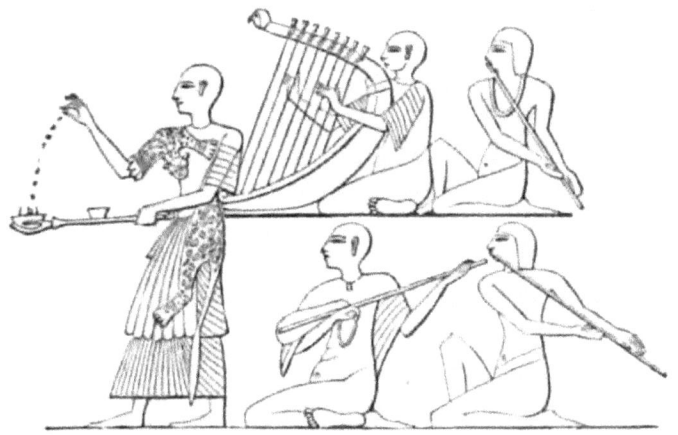

libraries. The priests also divine with curiously engraved bowls, and lamps, and with silver cups, as in the days of Joseph. By Isaiah they were called "charmers and men that had familiar spirits, wizards." In sickness they invoke the guardian spirit of that part of the body which is suffering, and as each member has its special physician, each priest-physician ministers at a special altar. The treatment of disease is, however, regulated by the books, and whoever departs from these directions is liable to be put to death, as he is held responsible for the condition of the patient. The physicians are supported by the public funds. The priest who fills teeth with gold, and he who mends a broken arm, he who cares for the lungs, and he who ministers to minds diseased, has every opportunity given him to perfect his knowledge by the examination of the bodies of the dead. He has at hand in the temple abundant balms and medicine.

The forty-two books of Hermes, the sacred writer, are the foundation of all libraries. They contain the wisdom of the past in rolls of papyrus twenty-eight feet long, having five hundred and fifteen columns, with thirty thousand characters. Much of the writing is in pictures. In such pictures the Hebrew letters probably had their origin. Beside these books, Cheops wrote on astronomy. Sethi I. had prepared charts of countries through which the troops marched, and plans of his Nubian gold mines. Menes wrote treatises on medicine, and Necho on astronomy. Histories of men and gods were added until, when the Persians entered Thebes, they found twenty thousand rolls of writings. It is evident that books must be numerous, since an exact account of public works is preserved, and revenues are recorded in all the detail of ponds paying in fish, lands in grain, marshes in cattle, and groves in various fruits. All cases of justice are conducted by written testimonies rather than with declamation, to prevent the play of sympathy. Decisions are also written, and, like every thing of public interest, are carefully saved.

The common people use signs sufficient for business in their shops and quarries. Many home-made writings are buried with the dead. The sacred language is kept a secret by the priests. The name for writing is the outline of a temple. Whatever has special interest will be copied from the ordinary language into more enduring characters of

## The Egyptian at Work. 117

this sacred text, and so be preserved. These books are sometimes models of style for the young priests; sometimes speeches to be learned for mental discipline. In the nineteenth dynasty, in a sort of psalm-like parallel, was written the experience of a soldier in the great wars of his day. I wish to depict to you the numberless troubles of an unfortunate officer of infantry:

While still quite a youth he is shut up in a barrack,
A tight suit of armor encases his body, the peak of his helmet
    comes over his eyes;
The visor is over his eyebrows, so that his head is protected from
    wounds;
He is wrapped up like a papyrus roll, and can hardly move his
    limbs in fight.
Shall I tell you of his expeditions into Syria, his marches in far
    distant lands?
He is obliged to carry water on his shoulder, as an ass bears its
    burden;
His back is bent like that of a beast of burden, his backbone is
    bowed.
When he has quenched his thirst with a drink of bad water, he is
    obliged to mount guard for the night.
If he meets the enemy, he is like a bird in a net, his limbs have
    no strength left.
When he returns to Egypt he is like a piece of worm-eaten wood;
If he is too ill to stand, they put him on the back of an ass.
His baggage is plundered by robbers, and his servant deserts
    him.

There are also religious romances, and volumes of law arranged for reference. Beside these we find reports from the chief of robbers, an officer recognized by the government. He restores stolen goods, when they are identified, for one quarter of their value. The business is so profitable that the regular robbers are well able to pay the expense of hunting down the irregulars, and delivering them to the state.

Memphis, Heliopolis, and Thebes furnish each thirty judges, who together form a priestly college. This noble body of select men care for the laws. The laws may be changed only by the chief priest of all Egypt. These judges are paid generously from the royal treasury. Many of their laws are most merciful. A plough cannot be taken for debt. No person can be seized for debt. Intemperance, perjury, false charges against the dead, and murder, are severely punished. The false accuser suffers the punishment he sought for the accused.

The judges wear, suspended from their necks, the image of Thmei, or "Justice and Truth," like the Thummim of the priest of Israel. This image is full of precious stones of different colors, and is used to touch those who are acquitted. By the record of the tribunal before which conspirators were brought in the reign of Rameses III., and the reports of the trial of the robbers who plundered the tombs in the days of his successor, these magistrates evidently do not bear the sword in vain. Spies have their tongues cut out, and murderers of their children are obliged to carry with them the dead body three days. The king alone can pardon one who murders a parent. The sentence for such crime is to be torn with sharp reeds, and burned on thorns. For severe punishment they cut off hands or feet. In the desert of Shur is a colony of criminals who have had their noses cut off. It is called the noseless city.

The priests have charge of building all the temples, since they are familiar with the wants of their order. Their training among the noblest works of art fit them for this labor. To them we trace the form of square pillars in the oldest temples, which imitated the piers of quarries within whose seclusion they first held the Mysteries. When they obtained larger resources they ran into a great variety of shafts and capitals, put gilding on purple bands, painted the shafts black and yellow, or red and blue, and stamped upon every building, whether it was a gateway and portico of a temple, or a playful summer house, the same style of sloping lines and reedlike mouldings. A delicate sense of fitness is seen in distributing the weights which rest on the capitals. The lines just curve enough along the walls to seem straight to the eye. Thus sphinxes and colossal statues, the columns, and the carving of foliage and faces, have a quiet and restful air which would seem impossible to obtain in such masses of stone.

The style of painting is kept by the priests within the limits of the most rigid rules. The figures make signs, not gestures. They have no feeling or sentiment. There is no unity of action. The parts of the figures might be exchanged in the groups at will. They stand straight before you, the faces always on one side. If many figures appear, they but cleverly multiply the first, and call it a group. They never think of variety. Yet the outlines are  grand, and simple. There is no doubt about the thought which they were designed to express. The freedom of the figures often found on the papyrus shows what they might do if only the laws would permit, and the ordinary panel painting is not without grace and spirit.

The discipline of the priests is severe. There are frequent days of fasting. Their beds are simple skins thrown on the floor, or on a wicker frame of palm branches. They are required so to regulate their diet "that the body may sit light upon the soul." Swine, sheep, peas, beans, leeks, onions, and garlic are forbidden, though onions may be offered to the gods. Twice during the day, and as often in the night, they must bathe in water tasted by the sacred ibis. Every third day they shave the head and the entire body. They wear on their feet only sandals of papyrus, and always dress in white linen.

The inferior orders of priests attend to music. To be "minstrel to Amun" is a title of great honor; but the ordinary musician, who uses maces, drums,

with bells, and cymbals, or joins in the chorus of the chant, has not great place or honor. There are vast numbers of these attendants, reminding one of the singing men of Solomon, the sons of Asaph, whose music was heard as far as Jericho when their voices blended with the hundred and twenty trumpets and harps.

Some priests keep the fragrant oils and ointments; others attend to the sacrifice, lead the sacred animals, carry the arks and images, arrange

## The Egyptian at Work. 121

the processions, keep the sacred robes, carry the sacred staffs or palm leaves, as signs of consecration, and the broad fans made of plumes and glittering with the gold of Meroe.

Women enjoy the service of the temple, and throngs of children take part in the service. The priestesses stand and cry from the temple porch, "All ye who are clean of hands and pure of heart come to the sacrifice." They carry about the streets in days of mourning the planteen and asphodel, whose blossoms are symbols of mourning.

The state pays all expenses of the temples, and demands no tribute of the priests. A third of the land is set aside for their support. As in Joseph's day, they may draw their supplies from the public granary. They are distinguished, even among Egyptians, by their serious, contemplative air.

The people believe that only the prayers of those who serve the temple find acceptance with the gods. They crowd to these holy places, where they see the priests eating the sacrifice of the altars, as a sign of reconciliation with the gods. They observe that these priests are blameless in life and conversation, rearing their families like other men. They therefore respect them as the key-bearers for good or ill of that door of Amenti, the unseen land, which all must enter. The gates of Osiris no man can shut if the priests bid them open, and no wealth or rank can open them if the priests forbid. Thus in religious affairs the priests are kingly in their power.

The king is himself a soldier. He is expected to lead the army in some campaign before he ascends the throne. If he can scatter an army of blue-eyed, golden-haired Ionni—the Javans of the Hebrews—and write on some far-off mountain, "It is I who have conquered this country by the strength of my arm," he is worthy of his throne.

Hardened by continual wars, the Egyptian has become the best of soldiers. His arms and discipline have gained many battles. With the chariots on the wings of the army, the light infantry in advance, the heavy-armed soldiers in the center, and his gods leading the way, he thinks he is invincible.

The soldiers of the Nile are far more merciful than the Assyrian. In the pictures of battles on the walls of Nineveh no cruelty seems too great, and after the strife prisoners are often cut to pieces and pierced with sharp stakes. The Egyptian saves those who lay down their arms, and sends them to the rear as prisoners. If the hands are cut off the bodies of the dead it is not from cruelty, but to witness before the scribes the number of the slain. In one of the naval fights of Rameses the ships and men on shore are represented as forgetting the battle to save the lives of their drowning enemies.

In peace each soldier receives six and a half pounds of bread, half as much weight of beef, and a quart of wine daily. He is allowed nine acres of land on which he does not pay any taxes. He cannot be arrested for debt. In return he is obliged to present himself, fully armed, at any time he is needed, for the field or garrison duty. His children are trained in military schools.

The character and position of the army shows us in what esteem the officers are held by the state.

## The Egyptian at Work. 123

One third of the land of Egypt is set apart for their support. They are as powerful in all affairs of this world as the priests are in those which relate to the unseen kingdom.

### V.

Just below the rank of priests and soldiers come the husbandmen. Great honor and no little state surrounds the brightly painted country-seats of those who keep the granaries of Egypt. The finest awnings, walls of brick and stone, towers and trellises, bear witness to the wealth and taste of the owners. The same fashions which invade the comfort of Thebes and Memphis rule here. The farmer, with his long train of servants, is a sort of  king. He may raise what he pleases, wheat, doora, or flax, so long as he pays tribute to the throne, which has owned the land since Joseph's day. Little clothing is needed, and the demand for food is not so severe here as in colder climates. The expense, therefore, of working the fields is light.

The cattle are well cared for if sick, and always sheltered during the inundation. They are usually driven to their stalls at night. Thus they were protected in part from hail and murrain during the plagues of Moses. Egyptian custom, as well as the Jewish law, commands that the oxen must not be muzzled when treading out the grain.

Vines are often trained on those trees which are cultivated for the carpenter's use. Other trees, raised for fruit, have their harvesting done by the

monkeys. The owner usually finds that his easy climbing servants look after their own interests, and make him spend much labor in saving a little trouble.

The sailors belong to the same general rank with the farmers. Many stories are told of the enterprise of these men of the Nile. One ship is said to have sailed by the great canal from the river to the Red Sea. Then the pilot steered southward past the copper mines, past the great ports which receive the Indian wares on their way to Thebes, until he found the shore on their right trending away westward. Again he pushed on till it ran northward. Three seasons they sowed and reaped on unknown shores, and took the harvests into their ship. At last the sun rose before them, and Ra seemed welcoming them home again. They recognized the dark waters of the slow-moving Nile, and set their well-worn sails to the familiar north wind. They had long since been given up by all their friends, for the sea is much dreaded, and Typhon, the evil genius, waits there, with storms and fearful winds, to destroy the sailors.

## VI.

The little shops of Egypt are hung like birdcages under awnings along the sides of the street. From these are sent forth the wares which are the envy of the world.

To walk from one quarter to another is a succession of surprises. Each quarter excels in some industry. Here are signet-rings, cut in fine-grained stones, so delicate that every edge and line appears to the eye perfect. Here is glass interwoven with delicate gold thread and bright colors, which hold their own through every pattern. Even delicate birds are copied in glass, scarcely an inch long, with all their plumage, and the very circle of the eye, perfect. Imitations of precious stones, glass beads, glass obelisks twelve inches high, glass gods arrayed in brilliant garments, red, yellow, and blue, are everywhere exposed for sale. They cover granite with glass, and even make glass which does not break though it falls upon stone. In vases the gold is sometimes placed between two glass surfaces, or rich colors are made to strike through the substance, and fragments of colored glass are joined together, though one cannot see how. Necklaces are made in the forms of fish, reptiles, and leaves. It was from these men the Israelites learned to engrave, in the wilderness, the "sardius, topaz, and carbuncle,"  and many other precious stones. And signets like the Assyrian rolls are cut in imitation of lion hunts and demons. We notice glass vessels which are filled with naphtha, and supplied with a floating wick. During the feast of Sais these lights shine upon every boat on the Nile. During all the night they seem like myriads of stars dropped down to witness the gladness of the people, while every column of the temple, and every cornice, answers with the same glimmer of lamps.

In working silver and gold this people leave all nations behind. They not only attempt borders  of various patterns, but work the forms of animals and foliage into baskets and vases. A fine appreciation of form and color seems quite their own. Had not a rigid law restrained the taste of the temple builders what might not architecture have become in Egypt?

The working of wood is also carried to great perfection. The tamarisks, and sycamore, and acacia of

their own country are greatly valued. Boxes, tables, doors, handles for tools, are made from them. But they are not satisfied without importing wood from the desert, from Syria, Ethiopia, and even Asia. Here is a table of ebony inlaid with ivory. A vine runs over one end. The royal basilisk is represented with sacred writing. Sacrificial joints are heaped on an altar, and an obelisk stands beside them. It will be used in the temple.

Often thin layers of costly woods, or pieces of carving, are fastened upon wood which is less expensive. In their love of rich furniture, common woods are painted to represent the woods of India or Asia.

Tongues and nails of hard wood are mostly depended upon for fastening boards, though fish glue is used. Axes, handsaws, wooden mallets, and chisels, planes, and a leathern nail bag, are the outfit of the carpenters. A stone is used in polishing. A drill is used for making holes. Covers of boxes and window shutters are made to slide in perfect grooves. The panels of houses are carved and painted with great animation, often with the figures of animals in profile, or gardens full of flowers.

But of all the work of the carpenters nothing is more entirely Egyptian than the inlaid harps which delight the court, and are heard in all the length of the land. The royal harper uses an instrument which perhaps better than any one thing beside represents the ingenuity and taste of the nation.

Many light and strong seats are made without braces, so firmly are the legs glued into the frame. A handsome pillow of painted cotton, or stamped leather, with a border of gold and silver tissue, or a lion's skin with the hair upon it, is used for a cushion. The corners are often fastened together and ornamented with metal plates. Sometimes the chair folds together, and is carried by a servant.

The ship-builders are a separate class. They nicely fit the boards which make the sides of the ship, fastening them with wooden pins. Acacia wood is mostly used, as it remains long unharmed by water.

The carpenters also build bridges for the canals. The two-wheeled carriages, decorated with colored leather, or leopard and fox skins, are drawn by oxen, and called Plaustrum. They make curious ends of cornices, carving them into the heads of birds and crocodiles. They also build sledges for bringing home such large game from the desert as wild oxen and wolves. The cooper supplies wooden measures for grain. Each branch of the business belongs to one set of men. Others are forbidden to interfere with it in any way.

The looms of the Egyptians, especially of the city of Chemmis, sent the finest of linen and woolen cloths to Solomon. Yet long before that day Egyptian linen was found in every household of the civilized world. The cool, clean linen tunic, fringed and knotted below the knee, called the calasiris, and the outer white woolen garment, were woven in every variety of pattern. But woolen seems rather for the streets. No one can be buried in woolen wrappings, or enter the temple with a woolen cloak. Cotton is also woven in upright or horizontal looms, five hundred and forty threads in a square the length of one finger. It is used much for coverings of chairs and beds. Strong bands, one or two inches broad are sewed on the edges of large pieces of cloth, to give them strength. These borders are often made of seven blue lines, with white or fawn color between. The threads are colored before the weaving, as we learn the women of Israel were accustomed to do in the desert. The eye can hardly follow the unbroken twisted linen through all the small figures in the cloth. They call the best work of their looms "woven mist."

They boast flax nets covering many feet of ground, which can be drawn easily through a finger ring. One man, they say, can carry a net which will cover a hundred palms. How grandly they embroider, the story of the tabernacle hangings, and Aaron's priestly robe, may well remind us. Gold and silver thread is in common use for such purposes.

The finest of the work is intrusted to men, though the wooden spindle, loaded with clay, is always in the hands of women. This spindle is often made of rushes with a loop in one end for securing the thread after winding. The men beat flax with mallets, and after the whole is softened draw out the fiber with hooks. After weaving, wooden rods are passed to and fro, and great weights give the cloth a shining surface. An uneven surface is obtained by depressions in the presses. Ropes are also made of linen, though more often of leather cut round and round the hide.

But in many respects the skill of the Egyptians who work in metals is most wonderful. The fine elastic bronze tools, which cut the hardest granite into delicate etchings, the coats of armor made of fine pieces of bronze like the scales of a fish, the swords and spears, are all wonders of art. The iron and tin which Moses took in the Midianitish spoils he had learned of these masters how to use. He had even learned how to turn gold to powder, or beat it into a leaf for overlaying the ark.

The people of Israel suffered even more in the mines under the Red Sea, and in the deserts and mountains of Sinai, than in the brick-fields. The Egyptian ladies were shining in the splendor of gold chains and ornaments, while the iron chains of these captives were eating their flesh day and night. Cruel taskmasters were over them. The prisoner was made to pound and wash the hard stone, break the ground with chisels and picks, and burn it in the fire, to make the vessels of the Egyptian feast more bright and beautiful. Their life was only a lingering death. Many of them without so much as a rag to cover them were painted a different color from the stone, that they might more easily be watched, and were then driven sick and weary into dark windings of the rock-cut chambers. Here the roofs were always liable to fall. A feeble light glimmered on their foreheads, in mockery of the sun their taskmasters gloried in. There the caves echoed their prayers, and the blows and curses of the overseers. How strange the contrast when these same hills trembled at the coming of the God of Israel. The nation so lately slaves were here made to feel that ten thousand angels ministered unto them. The rocks became for them rivers of water, and angels reaped for them harvests of manna from the unseen fields, while their Egyptian masters were mourning and groping in the tombs.

Every-where in the streets of the cities, and the

porches of the large houses, are scribes, who write petitions or receive accounts. They sit upon the ground with their writing-cases before them, their

reed pens in hand, and their bottles of red and blue ink before them. There are often two scribes writing at the same time, that the truth may be better known by comparing the separate accounts. The poorer classes hold them in great respect for their mysterious art of talking in silence, and in their presence put their left hand to their mouths as a sign of reverence.

It is interesting to see how many ways men find in the pursuit of a living. Some carry scales to weigh the drugs, or grain, or lambs, or poultry. A notary accompanies them to give the exact amount on a piece of papyrus. If they deceive, their right hands are cut off in punishment.

Some have mortars of stone, in which they will pound for a trifle the salt or seeds. Others go about repairing leather bottles, or making straps. A skin of dressed leather, a few threads of palm fiber, a stone for pounding seams, is at the same time their stock in trade and the sign of their business. The butchers wear a round steel in their apron for sharpening their knives. Menders of dishes carry bellows of goat-skins and a pot of coals. Armorers will hammer broken scales of breast-plates together, or mend knives. The justice, with an ostrich feather in his hand, tries small cases and hears appeals. The guilty men are beaten with rods on the soles of the feet, the women on their shoulders. Greater criminals are seized, and their hands are fastened together by oval frames.

Blind musicians take up their stand, and torment the passing crowd with flutes made of ivory and bound with bronze, or with pipes having four holes. Women and men with tambourines go dancing and waving green boughs, as in Judea, on their way to the tomb.

Hunters are leading dogs to the game preserves followed by their masters, who are dressed in tight clothes of 'dull colors. Others are leading the way for ambitious sportsmen, who ride in chariots with war-bows and metal-headed arrows in the quiver, to kill the Nubian lions. Others are quite content to stretch nets across narrow ravines, where they will drive the deer and gazelles, wild goats and sheep, or entangle the hyena, who devours the crops. Some go about carrying in wicker baskets ostrich eggs and plumes. Some have tame cranes and monkeys for sale. Some let out their wit for a price. They are decked in clothes of hide, and have tags at the elbows, to make cheap sport for the rich. Some collect eggs, which they will hatch in vaulted ovens nine feet high. Here, upon layers of bran, the eggs receive the heat of fires, and in eighteen or twenty days two thirds will be hatched and chirping. Some care for those unclean animals, the swine.

## VII.

Far below all these in rank are the brick-makers and shepherds. The shepherds are spoken of as "disgraceful men." The word shepherd signifies "disgrace." His life is protected, since he is useful to the state, but he can never own the land on which his flocks graze, or seek a more honorable pursuit. The priests teach him that only by his industry can he hope for happiness in another life, and it ought to be his pleasure here to labor for the king and his officers. They are unshaven, clad, like the oxen, in matting, live on coarse food others despise, are often deformed, and, what is considered worse, since they cannot afford the cheapest wig, must wear their own hair! If they fail to account for every sheep or goslin, every antelope in the herd, or egg in the nest, they receive no mercy. They cannot bear arms, learn a trade, or enter a temple. They are an abomination to the Egyptians, and scarcely recognized as human beings. No names of ancestors appear on their graves.

The brick-makers are also banished from society to the slimy fields and marshes. Walls of houses, cities, and palaces, temple inclosures and highways, are built of bricks. The demand for bricks is immense. Wars are sometimes undertaken to secure slaves for the

## The Egyptian at Work. 135

brick-fields. Whole villages are transported. It is evident by the lighter color of those brick-makers who are represented on the walls, and by their beards, that they were captives, not Egyptians. Nor do we see any Egyptian, except it be a criminal, employed in these tasks. A board shapes the bricks, a basket carries the clay. A rude hoe breaks the ground.  A stamp places the mark of the king on them, for brick-making is the king's monopoly. A scanty cloth is gathered about the loins, and a cap protects the head from the sun. Bending under the weight of bricks, beaten by the taskmasters, slipping in the slimy pools, the life of the brick-maker is always made miserable.

No king ever exceeded Rameses II. in his passion for building. He was the grand shoterim or master. While he swept with gorgeous robes and splendid retinue, with standards of plumes, into the temples, to thank the gods for making him so merciful and just and generous in his offerings of the golden wine of Lebanon and honey of Syria, the marshes of Goshen were full of suffering, dying men, crying to God for vengeance. No wonder his favorite throne is supported by figures of captives, wearing beards, with ropes about their necks. But these eastern captives were not left to their own weakness. The rod of a hated shepherd from Midian breaks the scepter of proud Rameses. His throne is humbled into the dust by the God of the brickmakers. The first became last, and the last first, in the eyes of the nations. The throne passed away from the thoughts of the world, but the sufferings of God's people prepared them to rule by their influence in the gates of their enemies, and of such a kingdom there is no end. Indeed, the greatest interest which clings to the throne of Rameses is gained by sympathy with those whom he despised and oppressed. The basest of people to the Egyptians was the chosen nation of Israel.

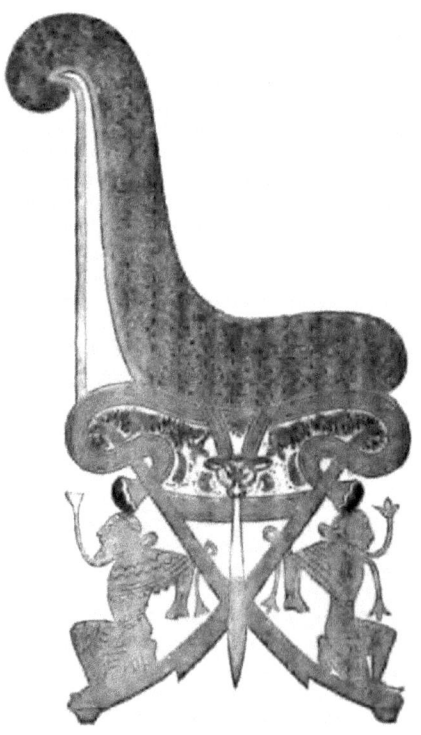

# THE

# RELIGION OF EGYPT.

## THE RELIGION OF EGYPT.

Religion claims the first place—Whence it came—The Gods—Sacred Animals—Sacrifices—Resemblance to the Institutions of Moses—Reason in it—A Fete Day.

### I.

THE Egyptian is in earnest when his thoughts turn to the gods. A serious spirit dwells in his solemn temples. A deep faith in the truths which are here taught has kept loyal the best service of the best minds in the land. The nation is entirely devoted to religion.

The king himself is the high priest, like Melchisedek and David. Yet the monuments represent him, when clad simply as a king, hastening into the temples, led by inferior priests. His hands are then laden with sacrificial flowers and fruits, as if he were no more than his princes, and less than the priests. His office as chief in the temple is the true dignity which gives Pharaoh authority with his people. It is because the throne stands in the shadow of the altar that men revere him as the visible Osiris.

The prosperity of the nation is believed to have had its rise in the days when the gods reigned. Though now invisible, they are still watchful. Nothing whatever, then, must be done to displease them. Every part of the Government in its relations to foreign nations and home rule is administered in reference to the good pleasure of these unseen allies. The arts and sciences are kept within the influence of sacred rites, and go forth every-where to carry with them the story of obligation to the gods. All days of rest are holy days. All processions are led by priests. The people are never out of sight of religious symbols and buildings.

## II.

The priests believe that the solemn rites of religion, and the truths they represent, as well as the names and offices of the gods, have never been changed. In the gray dawn of the world were established the festivals they now observe. The same overshadowing wings which we see were upon the

temple walls, and the same swift-moving, quiet spirit of light which enlightens us, was brooding over the nation when the gods dwelt among men. The same form of ark and the cherubim was borne through the streets which is now seen in the avenues of Thebes and Memphis. Religion has no story of change.

They even claim to have given to other nations their symbols. They say that long before Assyria

## The Religion of Egypt. 141

used its winged globe the Egyptians reverenced the same form. No one, they add, can see the sphinx

of Egypt without being reminded of the Assyrian image, which has the head of a man, the wings of an eagle, and the body of a lion. It may be a mere

fancy of the priests, but at least it shows their confidence in the antiquity of their own religion.

It would seem that in the day when Abram came into Egypt there were no idols. In the books of Moses Pharaoh uses the name of the one God, as if the sum of all religion was the reverence paid to this jealous divinity. Certainly the earliest temples had not upon them the likeness of any thing on earth or in heaven. They had no figures of gods and goddesses, nor worship of kings. The revelation which God made to Ham was undisturbed. There are pictures in the tombs of many slaves like Hagar, many flocks and herds, and all the order of government, which we should expect from the record in Genesis, but no idols. The number seven was sacred as a reminder of that primeval day in which the Creator rested. Indeed, the Egyptian week had always seven days. Evil was then but a darker shade of good, the night which brought rest after the day, the winter after the summer. For many ages evil was not considered the fruit of sin. Seth and Typho, Good and Evil, were represented together pouring consecrating oil upon the king, not in order that he should or because he must sin. The king cannot sin. But they knew how necessary it is that trouble or evil should go with prosperity in the forming of a well-developed kingly character. They even represent Typho instructing the king in the use of the bow, "teaching his hands to war, and his fingers to fight."

In what way came these lines upon lines, precepts upon precepts, to be engraven on every temple? How did the unseen God yield his throne to false deities?

It may be that Menes, the god and king, was Mizraim, grandson of Noah. Men revered, and soon worshiped, him as founder of the race. The more the nation went on, the greater seemed the number of those who were about the throne of Menes. In the mists of tradition, they seemed something more than human. They still call those who have departed Osirian, or godlike. It was easy to think thus of Menes. Horeb became the "mount of God" as Moses speaks of it, a place still sacred to the one God, and the gathering-place of all tribes from Ethiopia to Syria. Thus the places, like the men who made them holy by their presence, passed from ordinary associations and became divine. Soon after, in the desire for a visible deity, men began to worship the manifestations of the divine nature. The creature became more than the Creator, and as these forms of God's energy were innumerable men gradually lost the sense of his unity.

## III.

First, and most natural of all objects of love, was the ever-bright and glad sun. It was not to them a servant of God, shedding abroad the light and love of its master, but a visible god in the heavens. Some wise men like Job saw that this would lead them to iniquity, and so their hearts "were not secretly enticed, nor did their mouth kiss their hands to it when it shined." But others believed that in each of its different stages the sun was divided into as many gods. There is One, said the priests, who is "sole Generator in heaven and earth, who made all things, and is not himself made, but this sun is a separate deity with many manifestations." At high, triumphant noon he is Ra, at night he is Atum, or, as "producer of life," he is Kleper.

The hemisphere lighted by the setting sun is called Hathor, or Athor. She is represented by the symbol of a white cow with the sun between her horns. Ra nightly descends to her, and when morning appears he comes forth as her child. Ra now has renewed his youth, and is prepared to run his race. He is called the child Horus. His symbol is a boy on a lotus flower, which spreads its blossoms over the sacred lake. The cow, too, has changed her name, and becomes deified as Nub. She seems not unlike Neith, or Netpe, "the abyss and queen of heaven, the lady of dance and mirth, the universal mother of rejoicing earth." Her temples are all over the land. Her name signifies "I came from myself." At her great feast they yearly perform the mystery of Osiris in his death and resurrection. The lake in the temple inclosure bears the sacred boat of Isis, who, after long search, proclaims "The god is found." The over-arching heavens, full of stars, are but the garments, brilliant with precious stones, which are worn by this mother of the gods. Our best joys, they say, spring from darkness and sorrow, as the day from the night.

The sun under the earth is Osiris. His companions are the twelve hours, led on by Horus, son of Osiris. The employment of Osiris is to guide departed souls through the time between their departing from the world and their rising. He brings them on part way in his boat. He opens many gates, and finally Horus, his son, pierces with his spear Apep, or Apophis, the great serpent, the evil

## The Religion of Egypt. 145

one, as the rising sun pierces the mists with his rays. Then the day has returned. At his coming again Ra wears the serpent in his crown, as emblem of this final and severest contest with evil.

This Ra, or Phra, is worshiped in human form, with a hawk's head. The monarch is called Si-ra, child of the sun, represented by the sun's disc, and the goose, emblem of sonship. The word for king is derived from Ra, and who can forget the word Pha-ra-oh, the serpent and the sun, with the hawk wearing the crown of Upper and Lower Egypt. The name Osiris is never given to the living.

The father of Osiris, of "Ra in darkness," is represented as a divine breath animating nature. The gentle mist is his symbol. Did this worship spring from the high reverence in which the sons of Mizraim held that patriarch Noah? Was the ark that outlived the deluge the prototype of the sacred boat of this deity? Num, or Phtah, or Chunphis, the creative energy, gave life to the mother of the gods—as out of chaos sprang the earth. Perhaps he signifies water. At least his is the oldest name, and is spoken of as "the spirit without beginning or end." His symbol in the temples is the sun with overshadowing wings. Every one, as he entered the presence of the gods, could not fail as he looked upward to see this deity, who bears healing in his beams.

Num in Upper Egypt is called Kneph, and is represented in human shape with the head of a ram. This is the sphinx which is every-where seen in Thebes. Sometimes he is represented at a potter's wheel, fashioning the swiftly-turning clay into Osiris. The priests say that Chons desired to behold him, but was a long time denied the privilege. At last

the god clothed himself with the fleece and head of the ram just sacrificed, and so, hiding part of his glory, made himself known. To celebrate this revelation the king yearly at Thebes leads forth from the temples on the eastern bank of the Nile to those upon the west the gorgeous Naos, or ark, of this god, with the consecrated vessels. On their return they slay a ram, and having put the fleece upon the image of Kneph, bring to it an image of Chons, or Hercules. This story may be the dim suggestion of the glory of God, which no man is yet prepared to look upon in its splendor and live, but which may be seen, as it were, half hidden in the rites of sacrifice.

This same god is sometimes called in Thebes Amun, or Amun-Ra, king of gods, and is represented with the figure of a man seated on a throne, wearing two long feathers, and carrying the emblems of life and stability, a cross and a staff. It was from this name that Thebes derived its title of "No Amun." It may be that Amun represents the divine mind in operation, and wears a human form, since that is the highest expression we can have of God's work. Even when Amun is represented as moving over the waters he stands in his boat in the form of a man, and the asp, emblem alike of royalty and goodness,

## The Religion of Egypt. 147

spreads itself over him as a canopy. The use of the sacred boat for the gods is almost universal.

In Lower Egypt the supreme deity was Phtah, who must be some form of Ra, since he is represented as the father of all, fashioning all things by fire, or shaping them upon a potter's wheel. The kings of the Memphis dynasty called themselves his sons, and adored him as their lord. He is generally represented with his hands and feet half released from the bandages of a mummy. This may signify the first putting forth of creative power, or suggest that death cannot quite extinguish life.

The most human of all the gods, as well as the most exalted, are the three, Osiris, Isis, and Horus. This is the holy triad of all Egypt.

Each province or nome has its special divinities, whose positions in the mysterious court of Osiris are determined by the importance of its chief city. Every village, however, pays honor to Osiris, Isis, and Horus.

Isis has ten thousand names, as the priests say, and each represents some peculiar office. She is to be seen every-where. Her mother, Neith, is painted on the ceiling of the temple porches, inclosing the whole sky in her arms. Within her embrace moves the moon and stars. A similar idea of this all-inclosing being in the form of a serpent is seen on the ceilings at Nineveh. Neith is also seen as a human figure, pouring the water of life upon the souls of men from the branches of a sycamore-tree. The temple of Neith at Sais is the greatest in Egypt, and is open to the sky. It bears the inscription, "I am that was and is to be. No man hath lifted my vail. The first I brought forth is the sun." With so vague an origin Isis can hardly be expected to perform very distinct offices. Yet no goddess occupies so peculiar a place in the affections of the people. She is every-where the type of womanhood.

She is confused in later reigns with Astarte of Assyria. In both we see a female standing upon a lion. The Egyptian has two snakes and a flower, the stalks of which are twisted into the form of a ring. The Assyrian carries a ring alone, and is called Chiun by Amos. But the Scriptures have no words of severity for Isis. So far as she was an idol she was condemned; but no impure rites attended her service, and

## The Religion of Egypt. 149

the influence of her character was all for good. Her name suggested the fidelity and undying love of a wife to her husband, and their mutual love, which conquers all the enemies of life and happiness. The names which are given, and the stories which the priests tell, are all in her honor.

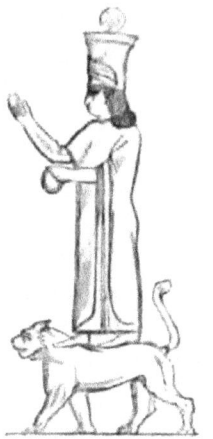

Every thing men loved in the earth about them, and the heavens above, were united in the character of Osiris. It is even said that he became king of Egypt, and taught the people how to care for the ground, and how to recognize the stars in their procession through the sky. Going abroad to extend his kindly kingly arts, his brother Typhon, or Seth the giant, the principle of evil, ascended the throne. When Osiris returned he was murdered, cast into a chest, and thrown into the Nile. Isis, his wife, was at Coptes when the messengers brought the tidings. She put on mourning, cut off her hair, and, attended by the jackal-headed god of the dead, Anubis, set

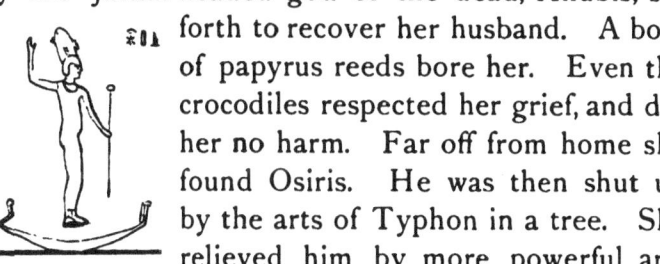

forth to recover her husband. A boat of papyrus reeds bore her. Even the crocodiles respected her grief, and did her no harm. Far off from home she found Osiris. He was then shut up by the arts of Typhon in a tree. She relieved him by more powerful arts than evil knew, for good, after all, is stronger than evil, and "Osiris was found." Their son Horus is represented by a house in the sacred writing. The homes of the people rejoiced in the care of these three deities. Every city claimed to be the scene of some act in this journey. When the new moon came up with a peculiarly bright star above it, they believed it to be Isis in her boat, still searching for Osiris. The dogstar was made sacred to her.

Horus was the last of the gods who blessed the throne. He wore the hawk's head of Ra. After him life became sacred, and mortals were able to reign, so lasting is the power of goodness.

Some say this story of the death and return of Osiris represents the receding waters of the Nile and their returning again. Their child is the spring, when the lotus flower, on which the young Horus is supposed to rest, blooms in the lakes. Others think it the diminishing of the sun's power when the November days have come, and with them the splendor of field and farm. Others still see in the story the representation of the constant strife between Typhon, or desolation, who robs the fields of life-sustaining moisture, and Osiris, or fertility, who regains his fields, and clothes them in living green.

With peculiar comfort those who have lost friends paint this tale both upon the bandages which cover the dead, and also upon the chests in which they lie. Especially when in the days of Solomon the belief in evil spirits increased, and the unseen world became full of terrors, they loved to think of Isis as the all-powerful queen. The walls of the Babylonians, with whom they are now brought in contact, are full of these tales of angelic strife with swords and daggers. The people of Israel had many a similar legend, like that of Michael, the archangel,

## The Religion of Egypt. 151

contending for the body of Moses. The Egyptians are continually gathering new impressions of the terrors which attend death, and turn for hope to the gentle face of Isis, which becomes each generation more frequent upon the temples and tombs.

Osiris is often represented with a whip, or flail, such as the kings carry, in his right hand, and a crook in the left. It would seem that he has more need of punishing than guiding. His crown is like the crown of Upper Egypt. His lower limbs are bound together as if he were still in the grave. His sisters, Isis and Nephthys, which may represent the companionship of the good, are still with him. They protect him with wings like cherubim, or they carry the sign of life, and admonish him not to fear. They always have the ostrich feather of truth, since truth is the best portion, whether it bring with it joy or sorrow. Soon Osiris will rise and wear the hawk's head, and be known among men again by the red disk of the sun. The king presents him ears of wheat, cut with a golden sickle, since it is Osiris who gives the newly-risen corn to the old fields.

There are hosts of other gods. Some native, some foreign, some brought in by compliment in treaties, some by conquest; but these are less known, and less honored. Every nome or division of country worship a triad of gods, who were believed to have a peculiar care of the name and its principal city. These gods are without history or adventures. They have no personal character, though they are greatly diversified in attribute and name. They are like spirits, to be feared and not known. The only human tie they recognize is that of parents and child. This seems to be the hold they gain upon the sympathy of the people. Whatever other apartments are built in honor of these triads, every temple has its birth-chamber. A child is ever the hope of the world. There is no god in Egypt, save Num,

## The Religion of Egypt. 153

whose parents are not known, and no goddess who has not carried a child in her arms.

Chons, son of Amun and Ament, represents the strength of the great god. He often attends Ra in his boat, as he sails round the world. He is confined in bandages like Phthah, and, like Egyptian princes and children of the gods, wears a long lock of hair over the left ear. At times he has the head of a hawk, upon which is the moon, as if some forms of sickness connected with the moon were overcome by him. He is called the "champion," the "Terrifier of Demons," and at Karnak is described on one of the walls as sent on a journey to deliver a foreign princess from an evil spirit. This is the inscription: His majesty Rameses XII. having gone to Naharina, the chiefs of each province prostrate themselves before him, and natives of lower rank, stooping beneath burdens of gold, of lapis lazuli, of copper and precious woods, draw near to lay them at his feet.

The king of Bouchten solicits peace. He brings his eldest daughter, young and handsome. She captivates the heart of Rameses. He gives her the title of Great Queen and the name of Ra-Neferu, and conducts her with solemn pomp into Egypt.

In the fifteenth year of his reign Rameses was celebrating, at Thebes, the mistress of the nations, the grand panegyric of his father, Amun, the sun, the distributer of thrones. Behold, a messenger of the king of Bouchten, with rich presents.

The envoy salutes the king, "Glory to thee, O sun of nine peoples; grant us the breath of life." Then, prostrating himself, he added, "The king, my master, sends me to thy Holiness because a secret malady consumes the sister of Queen Ra-Neferu: Wilt thou deign to send her one of these men around thee who know all things?"

The king called the sacred teachers of mysteries, the college of philosophers, and the doctors skilled in healing. "I have summoned you to hear and to obey. Point me one of you who is firmest of heart, quickest in understanding, most skilful of hand."

The scribe of sacred writings, Toth-em-hebi, bowed before the king, and was sent. But when he reached Bouchten he found himself inferior, and dared not enter the contest with the spirit which beset Bentenrest, sister of Queen Ra-Neferu.

Then the king of Bouchten sent, saying, "Sovereign lord! O, my master! deign to send a god."

Then his holiness, still at Thebes, prayed in the temple of Chons, "O, my beneficent Lord! I come to thee in behalf of the daughter of the king of Bouchten. If thou wilt command, I will cause Chonsou to be borne thither, endowed with thy divine power."

The patron of Thebes gave consent. Four times over he imparted a portion of his divine virtue to the god Khonson — Pa-ar-secher. Inclosed in a splendid ark, and placed upon a grand boat, and this upon a broad car, the god journeyed to Bouchten, escorted by many horsemen, riding on the right and on the left.

When, at the end of a year and five months, the god Khonson—Pa-ar-secher—arrived in the country, the king of Bouchten, with chieftains and soldiers, came forth to meet it, and, prostrating himself before the sacred boat, cried aloud, with his forehead in the dust, "Hail to thee who cometh to us by order of the king Rameses."

When the god came where the princess was, the spirit that beset her humbly cried, "Welcome to thee, mighty god, conqueror of those who rebel. The strong city of Bouchten is thy domain. Its inhabitants bow before thee. I am thy slave. I shall be no hinderance to the purpose of thy journey. I shall return whence I came. Only command the king of Bouchten to sacrifice in my honor."

Then Khonsou-Pa-ar-scher of Thebes said graciously to his prophet, "Let the King of Bouchten make a sacrifice honorable to this spirit."

The god Kohnsou and the spirit were thus talking together. The king, trembling in the midst of his soldiers, obeyed with rich offerings, and his daughter was instantly cured. Then the king, seized with great delight, said, 'I will not let the god go back to Egypt.' At the end of three years and nine months, the king, lying in his bed, saw the god leaving his ark, in the form of a golden sparrow-hawk, and extending his wings to fly toward Egypt. The king, awaking, was seized with inward sickness. He called the priest of Chons, and said, 'Make the car ready. Leave quickly.' So this god returned to his temple in peace, with numerous and costly presents, in the year thirty-three, on the nineteenth day of Mechir, of the King Rameses II., reigning eternally like the sun."

It was just before the journey of this ark of Khonsou that the ark of Israel returned from its exile in Philistea. With what contrast do the two stories come to us. The ark of the covenant was not allowed a single painting. Two figures of cherubim hovered over it. No army attended it. No chariots or horsemen were its escort. Kings did not fear at its coming. It was put away, with other trophies, in the temple of Dagon. But death went forth from that plain ark of shittim-wood, and the King of kings did it honor.

Thoth, son of Kneph, is god of the moon. His emblem is the ibis, whose black and silvery-white feathers suggest that luminary. The legs of the bird, with the perch on which he rests, form a triangle, and this triangle stands for his name in sacred writing. Wearing the head of an ibis, having a human figure, he attends the gods as a scribe, with his tablet, or roll of papyrus, in hand. (See page 194.) At times he wears the crescent of the moon. He is the god of letters, the teacher of astronomy, of music, and sacred worship. The lyre of three strings was his invention. He knows all languages, and is therefore the messenger of the gods. His wife, Saf, is "mistress of the writings, and president of letters." He is represented sometimes by a dog-faced ape.

Ma, or Thmei, is goddess of truth, a daughter of Ra. Her sign is an ostrich feather. Her image, with or without wings, having her eyes blinded as a sign of impartiality, is often held in the hands of the kings, who wear the title "Beloved of truth." The chief judge has such an image suspended from his neck by a golden chain. He touches the successful party with this in token of truth, saying by the gesture this judgment I give for you is of the mind, not of the sight, and is therefore true.

A similar emblem of the high priest of the Hebrews was called Thummin, "two truths." The Egyptians believe that the dead carry her feather as a sign of peace and of justification.

Beside these forms of god, or these gods, as they seem to the people, is Anouke, goddess of home and purity; Sabak, the crocodile-headed god of Ombos; Tefnu, daughter of Ra, with the head of a cat, or lioness; Pasht, avenger of crimes; Month, the terrible sun, shooting arrows of death; and a thousand others. Every day of the year and hour of the day, as well as every part of the heavens or earth, has its god. So completely is one surrounded by these beings that the mind becomes confused and helpless, and knows not what way to turn. Wise men from all parts of the world gather to study these mysteries, and meditate on the first cause, "the hidden" first principle, Amun or Kneph. How gloriously does this God, the only living God, creating alone heavens and earth, shine forth in his word given by Moses! Egyptian gods, save Osiris, may be to the priests mere ideas. It is likely that they are, since they exchange places, and powers, and names, so easily. Parents become children, and wives husbands, in different parts of Egypt. But to the people they are each different and true gods. It is for their sakes that the priests ought to rend the vail of secrecy, and destroy the idols.

## IV.

The love for symbols, which is the very soul of the religion of Egypt, carries the people still farther away from the simplicity of truth. They will not permit hideous forms, of shapeless wood and stone, to represent to them the attributes of their gods; but they consider living animals as the incarnation of deity and objects of worship. The priests, in the characters of such deities, wear the masks of crocodiles, and serpents, and birds. The king who leads the stranger through the magnificent temples reserves for the last the spectacle of the guardian deity! He advances with solemn air, chanting a hymn. He respectfully raises a splendid curtain, and lo! this god is some ibis or crocodile, wearing golden bracelets; or hawk, in his gilded cage; or cat, or ape! When these animals die they will be embalmed, and buried with every sign of sorrow. The same animal is often adored and killed in neighboring cities. The hippopotamus, sacred to the god of war in one place, is esteemed the evil spirit in another. At Hermopolis the ibis is a god. But at Brebastis, where the cat is worshiped, the ibis is killed. At Thebes the crocodile

## The Religion of Egypt. 159

is a deity, but at Hermopolis he is hunted and eaten in defiance, and at Elephantine all join in a yearly hunt to exterminate him. One city will often capture in derision the animals sacred to a neighboring city, and throw their dead before their rival's temple. Bloody fights sometimes result from this. One animal may be sacred, and not every one of his species. To kill a sacred animal, even by accident, is to be put to death. It often happens that great men maintain in their houses these creatures with the utmost devotion, and carry them, at death, embalmed with great cost, to the city where they are worshiped.

Three animals are most celebrated in Egypt as the very deity in the flesh. At Heliopolis the calf Mnevis is worshiped. 

His images, made of bronze or gold, are often covered with the wings of the great god Ra. The disk and serpent of Ra shine between his horns. His very name upon the walls of the temple is composed of the sun's disk, the vase of incense, sign of life, the wings of the good genius, the figure of the calf himself, with the emblems of honor and stability.

At Memphis similar honors are paid to the bull Apis, as the living form of Phtah, or Osiris. This bull is believed to be born of the lightning. When one such god dies in the order of nature, or by the command of the high priest, he is embalmed with magnificence, and buried in a coffin of black marble. The nation is in mourning. With every demonstration of grief he is drawn on a sled to the tombs, and laid aside in a truly regal sepulchre, twenty feet square, in galleries thousands of feet long. A successor is then sought. He must have a white triangle on his forehead, a half moon on his back, and a thickness under his tongue resembling a beetle.

When it is announced that another Apis is found, the land hails the tidings with cries of joy. He is fed with milk forty days, in a house facing the rising sun. A most costly boat, with a golden cabin, is launched for him. The finest food, the noblest attendants, the sweetest music is provided, and the nation keeps holiday while the priests bring him home in the first evening when the new moon appears. During his life warm baths and costly perfumes, crimson couches and truly royal apartments, are furnished by ample revenues. When Apis would be consulted, an omen is drawn from the choice he makes between two stables, or certain kinds of food. Or the priests bid the inquirer whisper his desires in the ear of Apis, and the answer of the god is given to him in the first salutation he hears on going out from the temple into the streets of the city.

Whenever the seven days' festival comes in honor of Apis, the spectacle calls into Memphis the people from many a city. The temple called the Apeum, with its grand court of pillars, is thrown open to the crowds of devout and eager worshipers. A royal guard of soldiers protects the god. A choir of women, singing hymns, leads the procession. The

## The Religion of Egypt. 161

army follows on behind. The people come out of their houses to welcome him. Even the queen performs the office of priestess and servant. Whatever children may feel the breath of the god are counted most happy, and are straightway gifted with prophecy. As the excitement increases, indecent dances and great madness of behavior become the order of the day. In the afternoon bulls are made to fight before the Apeum. The night ends in drunken feasts. Notwithstanding all this, the richest and wisest of the nation praise the greatness of Apis. The king hastens to present lotus flowers at his altar.

And when the overseers of the brick-makers were beguiled from their cruelty by the glitter of banners, and the pomp of the guards, by the canopies, and fans, and sacred vessels of the passing processions, the poor Hebrews must not be severely blamed if they, too, looked and admired, and came to think a golden calf a strong god, and a kind god to those who put their trust in him.

The priests say that Apis only signifies agriculture, and his worship ennobles fieldwork. They drown him if he lives beyond the twenty-fifth year. This is the Apis-Osiris who was worshiped throughout the whole of Egypt! Or, rather, this is the superstition by which the priests beguile the people into giving to and serving the temples.

Besides the calf Mnevis, and the bull Apis, the

goat of Thebes is eminent for the worship he receives. His sacred boat is four hundred and twenty feet in length, and is covered with gold without and silver within. (See page 163.)

The ape is sacred to Chons, and the cat to Pasht. The ass belongs to Typho, and the hawk to Athor. The dog is sacred to Anubis. Nearly every god has his animal. If any of them dies thousands of miles away with the army, they will be brought home to be buried in state. The fish are many of them sacred. The asp is an emblem of Kneph, and not only is cared for in temples, but is kept tame in gardens and houses. The harmless house serpent is respected all over Egypt as an emblem of eternity. The beetle is also sacred to several gods, because he appears at the rising of the waters, or, as some believe, because the balls he rolls up from clay, in which to place his eggs, resemble the earth. Even flies are reverenced. It is said that Thoth once escaped in the shape of an ibis. Therefore the very water tasted by the ibis is sacred.

For these animals great provisions are made of flesh of geese, roasted or boiled. To others, cakes smeared with honey are given. Perfumes, and beds, and baths, and costly oils are provided for them all both by fixed revenues and gifts. The care of the sacred animals is esteemed a great honor, and descends from son to son.

Nor is worship confined to animals. Many plants are honored with peculiar reverence, and happy are they who can sit under their shade.

## V.

The temple service includes the offering of animals, the pouring of wine and oil upon the altar, and the burning of incense.

Every victim is examined and sealed by the priest. A fire is lighted on the altar. The death-blow is given while the priest repeats the prayer, "May any evil hanging over us rest on this head." Then the head of the victim is sent away, the skin is removed, and the body placed upon the altar. About this gather the priests and people to eat with the gods, as a sign that the gods are by this sacrifice reconciled with them. Bulls are offered at Memphis, but cows are never brought to the altar. They are sacred to Isis. Sheep are offered, except at Thebes, where goats take their place during all the year, save at a single feast. At Mendes the goat is spared, and sheep are sacrificed.

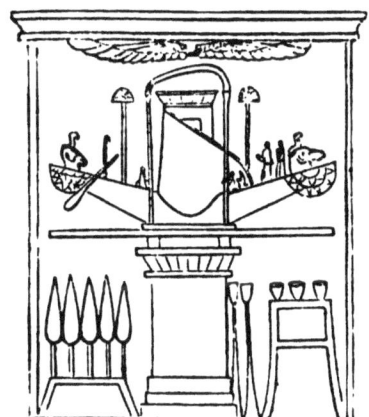

Sometimes the bodies of the victims, even oxen, are burned entire, filled with consecrated cakes, honey, raisins and figs, perfumes and oil. At the festival of Isis, while the sacrifice is being consumed, the worshipers beat their breasts. At other times there is glad music from harps, and flutes, and trumpets.

Wreaths of fresh flowers are frequently laid upon the altars, or made to crown the statues. Useful herbs and fragrant plants, fruits of fig-trees and vineyards, in baskets covered with leaves, are acceptable to the temple. Alabaster vases of sweet-scented ointments are also welcomed.  Beside these, garments, necklaces, bracelets, vases of gold, silver, and porcelain, inlaid tables, rosewoods, and, indeed, every gift which can enrich the treasury of the priests, are constantly received.  Processions bringing such presents are sure to find open the sacred doors.

Beside these are many emblematic gifts, made in performance of vows, or as tokens of a grateful heart. Here is an image of gold to Isis. It bears the form of the sacred cow, with the sun between her horns. The marks below may signify the hand which carries the plate for burning incense, and the vase out of which the wine is poured.  Here is an image of the jackal-headed Anubis, with the story of some recovery from death. A scribe presents a tablet and inkstand, a housewife a white cake sprinkled with seeds.  A shepherd brings a lamb, or milk, or honey, a poulterer fresh fowl, a gardener fine flowers,

## The Religion of Egypt. 165

or onions, which occupy a very prominent place in worship. Sometimes silver arms and legs, images of the members restored to health, are hung up in the temple.

## VI.

The worship of Egypt suggests the services which Moses instituted. The altar of incense, standing beyond the altar of burnt sacrifice, which was in the outer court, is to the Israelite and Egyptian alike

significant, of a step onward from material toward spiritual worship. The table of show-bread represents to the Egyptian what it does to the Israelite, a recognition of the divine care which gives fruitful seasons and bread-bearing harvests.

Children are led in bands to pray in the temple at certain festivals, and to praise Osiris, "Onuophris," "the meek-hearted, the manifester of good." During the festival of Pasht at Busiris, and Neith at Sais, all the people are required to gather together as they do at the great festivals of the Hebrews. The Nile is covered with boats. Flutes and clappers are in every hand. Wine and summer fruits are abundant. Jests and singing are the order of the day. Feasting follows the previous fast. Sacred stories are told. Offerings are made, and the people go home to their work with light hearts. The use of green boughs, and the season of the year, remind us of that feast of the tabernacles which Israel keeps when the harvest is brought safely home.

During the festival of lamps at Sais, on a particular night, every Egyptian, wherever he is—in the temple or by the way, in Syria or in Asia, on one of the great caravan routes in the desert or in the city—is expected to fill his vase with oil, and light a floating wick in honor of Neith.

Thoth has his festival, when those who attend eat honey and eggs, saying, "How sweet a thing is truth!" "The tongue is God."

Then there are many other mysteries, in part reminding the worshipers of some event in the history of Egypt, and in part celebrating the season of the year. At noon-day a procession starts forth bearing torches, and scattering flowers in honor of the sun.

Among the Mysteries is the representation at Philae of a brazen serpent hanging upon a cross, and worshiped by two priests. Could this in any way have been the shadow of that great day in the desert when the serpent of Moses saved the people?

The priests are believed to possess the art of knowing the will of the gods from the divining-cups. Joseph brought fear into the hearts of his brethren by referring to this well-known Egyptian custom. Such bowls, or cups, are of finest workmanship, and represent at least the wisdom of the workman

## The Religion of Egypt. 167

who made them. They have the holy beetle carrying a ball like the sun in his claws, his wings outstretched, standing upon a lotus flower. A similar beetle, with wider wings, forms a canopy, the ends of which rest on lotus plants. Beneath this are the

sphinxes in the unusual position of action—standing erect, one foot lifted above images and the wings elevated. Many mysterious lines and forms occupy the center and the rim. The shadows which come and go within these cups, and the position of certain drops of water or wine, are thought to be not less certain indications of the Divine will than the eclipse of the sun, or the discovery of new stars. All such divinations Moses sternly forbade. To use such cups was to be in danger of being cut off from Israel.

## VII.

There are many strange and absurd rites which dim the brightness of Egyptian wisdom. For some doctrines there is an evident reason, which partly redeems them from folly. The worship of animals teaches the people kindness. The cow is made sacred to preserve that useful helper of husbandry from destruction. Were it not for this the herds would become extinct. The ibis is honored because it helps destroy the very abundant serpents. The ichneumon eats the eggs of the crocodile, and thus earns a place among good deities. The ass is despised, as an emblem of Typhon, the awkward evil genius, who, as an ass, escaped once from battle. No doubt the training of horses, and consequently the love of war, is thus encouraged. For this reason, doubtless, horses were forbidden to Israel. The children of Abram were to be a peaceful nation, and stay at home. Even Solomon at his coronation was so meek and lowly, and obedient to the will of God, as to ride on a white mule.

It may be said in general of the beliefs of this thoughtful people, that they are intended as a discipline of the mind for those who study them. The laws of nature and of mind, so far as they are observed, and the wants of both worlds, are set forth in religious symbols, and in the relations which the gods bear to each other. The more simple rules which determine the policy of the country in treaties and in wars, as well as in managing the revenues and keeping the citizens in relations of mutual service, are all shadowed in the doctrines of religion. Very many forms of truths which are taught here in temples would elsewhere be learned in schools of philosophy.

But the fervent and superstitious minds of these imaginative priests have other beliefs, which grow up like seeds after the inundation. There is no possible explanation or excuse for them. All these beliefs, whether or not a reason can be given for them, turn away the thoughts of the people from the true God. They make the knowledge of religion the exclusive property of the priests, and all the consolations of religion become distant and cold.

## VIII.

The king, after many victories, has completed them all by a successful war in Ethiopia. He brings his gifts to the temples with the full splendor of the Egyptian religion. He is now not only the "visible god upon earth," but the priest who may walk with Amun, the "beloved," in the holiest place. Born of the gods, saved by the gods, he is something more than human. The city of Thebes keeps holiday in honor of his triumphal procession. As the sun rises, a burst of temple music welcomes his coming. Above the vast walls of a hundred temples rises the smoke of incense. A solemn prayer is chanted within the closed doors. Then the gates are thrown wide open. The military guards of each temple march forth and take their places, silent and motionless as statues, upon the right and left of the gates.

The morning breeze creeps up the Nile, and stirs the blue pennons which float from the staffs of the towers. A hymn is heard from the inner apartments, growing clearer as the doors of cedar wood, and embroidered curtains of silk, are opened before the king. Then he comes forth clad in a leopard's skin, which hangs loosely over his royal linen robe. A lion stands beside him. The ranks of priests, on either side the court, strike their harps and triangles. The pipes give out a shrill sound. The crowd answers with such a shout, and the martial roll of drums and trumpets so fill the air, that the rosy flamingoes start from the hidden pools by the river, the hoopoes sweep clattering into the sky, and even the quail are startled in the distant stubble-field.

The king stops, stern as the granite figures of his ancestors beside him. One foot is advanced in profound, almost scornful, repose. His beautiful profile is lighted up with a flash of conscious power. His small chin, slightly curved lips, narrow eye, broad forehead, high cheek bones, and wide, full chest, are known all over the civilized world.

The sacred scribe, with feathers on his head and in his hand a rule and reed, prostrates himself before the king. What are the commands of this son of the sun?

A chariot, superbly bright with gold and silver, at a signal from the scribe, drives out from the side temple. The charioteer holds the reins of the prancing horses, who are full of impatience, as if the drums were the signal of battle. Two princes seize their bridles. The king slowly mounts. Every step seems measured and considered. He waves his hand.

## The Religion of Egypt. 171

The princes stand aside. The chariot rolls forth. Then the cavalry wheel into line, company after company, this about the standard of an ark, that about a sphinx, and a third about the name of the king, shining in gold on a silken banner. The standard-bearers have been chosen for honorable conduct, and wear a necklace with a golden image of a lion, or sphinx, or some other emblem of courage.

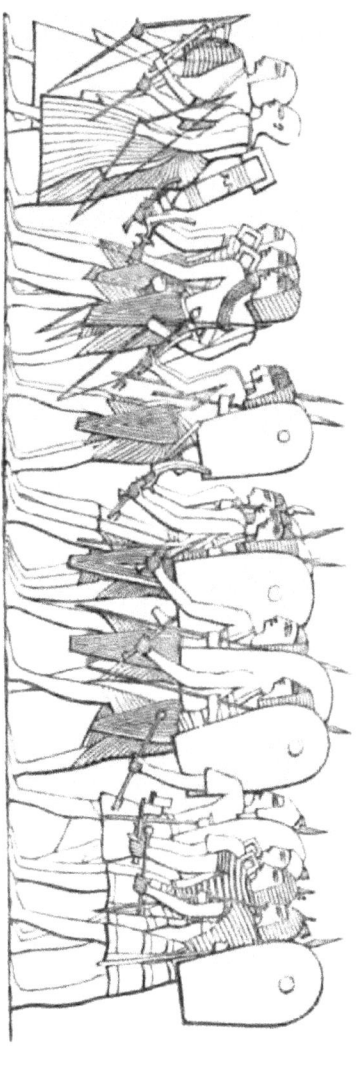

Here are the Hoplites, troops of the line, marching ten abreast. They form the center in the line of battle.

Their drums have casings of wood or copper, two feet and a half long, braced with cords. They are beaten with the hand or with sticks, and follow the standard-bearers. The trumpeters go before. The soldiers all carry green palm branches.

Some of the bowmen wear quilted helmets. The quiver is slung upon the back. They carry sticks of hard acacia wood, with which to knock down the enemy, or sharp swords, both for striking and piercing. Their arrow-heads are of bronze, or flint stones. They have no shields.

The pikes of the spearmen are six feet long, with metal heads, double edges, and shafts full of nails. They also carry shields of bull's hide, the hair outside, having a cross brace, and rims of metal or wood. They always wear quilted helmets and short tunics. Some also carry light javelins, such as Saul hurled at David. Others have swords two and a half feet long, with blades like leaves, thick at the center and tapering to a point. Others still have clubs ornamented with tassels, with a head of iron like a ball. One company carries a thick and straight bow, four feet long, a spear, and a hatchet which does great service in close conflict, or when gates are to be broken down. These are mostly heavily armed, and wear a breastplate and helmet of metal plates, not unlike the scales of a crocodile.

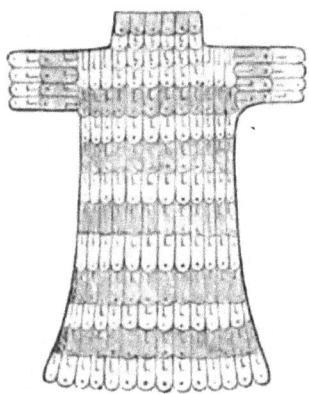

As the bowmen wheel into line in their chariots, they draw their arrows, two feet long, up to the ear. The feathered shaft is in a line with the eye. Then, suddenly relaxing the string with a twang like a hundred harps, they thrust back the arrow into the decorated quiver, and the bow into its leathern case, and draw their daggers. The people shout in applause, as if they, like the horses, felt

## The Religion of Egypt. 173

the glow of battle. The slingers follow, with bags hanging from their necks full of lead, and stones shaped like an olive.

With a great cry they swing their instruments thrice about the head, return the pebble to the case, and grasp their double-edged swords with the right hand. The officers carry swords whose handles are inlaid with costly woods, studs of gold, and heads of hawks.

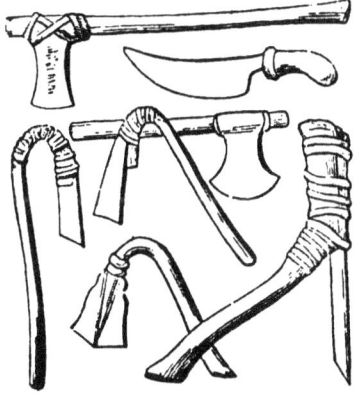

Some few carry a falchion called Shopsh, with a blade two feet long. The officers usually direct the march with a wooden staff, or by a signal from the drums.

But the most choice troops are the body-guard of the king, a thousand picked men, taken from the two grand divisions of the army, the Hermotybians and the Calasirians. These have pole-axes, with metal balls four inches in diameter at the broad handle which receives the blade. Their swords are not less than three feet long, and very slender. Their shields are immense.

Behind them appears the king's banner. This is the ensign of the empire. It bears the king's name, embroidered in gold. The staff is mounted with a golden disk of the sun. In battle, or on the march, it is never separated far from the king's chariot. In camp it marks the royal pavilion. It is to-day carried on a platform by generals of the army and admirals of the navy.

Here are chariots four deep, each drawn by two horses wearing plumes. The charioteer keeps them in line. The warrior beside him salutes the king by carrying the right hand to the left shoulder.

Behind these is an open space, into which wheels the chariot of the king. Rameses is shining like the sun, surrounded, like rays of light, with many royal fans of plumes. These fans are borne by princes, also resplendent as the morning clouds in Syria.

Then follow the conquered kings. Their hands are bound before them, and they have ropes about their necks. It matters little whence they came, or what their rank; whether they were a short time since supreme among the cities of Lebanon, or have been taken from provinces farther east on the Euphrates, or south from the lakes of Africa, or from the islands of the far Northern Archipelago, Rameses makes no distinction. All save Egyptians are accounted barbarians, and are dragged, a helpless spectacle, to adorn the triumph of the king. The light men of the North are in flowing robes, and the black men of the South in leopard skins. The men of Syria have fair blue eyes and long beards. They march with the Asiatic princes, who wear feather plumes, and whose half-naked bodies are painted in many colors.

Now more chariots and wagons appear, loaded with

## The Religion of Egypt. 175

rich spoils and tribute. They carry armor from the battle-fields, precious fruits, rare woods, curious animals, bags of gold dust, rich garments, and vases of perfume and ointment heaped together in studied confusion.

The members of the royal household come after them, sitting on platforms or ivory thrones covered with canopies of silk, or in stately chairs, carried on the shoulders of stout slaves.

Then we see the images of the king's ancestors, an innumerable train, and statues of the gods, which remind not a few of the processions of Bel with his thunderbolts, of which Isaiah speaks. Some of the gods are in tabernacles, some on sledges, some on simple platforms. All are attended by priests, who chant their praises and the honor of the king.

After these is the principal god, drawn in a splendid ark, glittering with gems and gold. An altar of burning incense precedes him. The figures of justice bearing scepters, extend their wings before and behind. Priestesses continually scatter lotus flowers and lilies over the sled. The attendants wear the masks of a goat, the livery of the great god Mendes, the god most honored at Thebes.

Embassadors, commanders of armies and navies, foreign princes, with varied costumes and noble suits of retainers, follow. Every tributary and friendly power, every great city from the oases and the Red Sea to the ends of the earth, wait on the king's pleasure to-day.

The Lybian and Phœnician allies, with foreign arms and native officers, bring up the rear. Their helmets are red, and green, and black. From weapon and shield the sun is reflected in dazzling splendor. We look in vain among them for the bow. This is the peculiar weapon of the Egyptian. The very name for a soldier in Egypt is the picture of an archer kneeling.

The last train sweeps by, and the chariots, always drawn by two horses, close the procession. These are the glory of the Egyptian armies. They sweep by in endless ranks, four abreast, filling the street, and drowning the very music itself with the rattling of wheels and the clatter of their trappings. One division carries bowmen, and another soldiers with spears and javelins, and a third, men with swords and shields. The light frame work of the chariot has an embroidered fringe on the outside, more for ornament than protection. The floor is an elastic network of thongs, closely braided, to lessen the jar as the chariot rolls over rough roads. The wood work is inlaid, painted and carved to represent sacred animals. A lion's head for a crest rises from the saddle, and the housings are gray, with tassels, and feathers, and rosettes. The horses themselves seem light as

## The Religion of Egypt. 177

birds and graceful as deer. They are proud of their masters and of their own splendid appearance.

The procession moves along the vast avenues lined with sphinxes, past the colossal doorways of temples gay with pennons, and the noble fronts of palaces hung with colored cloth. Thousands of men and women, dressed in their best robes, crowd the streets. The king looks on triumphs of sandstone, and marble, and red porphyry, black and rose-colored granite, until his heart is filled with delight. At length the open place before the main temple is reached. The bands now break forth in a noble challenge to the priests, who wait quietly within. The drums, covered with parchment, played with hand or stick, roll like a stormy shore. The braying of the smaller trumpets blends with the clash of cymbals. The brass trumpets, held with both hands, send the orders of the commander down the line, proclaiming that the march nears its end. Right and left the front ranks wheel. The king passes through his vanguard. He waits near the front gateway. Then the martial music melts into the solemn chant of advancing priests, who come to meet Rameses clad in linen robes. The bands of singers, and players upon pipes, and harps, and flutes, and bells, with the sacred clatter of the systrum, follow after.

The royal scribe, with the books of Hermes, the palm and the hour-glass, symbol of the astronomer's art, advances and proclaims the day fortunate. Rameses wears an apron tied in front and wound round the lower part of the body. The loose upper robe of fine linen has full sleeves. On his head are the sacred feathers, and he is still surrounded by the fans of office. The attendant carries a canopy above him. Its staffs are carved like lotus-stems, and the cloth is blue and sprinkled with golden stars. A second priest, with apron full to the ankles, held by a strap over the shoulder, bears "the royal measure," "the cubit of justice," and a cup from which he pours a libation before the advancing king. A third, like the others, wearing papyrus sandals, carries a water jar in his bosom. He represents Nilus. A fourth has loaves of bread, emblems of the sustaining power of a holy life. Another burns incense upon an altar. Then the challenge is given, not unlike that which is heard in holy Jerusalem, "Lift up your heads, O ye gates! The king of glory shall come in." "Who is the king of glory?" demand the priests. "The lord of hosts. He is the king of glory." The chant is ended. Through the opening ranks of the priests advances the sacred crescent-shaped boat, four hundred and twenty feet long, borne with poles upon the shoulders of twenty-four of the temple guards. Its stem and stern are resplendent with jewels and holy symbols, and its bearers have the peculiar robes and head-dresses of Amun Ra at Thebes.

The king descends from his chariot, and leads the way down into the forest of columns. Behind him are the captives and gifts, the royal household, and the priests. The soldiers rest on their arms without.

A confused murmur comes forth from the sacred courts, but the brazen doors are shut behind the king. Within the holy place the priests chant the record of marches and battles, and the goodness of the gods. The priestesses answer with temple hymns, to the measured sound of harps and viols

All the gods in order are represented by men who wear their masks. These move slowly before the king as he waits by the altar. Chons says, "We approach thee, to serve thy majesty, O sovereign lord Amun Ra! Grant a pure and safe established life to thy son Rameses, the lord of the earth, who loves thee."

Maut says, "I come to render homage to the sovereign of gods, Amun Ra, governor of the land of Kemi, in order that he may grant long years to his son, King Rameses, who loves him."

After these have passed, with similar words of honor is seen Queen Hofre Ari, praying, "I, the royal spouse, the all-powerful mistress of the world, bring homage to Amun Ra, king of gods and men. My heart rejoices in thy loving kindness. I leap with delight under the weight of thy favor. Accord to thy son, lord of the world, Rameses, established and pure life."

The great priest advances for his god Amun, and says, "My well-beloved son, receive of me pure life and long days. Joyously control the world. Thoth has written by thy name all the royal attributes of Osiris. All quarters of the earth open good gates to thee. Evil races lie under thy sandal. Force of thy arm, terror of thy name, the scythe of thy battle, thy whip and scepter shall rule in Kepi. The lady of the celestial palace hath prepared for thee a diadem of the sun, where I place this helmet."

Then proudly speaks the king, "I came to my father, Amun, at the end of the procession of gods, which he forever admits to his presence."

The priest stretches forth his staff of office to the

four quarters of the world. Four geese fly upward, and out beyond the city into the wilderness. They represent the four genii of the earth, Amset, Hapi Dawn, Mutef, and Keba-snuf. The king puts on his crown. He cuts the stalk of water-plants held before him, in token of rule over Egypt.

Then he retires to a side chamber, while the chanting of the priests and priestesses invokes the gods: "Accept the gifts of the king, O Amun Ra." Meats are offered and burned. Wine is freely poured on the altar.

The king comes forth. He is not the warrior now, but the high priest. A leopard skin alone hangs from his girdle, the head drooping over his right leg. His hair is plaited and braided. An asp with jeweled eyes is held by a simple band to the forehead. A wreath of golden lotus flowers encircles his arm. From his broad necklace hangs the characters which compose his title as priest. They are supported by vultures on either side. From his girdle, over his tunic of fine linen, hangs an apron embroidered with his titles as king. In one hand he carries an unbent bow. Silently he moves through the inner door. The trophies of war, and the figures of the gods, are carried into the treasuries of the temple. Only the prisoners and a few priests follow the king into the recesses of the temple through many doors, which shut their massive leaves behind.

An hour passes. The music within grows louder as it comes on from court to court. The gates are flung open. The soldiers spring to their arms. The measured chant is lost in the cry of thousands of loyal hearts. Rameses ascends, under the porch of

## The Religion of Egypt. 181

columns, a throne of ivory. Its arms are carved into lions, and its sides into sphinxes. The corners have the forms of Tmee, goddess of Justice, and Hormoei, sun-god of Truth. Twelve warrior chiefs lift the throne, and the procession is resumed in the order of the advance, save that the trophies and prisoners are no more seen. Those who have worked in the tombs remember the paintings of captives kneeling with arms bound to a stake surmounted by the head of the jackal, emblem of death. Others have seen the pictures of victims held by priestesses, the blood pouring from their heads into a brazier. Those who wait in the temple have shuddered as they have seen on the walls the headless figures, the sacrificial knife, and the names of foreign princes, side by side. But enough for the people that the gods declare themselves pleased with the sacrifice, and the land by these holy rites receives the powerful aid of the gods. They dare not ask the meaning of the sacrifice, and it does not concern them what the king does with their enemies.

When Thebes is silent again, the troops within the temple barracks, and the people within their houses, we may well remember how different is the religion of Israel, which has never inspired a war for gain, nor delighted in its solemn service in the shedding of human blood. Foreign conquests never disturbed the thoughtful, quiet ways of Israel. It became rather an honor to minister to the arts of peace and lay the foundations of the kingdom of peace. " He maketh wars to cease unto the end of the earth; he breaketh the bow, and cutteth the spear in sunder; he burneth the chariot in the fire.

The Lord of hosts is with us; the God of Jacob is our refuge."

In Jerusalem, "foundation of peace," the temple of Jehovah does not delight in trophies of war. The armor and chariots, the slaves and captives which adorn the temples of Egypt, have no place in the sacred courts. Whatever has been saved from the past remind the priests of the goodness of God, not of the power of man. In the holiest of holies, under the golden cherubim, rests the ark of plain shittim wood. Within the ark are the granite tables of the Lawgiver at Sinai. Even the pot of manna, and the rod of Aaron which budded, have disappeared. The old altar of incense and the table of show-bread stand in the holy place. The brazen serpent is elsewhere in the city. But the only warlike trophies of past days which are preserved are the five hundred golden shields which David brought back from the Euphrates when he smote Hadadezer, king of Zobah. Yet noble king David, because of this and similar deeds of war, could not even build the temple. His golden shields most appropriately were hung on the towers which Solomon built for his Egyptian wife. It is indeed true that "the shields of the earth belong unto God," but they must not be seen in his temple. No sound of war may come thither. No signs of human pride may rest there. No voice of praise for human service becomes this place. "But the Lord is in his holy temple; let all the earth keep silence before him."

AMENTI.

## AMENTI, THE LAND OF THE DEAD.

The Future always in mind—"Book of Manifestation to Light"—Embalming—Funeral—Tombs of the Poor—Tombs of the Kings—Pyramids—Sphinx—Extent of the Tombs

### I.

THE gateways of the temples are to the Egyptians the shadow of that entrance by which men pass on into the land of the dead. He who runs may read upon these carved stones the story of offerings received and services performed by nobles and princes in this world, in the hope of an entrance into the life to come. There are also figures of gods and goddesses, whom human eyes have never yet looked upon, but who have revealed themselves to the priests, and are always waiting to meet the soul when it is summoned away from its pleasant gardens and cheerful house. Whether it be a king who passes into the temple to do sacrifice, or an embassador on his way to India, or a prisoner chained to the chariot of a superintendent of Nubian gold mines, or a Hebrew shepherd, to each the same picture-language speaks from the gateway of a future existence. The overshadowing wings of this entrance to the temple are the pledge of care; the globe, of the light which will shine along the way; and the serpents, of the wisdom which will guide the soul through all its journeys. Nor is it the entrance alone to the temple which becomes associated with the future. The more the people hear of its secret chambers, its uncounted treasures, its deep dungeons, its society of noble men, and its strong towers, the more are they impressed with the necessity of serving, through the priests, the gods themselves. Whatever is given to the gods seems saved from destruction. Whatever fires are lighted on the altars are sure to shine into the land of shadows. Whatever deities are remembered by the costly shrines, gilded arks, cedar boats, and rare perfumes are sure to keep them company when friends and priests shall both be left behind.

The great truth which is familiar to all the Egyptians is, that the soul is formed in the image of Osiris. The body is honored as the dwelling-place of this great god. In this life there is a distinction in the same man between the divine and human. The king in his human nature pays homage to his divine soul. Whether it be the good soul of king or slave which goes away from this world, it enters the presence and becomes a part of the great god. It is Osirian. The body is also to be honored, since some time, if it be properly cared for, it will complete in another world, the joy of the soul. It becomes, then, the great desire of every one to keep the soul in good favor with the god, and to have the body prepared after death for its long rest.

"The buildings we use are inns," they say, "but the proper house of men is the tomb," Throughout an Egyptian's life the tomb is ever kept in mind. If he buys, or builds, or sits at the feast, he is still thinking of the place of his final rest. Whenever he sees sacred symbols, holy figures, fine colors, or quarried stone, he is mindful of the adornment or building of that house which is appointed for all the living. Every stately ceremony in some way sets forth the court of Osiris, or the procession of gods in the land beyond the gateways of Amenti. If he goes out in the early morning to the meadows west of the city, he sees a hungry crowd of the poor devouring boiled meats which are placed there during the night by the priests. " It is the table of the sun, and is supplied by the earth," he is told. But the table is spread among the tombs in honor of Ra-Atum, the sun in darkness, the soul in death. If he studies in the temple, the books he uses are illustrated by pictures of departed souls. The trials he must meet, and the courage which will be required, are constantly impressed upon his mind. There are not half-furnished troops to be overcome, or half-defended cities to be stormed; but his enemies will be spiritual, and he must meet them all alone without allies. The coming of the sun through the gates of the morning is the type of the new life which comes forth from death. The sun drops down behind the western hills and has entered another valley, in which the celestial Nile flows with broad, and deep, and sweet waters. This is the path he also must take in his last journey, and no labor is spent in vain if it may make that untried way safe for his feet.

## II.

The learned class carefully learn those mysteries relating to death which are written in a book called "The Manifestation to Light." From its sacred characters and bright pictures they regulate their lives, in hope of another existence. They are told what ceremonies should be paid to those divine souls who have gone on before them, what order is necessary to the funeral, and what hymns, confessions, and answers will secure them the favor of Osiris in the day of judgment. This book they desire to have buried with their friends. If they cannot bear the expense of the entire ritual, a part will be of great value. If none can be obtained, they will write with their own hands in rude characters some part of the service which relates to the final journey, and fasten it with gum to the folds of the mummy-cloth.

It would be strange if these Egyptians were not devout. They are taught from infancy that a good life secures a dwelling-place with the gods. They live under the shadow of the tombs. They walk among the graves of their fathers. They spend all their resources in providing a sepulchre for themselves. The book of which they hear more than all beside is a funeral ritual which has come to them with the approval of past generations. They are never allowed to forget that they are immortal if good, or, if bad, the fires of punishment, which will ultimately consume them, will appear endless. The

## Amenti, The Land of the Dead. 189

very mystery of the soul in relation to the body adds to the solemnity of such an immortality.

With the "Book of Manifestation to Light" to guide us, let us follow the wanderings of the good on his way to Osiris. The departed soul opens his eyes to behold the god of the dead. He pleads for entrance into the dominions of this deity. He declares that he has led a good life. There is about the god a great cloud of souls who have entered before. They are the companions of the god, and attend his movements. Filled with sympathy, they repeat before their king the petition of the supplicant. They wish the soul to join their company. A voice now is heard from the earth. The priest at the altar intercedes for the soul. The good deeds of service and the gifts to the temple are remembered. At length the god of these lower regions answers, "Fear nothing in praying for endless life for thy soul. It is permitted thee to pass the threshold."

The soul, reassured, draws near Kar-Neter, land of the dead. He sees the dazzling sun in the lower hemisphere, and sings a hymn of adoration. He calls on the brightness to come no more from without, but to kindle a light within him. One by one he invokes the gods who preside over the feet, the legs, the thighs, the body and arms, the head and the forehead, to release him from the wrappings of the dead. Each one performs his office. At last the soul is freed. Then he takes the sacred beetle, which he had placed on his body at death, and holds it above his head as a pledge of life. The dread portal respects the sign, and permits him to advance unharmed. Thus the soul is prepared to enter the land, through which he must pass to reach Osiris.

The journey now begins. The soul has adored the sun with litany and invocation, and will no more suffer for want of light. Religious knowledge is henceforth the food which will supply him with strength. He will not need such grain or fruit of earthly harvests as many other nations bury with their dead. "Knowledge is *sbo*, 'food in plenty.'" He who has not knowledge cannot have life. It is knowledge alone that is fitted to receive this eternal life. All things else must perish.

The soul labors to find the meaning of sacred symbols. Happy is he who has studied those things in the temple. His labors are easy. Sad the work which now attends the idle or thoughtless.

Meanwhile on earth the living are addressing, in his behalf, prayer to Thoth, the guide of the dead. In every petition allusion is made to the conflict between Osiris and Typhon, how the god once suffered, and was tried, and knows therefore how to deliver those who follow after him. At the close all join together, the priests, friends, and departed, "Aid us, O Thoth, as thou didst in that solemn day help Osiris and his son Horus, avenger of his father."

Mysterious changes come over the soul. The enemies of Osiris become its enemies. Many other spirits, who seem to seek his destruction, are only sent to try his valor. There are crocodiles coming out of the land and water, daring him to fight. Tortoises and serpents creep up to dispute the way. Terrible sphinxes, gazelles with wings; Sak with a hawk's head, the body of a lion, and a tail like a

## Amenti, The Land of the Dead.

lotus flower; and the square-eared hippopotamus, known in Numbers as the unicorn of Egypt, appear to the soul. All manner of strange beasts defy him to combat and insult him. At each of the fifteen gateways he meets a separate deity with a drawn sword. He must prove to each of these sharp-sighted gods his good deeds and knowledge of divine things.

Finally he wins or forces a way through them all, and, full of joy, sings a song of victory. He likens himself to the gods who have entered into his body. The divine nature begins to triumph in him. " My hair is like that of Nu, (the firmament;) my face is like that of Ra, (the sun;) my eyes are like those of Athor, (the evening.") He glories in his strength as if it were the strength of Set. He rejoices in the very trials by which his valor is now made manifest.

He is weary, for he is still far away from Osiris. He therefore rests. But rest is not idleness. He still gathers strength, and satisfies his hunger by knowledge. He would have died of starvation had he gone aside in the desert, and even now he cannot live but by obedience to the divine truth. The goddess Nu gives him, as his reward, refreshing waters from the tree of life. He sets forward on his journey anew, holding conversation by the way with the divine Light, who instructs him.

For a long time Light is his guide. It helps him in his conflict with Apap, or Refrof, the enemy of the sun. This is the last great enemy—death. It is defied and overcome. Then the sublime mysteries of nature strengthen and prepare the soul for the indwelling of Light, and Light strengthens it for a conflict with death.

A series of changes now take place, through which the soul becomes more and more elevated, and fitted for the remainder of its trials. As the sacred animals are symbols of divine attributes, so the soul is changed into a hawk; into an angel or divine messenger; into a lotus; into a god Ptah; into a heron; into a crane; into a human-headed bird, which is the usual emblem of the soul, (see page 206;) into a swallow; into a serpent; and finally into a crocodile. At each change he becomes more like Osiris, who is himself in all of these forms of life.

The soul has passed through its former troubles as a disembodied spirit. In some way not known, the body is now necessary to the progress of the soul. Alas! if by the carelessness of the priest or poverty of the family it has failed to receive the proper care. No knowledge will supply its place. The more perfect the foldings of the bandages, the more care the priests have taken with the successive folds of cloth which have been glued together, the finer the plaster surface above these and the colored symbols, the happier shall be the progress of the soul hereafter.

It is doubtless in view of just this most important stage of the journey that Isis is described so carefully as gathering together the parts of the body of Osiris. There is no part of the story upon which the priests dwell more than this.

Having proved himself worthy of the trust, the body is now restored to the soul. The prayer which was uttered long ago in the temple is answered: "O that in the dwelling of the master of life I may be reunited to my glorified soul! Do not order the

## Amenti, The Land of the Dead.

guardians of heaven to destroy me and hinder the eye of Horus from preparing my way." Horus regards him now as he never did in the land of the Nile. He is a brother, rather than a servant.

He passes through the home of Thoth, god of learning, who comes out to meet him, and offers a book which contains fresh knowledge for the way which yet remains. Beyond this dwelling the soul approaches a broad river. The happy fields lie upon the other bank. A false boatman offers him passage, hoping to bear him to the east. But the soul, having fed upon the book of Thoth, with great discernment sees the danger, and drives the tempter away with reproaches. The true boat appears. He enters and sails to the west, where the way lies toward the sun in the lower world. The divine boatman plies many a question. Each part of the boat cries out, demanding its name and meaning, in twenty-three questions. The mysteries of life and death are set forth under the figure of this boat. The soul passes the ordeal and reaches the land, beyond which lies the valley of Aoura, or Balet.

A serpent, thirty cubits long, is on guard at the northern entrance of the valley. At the other extremity is a lake. It is another Egypt with its dreaded northern sea where the evil serpent lies in wait, and its quiet southern waters, full of rest and wonderful for beauty. Osiris is among the canals, sowing and reaping. Lo! what delight to find that this labor is all for the soul. The bread of knowledge he will so much need is being prepared for him before he feels the hunger of his divine soul.

Anubis leads him to the house of double justice.

Osiris is seated upon his throne carrying a staff and whip. A lotus lies on the altar before him. The lotus is the only flower of Amenti. Attentive to the verdict, Thoth will enter the record on his tablet. The soul approaches, attended by two figures of Truth or Justice, each wearing the ostrich feather. They are like the Hebrew Thummim, or "Two Truths." They stand at the entering in of the gates. Horus, son of Osiris, and Anubis, attend the weighing of the soul. The good deeds of his life are put in a jar. The weight in the balance is the ostrich feather, emblem of truth. Four genii of the dead sit patiently waiting for orders from Osiris. Before the great judge is the terrible beast Cerberus, "the devourer of the wicked," who protects the throne from evil souls. The wicked can never enter the land of the good. Behind Thoth, seated on a crook, is a figure of Harpocrates, showing in the figure of a child that one must be born again ere he can enjoy the immediate presence of Osiris. It also shows how there may be a change in the relation of the soul to its god, becoming as a child again, and yet without death.

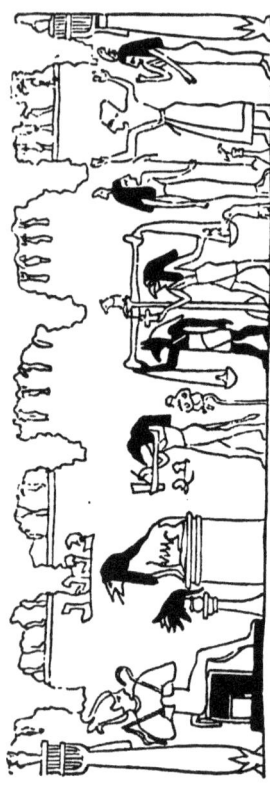

But the most solemn part of all is the questioning

## Amenti, The Land of the Dead. 195

of forty-two triers. Can the soul give proof of a right mind and correct life? "I have not blasphemed. I have not stolen, stirred up trouble, been idle, or intoxicated. I have not made unjust commandments, shown improper curiosity, betrayed secrets, wounded any one, or made them fear. I have not slandered, envied or spoken evil of king, or father, or any one. I have accused none falsely. I have given offerings due the gods, food to the hungry, drink to the thirsty, and clothes to the naked. The stones for the mooring vessels have I not injured, nor have I disturbed the canals, or stolen sacred fish, or herds, or offerings, nor defiled the waters of the Nile."

The forty-two assessors are satisfied. Osiris pronounces, "Weighed in the balances and found sufficient." Thoth records the decision. Thoth is the emblem of that part of our nature called the intellect or conscience, which has now been weighed. The meaning may be that the soul will approve or condemn itself in the balances. The soul enters the land of happiness. It is at this point the dead is called Osirian, and on the walls the departed, with their wives seated beside them, receive the offering of onions. (See page 196.)

Then the soul traverses in company with the sun-god the tabernacles of the heavens, and explores the very sources of light. A god himself among gods, he dwells forever with the blessed, and shares their society. The great Osiris converses with him as they walk together, and round about them both shines a light, as if from a common disk. The accepted soul no more puts his right hand over his left shoulder, or kneels on one knee, as signs of a lowly spirit. He no more pours wine on sacrificial altars, as a token of impurity. The soul in his glorified body is like the deity in nature—above all weakness or sin. It receives the sacrifices paid to gods.

But even here idleness is banished. The moment the soul disembarks from the sacred Nile he becomes blue, and takes up the labors of the sun-god, or the blue Nile god, who becomes his companion. In his right hand is a hoe, and over his left shoulder hangs the seed basket. Or, if some other trade than the farmer has been his employment, his tools, which have been buried with him, will share some form of pleasant work in the celestial country. Yet every trade will at times give place to the first and most godlike employment of caring for the fields. Over the door of the house is written, "Take your sickles, reap your grain, carry it to your dwellings, that ye may be glad therewith, and present it as a pure offering to your god."

## Amenti, The Land of the Dead. 197

But there are other souls who cannot be colored blue. The scepter of Osiris gives token of rejection. They are weighed and found wanting. These wicked souls may, if they have small faults, be guarded by four genii, and through fire become purified, and thus at last enter "Pleroma." The happy souls are then fed with delicious food by Osiris, who is ready to forgive and anxious to be the guide and companion of all who forsake the evil gods.

Those who have been exceedingly sinful, and have indulged in low pursuits, are judged out of their own lives. What they once associated with, determines their future. A transformation takes place before the throne of Osiris. They are changed into swine, and, under the care of two monkeys, Thoth or Time's servants, are ferried back to wander on the shores of the lake. A man cuts away the ground behind them with an ax, to show that their fate is hopeless. Such subjects are often represented upon the tomb, (see page 218,) and are in striking contrast with those spiritual beings who guard with outstretched wings the ark of the gods.

Other souls undergo frightful torments. Their arms are bound tightly about their breasts. Their heads hang, half severed, over their shoulders. They are crucified head downward. They are dragged over the ground, plunged into hot cauldrons, bound to stakes, and covered with wounds, scourged and torn asunder. This ghastly, melancholy company is guarded by evil spirits who are at the same time their executioners. Their place of punishment is described as dark and silent, and therefore joyless. " They do not see their great god.

Their eyes do not drink in the rays of his disk. Their souls are not illustrious in this world. They do not hear the voice of this great god who towers above the sphere."

Some souls seem to be utterly destroyed. Their heads are severed on the block of Hades. The evil spirit which has betrayed them now returns and enters other men, bringing them into unclean places and luring them to evil.

But for most souls a way is kept open through many animals back to a new trial as men. This part of the book "of manifestation" is exceedingly obscure.

## III.

The narrow and crowded valley of the Nile has no room for the dead. Even if there were room, the shifting channel of the river would give them no hope of a continual rest. Nor does the desert beyond the hills offer a secure grave among its shifting sands. There the winds and the jackals are ever at work. The building of tombs on the edge of the desert, which happened later (see page 199) in the day of the Pharaohs, seemed neglectful of the solemn rights of departed souls. The mountains alone were the only proper refuge for the dead.

If the bodies of men and animals should be simply buried out of sight, in the ravines and caves of the hills, the air would be intolerable. The caravan routes, which wind in and out among the mountains, and the villages which cluster at their base, would be deserted.

## Amenti, The Land of the Dead. 199

The Egyptian therefore preserves the bodies of the dead from destruction. This is called embalming. Not men alone, but oxen, dogs, cats, birds, crocodiles, beetles, and even eggs, are carefully prepared to escape the sentence, "Dust thou art, and unto dust shalt thou return."

The custom of embalming doubtless sprang from the necessities of the country. It, however, soon received the sanction of religion. The priests became the embalmers. The condition of the departed soul was closely connected with its faithful performance. None were permitted to evade its duties. The State provided for the poor.

When any one dies the priests are at once informed. They come to the house of mourning with various patterns in clay or wood of different kinds of embalming. A selection is made. The body is then taken to the temple. The priests receive it with every demonstration of grief. It is strange, since the profits of their work is in proportion to the 

wealth of the dead, that they should utter the saddest cry for the richest comer. It is possible, however, that they reckon these cries as part of the expense of the embalming, and only to the friends of the dead has it the sound of sorrow.

Twice a day, during the seventy-two days the body remains at the temple, chants are sung and prayers are repeated for the departed soul. Hired mourners, who measure out their despairing wails by their hope of pay, go about the streets rending very carefully their garments, throwing dust very sparingly upon their heads, gently beating their breasts, and lavishingly praising the departed. Their cry is, "Ho, ye that pass by, see if there be any sorrow like unto my sorrow, wherewith the gods have afflicted me in their fierce anger." They challenge any man to speak ill of the dead. He had no faults. If half the kind things said by hired men and strangers after death were judiciously said by friends during life, men would be encouraged to become the most deserving and happiest of beings. But it seems to be necessary to die before one is appreciated.

While the mourners go about the streets the priests have quietly commenced their labors. If the embalming is to be costly, and worthy of a prince or priest, the perishable parts of the body are carefully removed. The brains are drawn out through the nose with a wire and placed in a jar with perfumes.

## Amenti, The Land of the Dead. 201

A priest takes a sharp stone, brought from Ethiopia and, making a wound in the side of the body, runs quickly away, followed by the formal imprecations of the priests. The lungs, and whatever else may be easily removed, are taken out, washed in palm oil examined to see if there be any sickness future treatment may remedy, and then either returned or placed in separate jars and sealed. The covers of these jars have heads representing the four genii of Amenti. The lion-headed, or jackal-headed, Smautf

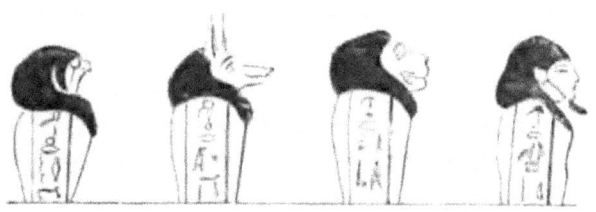

guards the lungs and heart. The human head of Amset keeps the stomach. The ape-headed Hapi contains the smaller parts. The jar of the hawk-headed Kebhusnof is reserved for the liver. These jars differ in size and material. Some are of alabaster, twenty inches high, and are covered with inscriptions and figures of the sun or sacred beetles. Others are of limestone or wood. They are especially interesting as in some way suggesting the four spirits of the unseen world which Ezekiel saw about the chariot of the Almighty. An image of the eye of Osiris is immediately placed over the wound in the side. This is sewed up, the whole body having been filled with pounded aromatics, myrrh, cassia, and fragrant substances. It is then placed in a bath of natron seventy days.

When the body is removed from the natron it is washed in palm oil. The face, eye-lids, nails, or whole body, may be covered with gold-leaf and wound with bands of fine linen smeared on the inner side with gum. The limbs are bound together, and even the face is carefully concealed. The very sawdust of

the floor is taken up and tied in linen bags, to be buried with the mummy in vases. Within the folds of the linen are placed many articles of value, especially the images of the gods and the sacred beetle. The signet rings are usually buried with the

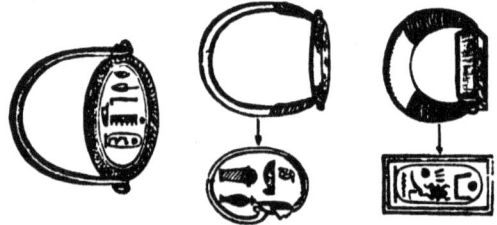

dead. The rings in Egypt make the signature, which in other nations is accomplished by writing, on documents or doors closed with wax or clay. These rings

## Amenti, The Land of the Dead. 203

are of the finest workmanship, and some contain small openings in which perfumes were placed.

When the bandages, which are often a thousand feet in length, are completed, a cover of pasteboard is made to fit the form and to represent the features. Over this is placed a thin coating of plaster to receive the sacred writing and holy symbols. The whole is sewed together on the back, forming a tight envelope. The most frequent subject which is represented on this covering is Netpe, or the winged sun. The outspread arms of the goddess seem to protect the sacred body. Gold-leaf is lavishly used, and eyes of brilliant enamel or glass, with the careful imitation of hair, are added to restore the likeness of the dead. A network of colored beads is spread over the breast, and sometimes over the entire body. The devices worked upon this are of great variety. The faces of men are painted brown and the women olive green. A second or third case of pasteboard is sometimes added, covered, like the first, with the story of the man's life, his services to the gods, and his hopes of the world to come.

The body is now ready for its outer case of wood or stone. In olden times a door was represented at one corner of this chest. At one end is Isis, at the other is Nepthys. Isis sometimes is represented embracing the feet of the dead. Lines of hieroglyphics repeat over again the good story of the life now finished. The face often appears in relief, a faithful copy of the face upon the cover within.

There are far less expensive modes of embalming. Less costly spices, and sometimes only bitumen, are used. The jars may be earthenware. The figures of these gods are often made of wax, or their outline alone is buried with the dead, engraved on a metal plate. The sarcophagus is very plain, and contains a fragment of the funeral ritual, or a few ear-rings or porcelain images. For the poorest no coffin whatever is used, and the bandages are exceedingly coarse. "Gilding and painting" are never bestowed upon the poor! But for this reason they are left undisturbed. The sacred beetle does not shine upon their breasts, nor does Isis and Nepthys appear supporting a canopy over them. Nor do the other gods pray for their protection. But the very absence of such signs of wealth is their real safety. The spoiler of tombs knows that no wings of gold or silver, inlaid with precious stones, no chains or signet rings, are to be found upon them. There are compensations in the severest lots. Poverty and disquiet, and hard labor, and humble burial, may secure repose in "the everlasting habitations." What does it matter if the priests hastily perform their unpaid services by plunging the body of the shepherd in liquid asphalt, or dry it with common salt, or fill it with chips of bitter wood and ashes? Of what consequence if the sacred cat receives thrice the care of the servants who feed it? After it is all over the body rests well, and the priests do not envy it the pittance of linen which they have bestowed upon it.

But the bodies of all men are sacred. To injure any is sinful. The eye of Osiris is placed over every opened side of the mummy. The same time is also used in embalming the poorest and the richest.

## IV.

The mummy is delivered to its family. Upon his chin is the beard of the gods, turned at the end, since he is now presumed to be in holy company. During life he wore a beard of false plaited hair scarce two inches long, square at the bottom. The king alone is permitted to fasten to his chin a long beard. The body is bound up to resemble the form of Osiris.

A service is performed, and the household worship the mummy. A priest with a leopard skin comes in to minister at the altar. Vows are made, which will be paid to the temple if the great Osiris, or Anubis, will grant safe burial. Incense and libations are freely offered. The friends pray to the dead, and embrace the body with every sign of grief and respect.

The great question now arises, Shall the mummy be buried at once? The desire of keeping each other company in the tomb, or the unfinished state of the tomb itself, or the mortgage which remains upon the body from too costly preparation, may determine the family to build a closet and keep the mummy for days or years in the house. The dead are then placed upon a sled and drawn to the altar from time to time. Or the doors are thrown open, and garlands, wreaths, cakes and fruit are laid before it, precious oils are poured over it, incense burned before it, while prayers are read from rolls of papyrus. These offerings for the dead, both in the house and in the tomb, were strictly forbidden by Moses. To the Egyptian they were a reminder that the departed soul has still its journeys and its hunger.

It is always thought best that the funeral should take place at once. Such is the usual custom. No man can receive honorable burial if the body of one who depends upon him is still journeying among his creditors.

When the time arrives for the funeral the priest who wears the leopard skin gives the order for the procession. The priest who wears the mask of the

god Anubis, guide of the dead, gives up the body. The soul in the form of a bird, Bennu, with a human head, is still, as they believe, hovering over it with the cross and circle, emblems of life and of its journey. The body will, they say, rise with him, and "the vital spark lingers in his members." His favorite couch, fashioned to represent the head and body of a lion, can no longer detain the mummy.

## Amenti, The Land of the Dead. 207

He is laid now in his outer case of stone or wood, curiously engraved. This in turn is placed in a sacred boat, drawn on a funeral sledge by four oxen and seven men. Upon this sledge the nearest relatives stand or sit weeping.

The procession is ready. The servants lead the way with tables on which are heaps of fruits and flowers, vases containing ointment and wine, young geese and joints of meat, napkins and wooden tablets. Then appear the images of the gods, borne on platforms by the priests, or in closets with folding doors. They also carry the various weapons, staffs, sandals and fans, collars and necklaces, which were used by the dead. His empty chariot follows. Another chariot is driven by the servant as he walks beside it. There are couches, offerings, altars, gold vases, images of ancestors. Then come the various tokens that the dead once was in attendance at the palace. All these are guarded by priests and servants, who carry napkins over their left shoulders. Now appears the funeral

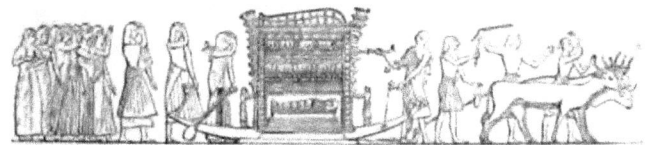

boat upon a sledge, the panels of the cabin richly ornamented. The abundant supplies of lotus flowers, heaped up in front and rear, proclaim at once the importance of the dead, and his present journey among the flowers of Amenti.

The lower part of the cabin is left open to show the splendor of the sarcophagus. The children of the family hold up their hands in prayer to the departed. Upon the prow of the boat is always the mysterious eye of Osiris, like that which was placed over the opening in the side of 'the body during its embalming. The prow and the stern of the boat are carved into the familiar lotus flower, in memory of the voyage of Isis, and perhaps of the boat of the great spirit Khem, who moved over chaos and subdued its waves into patient canals, and its hills into gardens. Images of blue pottery representing Osiris, and birds emblematic of the soul, are carried by inferior priests. A company of men, friends of the dead, follow with long staffs, the peculiar mark of an Egyptian gentleman, in their hands. Then appears the priest with his roll of papyrus full of the record of the good deeds of the dead, who must soon pass the ordeal of the judgment.

Servants scatter an abundance of palm branches along the way, to make the sled glide more easily. The drivers urge on the slow-moving oxen. A priest holding a bottle of water sprinkles with a brush the passers to prevent the "evil eye" of envy. If for any other reason the sled stops, another priest is ready with ointment, which he pours on the ground, and with fresh cries of sorrow the procession starts on its journey again.

Behind the sled are the mourning friends, filling the air with shrill cries, and casting clouds of dust into the air. The hired mourners behind them take up the cry. Then come more servants, with yokes from which hang baskets of earth, flowers, and jars of water. With these they will make a garden about the sepulcher. Here and there in the procession,

## Amenti, The Land of the Dead.   209

but always before the funeral boat, appears the priest with incense. Boys clothed like priests, with a leopard skin, having shaven heads, occasionally strew flowers in the way.

They pass out of the western quarter of the city, across the plain, and reach the shore of the sacred lake. Here beneath the trees are many beautiful chapels. Before one of these the priest gives the signal to halt. The funeral boat is taken from the sled. Its cabin is painted to represent the dead. The husband is now reunited with the wife who preceded him in the journey to the land of spirits. They have an altar before them with a palm branch, a joint of meat, cakes and fruit. Before the cabin is

the altar with sacrifices. Affectionately they sit together. Such is the belief of friends; but the forty-two assessors are there, and have yet to pass sentence. The priest before the cabin reads from a long roll of papyrus the good deeds of the dead, and offers upon a table yet other gifts to the gods in the name of the children. There is a great silence as the trial proceeds. Any one may accuse the dead and the judges will listen. If, however they speak falsely their punishment will be exceedingly severe. The friends plead with the judges not the noble birth, but good life, of the dead, for all the good are noble after death.

Then, as the drone of the chant and the cloud of incense cease together, is heard for the dead a voice crying, "I have not disturbed the gazelles of the gods in their pasturage. I have not netted the water-fowl of the gods. I have not caught the sacred fish of the gods." Appealing to each of the forty-two triers, who represent the avengers of as many sins, he addresses each in this manner: "O thou that destroyest peace, I have not stolen! O thou that smitest hearts, I have done no murder! O thou of the two lions' heads, I have not falsified measures! O thou of piercing eyes, I have not played the hypocrite! O thou avenger, I have not robbed the dead!" Then, again, after these negative declarations, follow the list of good deeds, which end with a prayer for a merciful trial in the balances.

It all reminds us of the words of Job: "Is not destruction to the wicked? Doth he not see my ways, and count all my steps? If I have walked with vanity, or if my foot hath hasted to deceit, let me be weighed in an even balance, that God may know mine integrity. If I did despise the cause of my man servant; if I have caused the eyes of the widow to fail, or have eaten my morsel myself alone, and the fatherless hath not eaten thereof; if I have seen any perish for want of clothing, and if he were not warmed with the fleece of my sheep, this were iniquity to be judged. If my land cry against me, or have caused the worker to lose his

## Amenti, The Land of the Dead.

life, let thistles grow instead of wheat, and cockle instead of barley. The words of Job are ended."

There is no reply from the judges, and none from the crowd. Nor would any ordinary sin be urged when so great a multitude of friends stand about to punish the false accuser, or cry down the true witness. Yet as such things do happen, even happier than one's birth is thought to be the day of his burial, and no warrior or king boasts until he puts off his armor at the tomb.

In the funeral before us great is the cry of joy and relief from all the crowd.

The shame and disgrace of a refusal would be excessive. They must then take back the body to their homes until the gods or men are satisfied or silenced. But no magnificence of a lotus funeral would atone for the first failure. No devotion of friends or prayers of the priests would remove the sorrow of this day of disgrace before the multitude on the banks of the "lake of the nome."

Some, from extreme poverty, are obliged to be buried on the shore, but this is also greatly to be dreaded.

It is not the prince or the beggar alone who must pass this ordeal. There is none exempt here, or in the trial of Osiris. The king himself must have the piece of money in his mouth as a sign of acceptance, or the tomb will not open for him. His deeds must win the favor of the judges, and the acclamation of the multitude. Some have failed, and, like Joash and Manasseh, have not come to the sepulcher of their fathers. Not one has entered who has not appealed to the people as Samuel did: "Witness against me before the Lord: Whose ox have I taken? or whom have I defrauded? whom have I oppressed? or of whose hand have I received any bribe to blind mine eyes therewith? And they said, Thou hast not defrauded us, nor oppressed us. And he said, The Lord is witness against you. And they answered, He is witness."

The formula of address, and the decision of the judges, are usually painted at the very entrance to the tomb. The address is, "O thou sun, our sovereign lord! and all ye deities who have given life to man, receive me and grant me an abode with the eternal gods."

The ordeal is past. The dead needs not to be returned to his house, nor will he be buried on the eastern shore. The coffin is placed in the baris, or sacred boat, in charge of the steersman Horus, and towed by a larger vessel, which has both sails and oars, moves across the water. The boat is shaped at either end like a lotus, and always has upon the bow the eye of Osiris. The mourners, and altars, and offerings follow in other boats; some silently, others with noisy demonstrations of grief. From the chief boat, between two figures of Isis and Nepthys, who, as the representatives of the Beginning and the End, watch over worthy lives, the priest is throwing incense on an altar.

The western or sacred shore is reached. A crowd of people are in attendance. The body is again drawn by oxen on the funeral sled. The crowd follow after. They are the poor, who increase by their numbers the procession of mourners. They will receive for this service the offerings which will

## Amenti, The Land of the Dead. 213

complete the funeral rites. Many of these carry their children in shawls on their backs.

At the foot of the mountain the funeral sledge stops. Once more the altar sends up clouds of smoke. Once more the mourners break out into unrestrained cries, and clasp the sacred body. Once more prayers are recited, and the body anointed. Then the sycamore doors of the high pyramid are opened at the command of the priest who has charge of the tombs. Within the door is seen a small chamber. There are arranged about the sides chests of rare woods, containing jewels, and garments, and writing-boxes full of papyri. Tablets are cut in the wall with funeral subjects painted upon them. The winged globe is above the entrance. Just opposite the door are large stone figures of the priest and his wife sitting side by side. These were the builders of the tombs, and are waiting to greet, one by one, their children in the generations which follow after them. In the center of the chamber is a pit eight feet square. The servants descend and light the lamps in the niches. There are now seen shelves full of brightly-painted coffins, all as fresh as on the day they were placed there. Beside one rests the model of the sacred boat he commanded. By another are the leathern sides and inlaid top of a scribe's case. By a third is the fan carried before an ark of Amun. By a fourth, still smaller, among heaps of little porcelain images of the gods, is a shapeless, gaudy, broken doll. By another the shield, but not the weapons, of a soldier. No sword enters here.

There are no wars in Amenti. By another sarcophagus is the palette of the painter.

Into one of these niches the dead is lowered. The casing shows a procession of gods. The breast is covered with wings. The hands grasp the signs of life. A calm, quiet face stares patiently upward.

The frames with meat and wine are brought into the tombs. The altars of incense are lighted. The precious gifts are laid aside with the treasures of former days. The chanted prayers are broken with the lamentations of friends. Fresh flowers are scattered about, and the ceremonies are over. The friends throw a few shawls over the other coffins, and go out.

The priest shuts and seals the door. The crowd go away, each carrying some money, or fruit, or part of the offerings.

A few friends remain to make another garden at the gate of Amenti. Soil has been brought from the valley, as a part of the procession, and jars of water are poured upon the handful of flowers, now set out in order. The favorite plants of the dead are still believed to be precious to him. At least they are a comfort to the living.

But with all their efforts flowers will not bloom at the gate, nor will these places be made attractive to the living. Prayers will continue to be offered, and for a little while these fading flowers will be watered, but the most sorrowful of all the friends are turning to their duties and amusements. They shave again and put on bright robes, for the days of their mourning are ended. They go in and out before Pharaoh with as cheerful a countenance as if they had never been in the shadow of the domain of Athor, " President of the West."

## V.

The tombs of the poorer people are little beside rough-hewn chambers. Like the tombs of the higher classes, they are usually high up in the western hills, though sometimes they are mere pits in the plain, or recesses in the side of the rock. There the dead are all crowded together until a pit is full, and then it is sealed up with masonry, and another opened.

It would be difficult to imagine the immense number of these chambers, or their countless heaps of mummies. Passages and walls pierce the mountain till it becomes like the comb of bees. No painting adorns the walls. No outer chapel marks the entrance. These vast armies of the dead which enter every year are truly at rest in coarse mats and bundles of palm-sticks. They lie with faded flowers. There is no object in disturbing their unadorned houses.

But the richer class are not so secure. A tomb may for many reasons be resold by the priests. A failure of a son to meet his obligations may not only deprive his father of his sepulcher, but even of his coffin. One name is sometimes erased from a tomb and a sarcophagus. It is then sold to another, and the dead must lie in humbler places. Or if there be a demand for a tomb not readily furnished by the priests, a family which has passed away is quietly removed, and new tenants occupy the house.

These tombs are always kept ready for use. The walls are painted in every variety of detail, giving a short epitome of life, which is always described as remarkable, then leaving a space for the portrait, name, and deeds of the occupant. It often happens that a space is left alone for the name; so much alike, after all, are our lives, which we imagine in our loves and sorrows to be so peculiar. But a costly tomb, with three or four upper rooms and as many pits forty feet or more deep, having recesses both at the sides and at the bottom for one large family, is usually made by the owner, and ornamented strictly with reference to his life and pursuits. Some of them are even more costly than that of the kings themselves. The rooms are connected with one another by wooden doors turn-
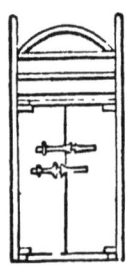
ing on pins like those of a house. They are secured with bolts and bars, and sealed with clay. These are opened only for funeral rituals when a new member of the family goes down to the "sides of the pit." Then, indeed, all the echoing chambers seem to cry out, "Art thou become as weak as we? Thy pomp is brought down to the grave." The exteriors of such tombs are often of great beauty, and cut in the rock itself with noble pillars and cornice. (See page 218.)

## Amenti, The Land of the Dead. 217

They are sometimes lined with Syenite granite, and serve at first as homes for those who afterward use them as sepulchres. This double service of the tomb is not, however, common, as they are usually remote from the cities.

### VI.

The kings at Thebes lie in solitary tombs higher up among the hills than their subjects. They are in an utterly desolate valley where no blade of grass ever softens the rays of the fierce sun. " The kings of the nations, even all of them, lie in glory, every one in his own house." They that were wont to " shake kingdoms" "go down to the sides" of the pit. The passage leads down from the entrance into the mountain by a long inclined way. This becomes a flight of steps. Then there is another inclined way ending in a chamber. Under this sinks a deep pit. Passing beyond we enter a pillared hall. Still farther within the mountain is a second hall. Returning to the first hall, the way goes still down another flight of steps, and by another sloping passage, to a floor which is half descending, half level. Then there is another chapel; a yet greater pillared hall, leading to the largest room of all, which has a vaulted ceiling. But the king evidently intended to have gone on far beyond this. One chamber is almost finished. Part of it is covered with figures laid on in red, and corrected, re-drawn, and then half painted. From the great chamber is an unexplored passage, or a driftway, still downward. Such is the tomb of a single king, reaching three hundred and fifty feet into the mountain.

As soon as a king ascends the throne he begins to prepare his final resting-place. The place is chosen. The chisels of the workmen are heard incessantly till the hour the king dies. The rough walls are covered with stucco to receive the painting. Bright red and blue colors adorn the walls. The subjects are partly social, but mostly religious. Among these latter the boat and serpent of Kneph are most frequent. There are winged serpents, human-headed serpents, serpents with legs, sometimes stretching across the ceiling, sometimes embracing the dead in their folds, sometimes rising as they are guarding the cherubim, sometimes carried on the shoulders of priests. They reach down the sides of the galleries,

## Amenti, The Land of the Dead. 219

stand by the ends of the corridors, move in and out among the constellations on the walls. They are worshiped, crowned, and some of them are even pierced with the spear of Horus.

Here and there a ray of thought appears struggling through these clouds of deities. A serpent, emblem of time, draws its folds about a garden, dividing its life from the death of the desert which is about it. There is a single way of departure for the soul out of the garden. The body of the goddess Neith, presiding over the firmament, reaches through the center, making day upon one side and night upon the other. In the east, with the darkness about it, the infant Ra, the young sun, emblem of human life, is launched by his mother upon a stream. He is yet in darkness. A bark like the ark of Moses, before his face was light to the world, bears him onward. At every stage, mingling with the nations which live on the banks, the brightness of Ra grows with his need of shining. All about him are now watchful spirits. A star marks each hour which hastens toward the dawn. At the seventh hour he seems mindful of danger, and sounds for the shallow places. At the ninth hour he shares his boat with a heavenly pilot, for troubles have now multiplied about him. He comes to the twelfth hour, and the star gives place to a globe. This, too, is past, and he is out in the great and troubled sea in full day. New trials beset him, for mild Tethys, wife of Oceanus, invites him to rest from his labors. But the journey is not ended. Backward he turns, seeking the home of his childhood. The burden and heat and toil of life are upon him. Celestial deities take pity on him when the dangers are too great, but leave him when he is able to labor alone. At last the globes are finished, and the stars seem ready to rise in the darkness. He leaves the garden. The voyage of life is over.

Besides these subjects are groups of gods in solemn, silent council—all the abominable beasts and creeping things, and the many idols Ezekiel saw portrayed when he had digged in the wall. There are deities forming men of clay on a potter's wheel, moving over the face of the waters, and watching the arts of men, in all variety of enormous, fantastic forms. There are men, black, yellow, white, red—Africans, Asiatics, Northmen, and Egyptians. There are vultures, apes, lost souls, in the form of pigs, ferried back to earth, and endless columns of sacred writing. Within all this, among the grandeur of the pillared halls, rests the king in his transparent sarcophagus of oriental alabaster.  The sides of the funeral case are but two inches thick. Without and within are most delicate cuttings, representing funeral processions and religious ceremonies, in hundreds of figures not more than two inches high. At the door, as if keeping guard, are the figures of fan-bearers and servants, arms and standards, harpers and trumpeters. They seem busy, watering flowers, preparing the table for the king, leading in the bearers of tribute, building the palaces, and amusing the leisure hours of their master. But how silent and quiet the place when another king demands the thought and care of the living! He who was worshiped as the visible sun upon the earth, surrounded by great men and lords, lies in the feeble flicker of a few lamps. Even these will soon languish, fade, and die! The rich and the poor, king and servant, lie down alike in silence and darkness.

How wonderful it is to see the temples dedicated to the gods rising in each reign, corridor beyond gates, and halls beyond porches; but these tombs, built for the resting-place of a single man, are the work of his own life. Not even the king's son extends the work of his father. He who lavishes all the treasures of Egypt one day on his burial-place, the next day cannot command a single mason or painter. The gods only are great in power, since their influence lives forever.

## VII.

Among all sepulchers the pyramids stand unrivaled. They are mountains of cut stone rising from the edge of the mysterious western desert. To the Egyptian they seem like the portals of Amenti. The word pyramid means "lofty," and has, from the resemblance of words, been thought to be the "desolate places" for which Job longed when he said: "Then had I been at rest with kings and counselors of the earth who built *pyramids* for themselves.... There the wicked cease from troubling; and there the weary are at rest. There the prisoners rest together; they hear not the voice of the oppressor."

What weariness did thousands of prisoners suffer to provide a place of rest for one king of Memphis!

A vast causeway, eight miles long, was built from the eastern quarries to carry the stone to these hills. This occupied the labors of a hundred thousand men for ten years before the inclined way, fifty yards wide, and sometimes forty feet high, was built, and polished, and covered with sculpture. This labor alone would have raised the walls of Jerusalem twice over. Twenty years more were given to the g eat

pyramid, a mass of stone weighing not less than six million eight hundred thousand tons. A wall might be built with this, six feet high, to inclose the whole land of Egypt, run from Memphis to Babylon and back again, and still have left enough of stone to reach to the Black Sea. Add to this the labor of reducing the mountain on which it stands! There it towers twice and a half as high as Solomon's proud porch!

## Amenti, The Land of the Dead. 223

The mind which could plan such a work would hardly seem human but for the very smallness of the chamber, a mere rent in the mountain of stone, which was enough for its rest. It was human, too, in its desire not to be forgotten, in its challenging the praise of men who should come after it.

Once the sides were not covered with polished limestone, but rose in more than two hundred layers or stages. It was, perhaps, the earliest manner of building. Certainly the pyramid was old when Abram sat under its shadow. It may even in some way have been the imitation of Babel!

It is not unlikely that during the life of its builder the priests climbed its sides to worship the sun, or watch the stars. Certainly, the construction is upon such principles as suggest its use in observing the movements of the heavenly bodies. Unlike the temples, the sides of the great pyramid correspond with the four cardinal points. The Babylonian temples correspond in their angles with these same points.

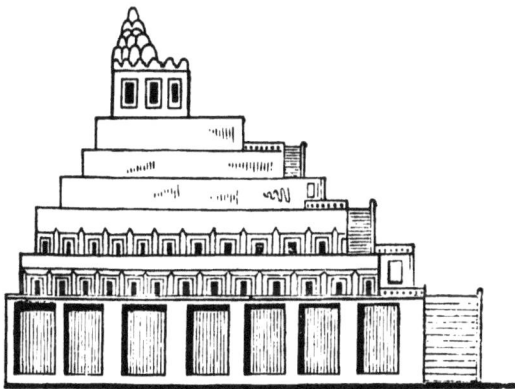

The Assyrian temple of Belus was in the manner of ancient Babel, a tower built on stories, not to climb above the floods of a new deluge, but to worship the gods who could save them from the deluge. The seven platforms at Borsippa rose with different colors in honor of the seven planets. The lower stage, like the Egyptian, was an exact square, made dark with bitumen to represent the color of Saturn. Above this were the orange-colored bricks, where Jupiter's altar stood. Then a bright red platform was dedicated to Mars. Still higher the sun was worshiped on bricks covered with gold. Above the sun was the pale yellow stage of Venus. The priests next came in their ascending to the blue bricks of Mercury, which had been heated into slag by fires. But the highest of all was the silver platform of the moon, with its observatory for the astronomers, its watch-tower for astrologers, and its shrine for the priests. The vaulted apartments, brilliant with paintings, colored tiles, and ivory, though braced with cedar, and

cypress, and bronze, have quite fallen. The confusion of religions at Babel has overtaken the temple

## Amenti, The Land of the Dead. 225

itself, and it stands in a solitary valley a mound of bricks furrowed with rain.

The Egyptian pyramid, more than three times its height and thrice its breadth, was plain and somber, according to the habits of the people who reared it. But the pyramid remains almost unharmed.

No doubt we may learn something of the use of the latter from the former. The grand entrance of the tower of Babylon was on its north-east face; at Memphis on the north. The platform on the summit of both must have been nearly alike in size.

Beside the great pyramid nestles the pyramid-tomb of Rhodopis. She came a stranger into Egypt, with her mother. Like Ruth, she was rewarded for her filial devotion by marriage with the ruler of the city. Here she rests beside the king at Memphis.

The third pyramid, most sumptuous of all in its ornaments, was built by Mycerinus for his only daughter. When she died he buried her in a sarcophagus made like the sacred cow of Isis. The case was of wood inlaid with gold. Every year, in obedience to her dying request, she was brought out to see the light of the sun, which had made her childhood so full of happiness. The lower part of this pyramid is covered with red granite. A sloping passage leads to the chambers. The door is blocked by three immense stones like the triple portcullis of a city. The whole is richly covered with sculpture.

There are more than sixty pyramids beside these, standing like sentinels along the edge of the desert. Each has its story, but this story, like the history of those who once imagined they stood in the center of the world, has passed away from the knowledge of men. It is even a matter of dispute in what age they were builded.

The name Memphis is but another word for Men-ofie, "the haven of the good," "the land of the pyramids." It is singular that the city which was so full of life should be known by the name which describes the home of the dead.

## VIII.

What the pyramid is among tombs, the sphinx Har-ma-chu, "the sun in the horizon," is among images. It is hewn from the solid rock, the strata of

which are still seen. One of these forms the mouth. With the head of a man it has the body of a lion.

## Amenti, The Land of the Dead. 227

Between the front paws, which are stretched out before it, stands the temple. Forty-three steps lead to this platform. The summit of the head is fifty-six feet above the temple. A royal helmet rises nearly half this height still above it. The entire body is one hundred and seventy-two feet in length. The cruelty of the shepherd kings, and the relentless sands of the desert, have alike failed to destroy the tranquil and gentle blessing of that face. The mourning people of Memphis go out to Amenti and look up for courage into this countenance, which seems to be watching for the signs of the east, those signs which will attend the rising of the soul in new glory.

There are other noble temples under these hills. Serapis, Anubis, and the god of healing, have great corridors and gateways, but none of them have such a throng of worshipers as this sphinx, the quiet guardian of Memphis. Behind the temples rise the long lines of pyramids of white and smooth marble, or yellow limestone, or the dark red granite, but the immense masses of stone weary rather than console. From one to another the stranger goes along the dromos of sphinxes. The seven statues of king Chephren, the labyrinth of chambers Cheops built, the vast walls raised in honor of the sun on the horizon by Tothmes III., bewilder him, but he returns to the sphinx with a feeling of friendship and love. Its sweetness and serenity are the counterpart of the sublime pyramids. Both of them seem to need the other, and together they stand to watch over the tombs. The rocks beneath are full of the dead—men, oxen, reptiles, birds, and insects—a quiet city to which all Memphis sends its citizens, as each generation comes to bury that which goes on before it.

## IX.

There are five miles of mountains filled with tombs at Thebes. There are sixteen miles at Memphis. No wonder Hosea says of the disobedient Israelites, "Egypt shall gather them up. Memphis shall bury them." Every city, save a few on the eastern shore, had its western lake and burial-place. Here they put away the dead with a silver or gold plate as a gift to Hermes, who guards the brazen gates of Cocytus, and leave them, like the beetles they worshiped, to sleep out the winter of death.

To die and have no pictured tokens of other days about him is to the Egyptian the severest punishment the gods inflict upon men. What wonder, then, that the Hebrew laboring at the stone borders of the temple lakes, or working in the fields and watching the state and pomp of these funeral processions, knowing that the taskmaster would do no injury in the long night of rest before him, came to think of death as his great joy. Then even the Egyptian would embalm him, as certainly though not as finely, as they did the precious body of Joseph, which was the bond of union in all the tribes. Its gilded and painted coffin was the pledge of Joseph's love for the sepulchers hewn in the Land of Promise, where the cool oaks of Hebron drank in the sunshine and the rain, where the vineyards of Eshcol gave a goodly smell But when Joseph's body seemed to have no prospect of rest in its wanderings, when only a waste and howling wilderness received the embalmed body of friend and child, how bitter, though natural, the taunt which broke from his lips: "Are there no graves in Egypt, that thou hast taken us away to die in the wilderness?... Is not this the word we did tell thee in Egypt?...Let us alone...better for us to serve the Egyptians than that we should die in the wilderness." And so they looked back to the fields above which they saw the winged globe and the gateways of Amenti—the land of rest.

How gracious was the answer of Jehovah. He did not despise their fears, nor forget that all their lives they had been in bondage. Like one who in all their afflictions had been afflicted with them, he turned their anxiety into hope. "You have been wont to believe you had no place in Egypt. You have longed for the mysterious land of Amenti, where Horus would lead you to a country of rest, and, slaying your enemies, be your avenger. Now, fear ye not. Stand still. The Egyptians whom ye have seen to-day ye shall see them no more forever." Like the gateway of the tombs, stood up, on either side, the waters. Like the mysterious land through which the soul was believed to journey, opened the desert. Down into the shadows, silently as a funeral procession, passed the frightened host. On the further bank they sang in triumph, as the soul is believed to sing at the gate of Kar Neter. The journey had its trials and its enemies, as the soul has its foes on the journey to Osiris; but the old enemies never found them out, and the bondage of taskmasters never disturbed them. They were dead to their old life, and on the threshold of the new. It was at the Red Sea that the influence of the funeral rites of Egypt was forever broken in the mind of the Hebrews. At some graves were doubtless heard bitter reproaches, because all sepulchers were denied them. There were burning hearts when the cloud moved on from the places grief had made sacred, but the people never went back to the worship of the deities of Amenti.

The Greeks, in their customs, show us what Israel might have been. The river Styx, over which the souls were ferried; the obolus, placed in the mouth of the dead; the robes, the earthen vessels, the honey cake and sacrifices placed on the tomb; the hired mourners, the funeral oration, the image of death as a journey, and the garlands put upon the grave, were taken to Greece from Egypt. When this people were in the land of the Nile they were very particular to be embalmed, and built tombs like the natives. In one way beside the influence of the Egyptians among the Greeks is seen. They both thought the departed would need light. They therefore, last of all before they went out from the tomb, trimmed and renewed the lamps, and then bade farewell to the travelers who had gone on into Amenti.

# STORY OF EGYPT.

# THE STORY OF EGYPT.

Egyptian Annals Unreliable—Menes—Whence the Race Came—Early Civilization—The First Kings—Thebes Appears—The Middle Ages—The Shepherds—The Restoration—Tothmes III.—His Successors—Rameses II.—The Decline of Egypt—Assyria in Egypt.

## I.

THE priests always entertain strangers with what they call the history of Egypt. When, however, we pass from Heliopolis to Abydos, or on to Thebes, there is such difference in the lists of kings that it is evident no single account of past days can be entirely trusted. Rameses II is represented on a tablet at Abydos paying honors to fifty ancestors. But when we compare the record of this noble society of kings with similar tablets on the walls of Karnak, where Tothmes III. makes an offering to his fathers, some names are omitted in each which are found in the other.

The same thing is true of the books which are preserved in the sacred libraries. If we consult the priests of Memphis, they magnify the number and deeds of the kings who ruled in their city. If we listen to the priests of Philae, we might suppose the dynasties of Memphis were of little consequence.

Nor is it names alone that trouble us. The years of the different reigns are in equal confusion. Immense periods of time are given to favorite rulers, and very naturally the days of oppression are forgotten, or reduced to a very small limit. They seem to think that when time passed wearily a record of it would only perpetuate a heaviness, and ought therefore to be forgotten. Whereas a brilliant reign needed to have ascribed to it fabulous numbers of years to give the true impression of its greatness. Then they do with history what they do with statues. That which is farthest from the eye is made larger than a true proportion, that when the whole is seen in its place the appearance may be just. Egypt is to their imagination not only a colossal figure, as it certainly is in the view of all the world, but also a figure of perfect symmetry. The latter claim we can hardly acknowledge. Yet none can correct the assertions of the priests, since they only observed the events which they describe. With these difficulties in our way, we can only attempt, in the place of history some fragments of the story of Egypt.

## II.

There were, say the authorities, first of all, the reigns of gods, heroes, and shades, the last of whom was the favorite deity Horus. The first king was Menes.

They thus confess they know nothing of the early days of Egypt, or they describe the rule of the priests under the names of the gods. We are the more inclined to believe in the rule of the priests, since Menes was condemned by them. They say he was hated because he introduced foreign luxuries and ruined the simple ways of the people. If this were true, the temples would have been first to praise him, since they would have received the greatest benefit from the arts of which he was the patron. It is much more likely that this people at first, in true patriarchal way, obeyed the oldest child in the different families as a priest. They believed that in ministering at the altars of the gods the "first-born" became acquainted with the will of heaven concerning men. After a time the tribes doubtless lost something of the family relation, and moved more in harmony as a nation. Then the strong desire which made the children of Israel dissatisfied with the simple ways of their temple-loving and retired priests, and seek for a Saul to go in and out before them, led the Egyptians to clamor for a king. Menes may have consolidated the four tribes of Mizraim, the Ludim, the Pathrusim, the Naphtalim, the Annamin. In setting up the splendid throne and court of a monarch he would naturally gather warriors into his council. The priests, feeling their authority lightened, would hate the usurper.

## III.

The Egyptians doubtless came from Asia. Some have believed they followed the Nile from Ethiopia, But in the earliest monuments the tribes of inner Africa are represented as socially and intellectually far behind the Egyptian. Besides, the language, shape of the head, features, color of the hair, and all marks of nationality, identify the Egyptian with the tribes of the East, not with the rude races of the South.

There are many other indications of the common

origin of the men of the Euphrates and the Nile. Some of these we have already noticed. Others will continually appear. Indeed, it is impossible to be long in either country without being reminded of the other.

There is the god Nisroch of Assyria, whom Ezekiel describes as "a great eagle with great wings, long-winged, full of feathers, which had divers colors. He came unto Lebanon and took the highest branch of the cedar."  In one hand he carries the sacred cedar tree, and in the other the basket. He is one of the most prominent figures on the earliest monuments, and stands in colossal proportions guarding the entrance of palaces. He is spoken of as a great conqueror, eternal dispenser of all good, the best of the good, the wisest of the wise, the father of equity, self-taught, the inventor of sacred philosophy. Nisroch is alluded to in II. Kings in describing the fate of Sennacherib, who when worshiping in the house of this god was killed by his sons. The titles of Nisroch are the attributes of Ra, or Osiris, whose hawk-head appears in every conflict, and whose goodness and wisdom are the theme of so many inscriptions. It was natural that both nations should adore the sun-god, but it can hardly be an accident that they should worship him under the same figure.

The sacred bulls, sometimes with wings and sometimes human-headed, are another point of resemblance between the two nations. Their figures are at times embroidered with the sacred tree upon the king's garments, and sometimes on borders of the ceiling of the palaces and temples. These bulls are strangely like the sphinxes of Egypt. In both countries they are the impersonation of the kingly power and intelligence. Still more wonderfully do these Assyrian bulls resemble the great bull of Memphis, the renowned Osiris-Apis.

The sacred cone which Nisroch carries as the fruit of the sacred tree is always put upon the staff which bears in the sacred procession the leopard skin of Osiris.

Still another point of contact between the nations appears in the manner of building palaces and houses about a great court. The Egyptian made his columns much stronger, and the cornice heavier. The lines of his building slope inward as they ascend. The material he used was solid stone. The Assyrian built with a love for lighter material and more cheerful architecture. About the base of his buildings are fine alabaster slabs. The walls are usually made of brick, and the pillars are covered with stucco. The fretwork along the sky line is broken. Stories are built one upon the other. But we gain, after all,

238 *Egypt.*

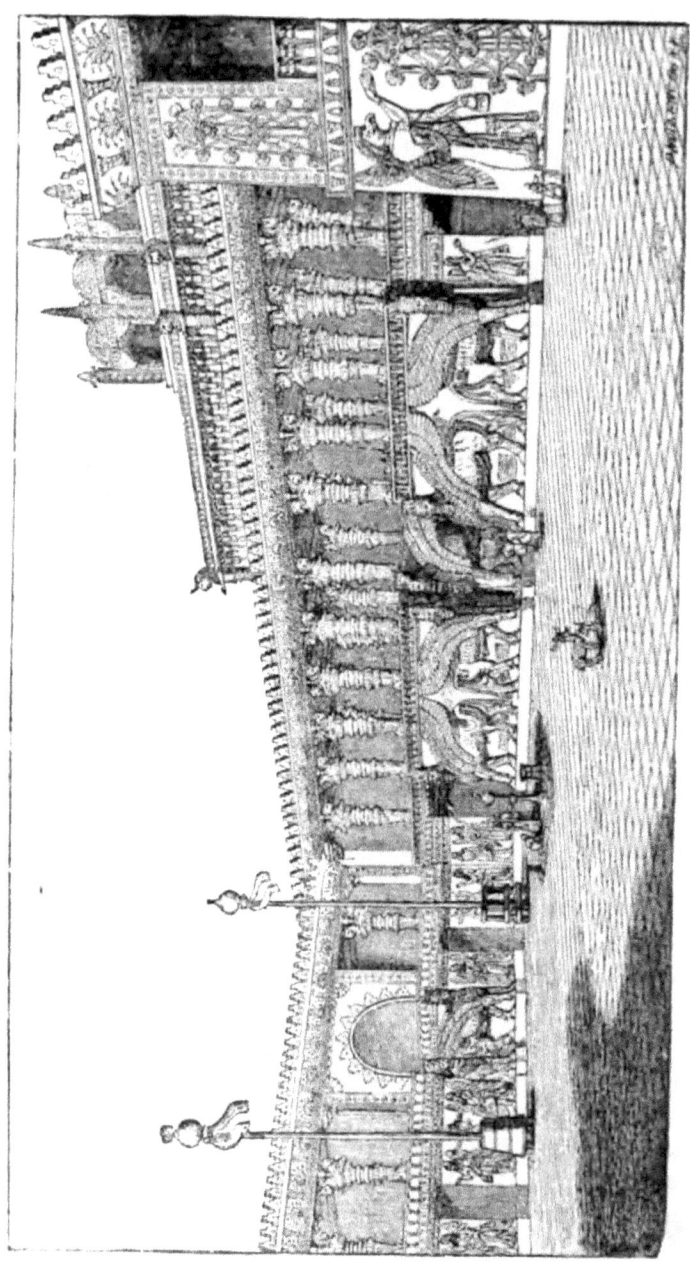

our true ideas of the spacious courts, of the brilliant decoration and sculpture of Egyptian palaces, from what is far better preserved for us in the ruins of Nineveh. As we look into one of these Assyrian palaces we can easily imagine the little group who are here offering morning incense to the human-headed bull to be the courtiers of Menes in one of the palace temples of Saïs, adorning the form of a bull, Osiris-Apis.

It has been said of the early Egyptians that they were rude, and lived in caves. A better acquaintance with the tombs of the early kings shows us that the roofs are carried on stone beams and decorated with narrow horizontal bands. These are clearly imitations of palm and sycamore beams. If they prove anything, they show us that the Egyptians fashioned rock-cut tombs after the manner of their dwellings, and did not live at any time in caves, Rather like the Assyrians, who loved the broad plain, and built at a distance from the mountains, they had houses of clay supported and roofed in by wood. This, too, better harmonizes with the cheerful, sunny temperament which is common to either country.

## IV.

The sun of Egyptian civilization seems to have risen in full splendor. The most ancient tombs do not show us in their paintings the timid efforts of a wandering tribe contending for a place of rest, and gaining little by little the knowledge of how to gather from fields and forests the comforts and

240                 *Egypt.*

luxuries of life. We see no horses as yet represented. Asses are the only beasts of burden. But otherwise you might imagine yourself, as you look on these pictured walls, among the people who followed Tothmes III.

Men are working in the fields without swords or shields, safe from that fear of violence which usually throws a shadow over the beginnings of national life. Wheat and barley are reaped, and corn and rice are sown in the gathering waters. The husbandmen are pushing their boats over the fields in the inundation, and driving home the swimming cattle. You think of the thrice-told story of later days, when a sailor, afraid of shipwreck, turned farmer, and was drowned in his own fields. The cotton, too, "the fleece of the trees," is sown, and woven with gold threads into the breastplates which were so famous long afterward.

Cactus trees are trained in arbors. Palm trees are planted for wood and fruit. Laurel and willow

## The Story of Egypt. 241

flourish with the papyrus by the brooks. Athul and acanthus trees line the gardens. Indeed, they seem fully to understand what the warm and dark mud can do for them, and, like lords of the soil, bid it quicken every living thing that man might enjoy. When the tender grass withers, and the waters fail, and men breathe with difficulty the sickly air; when the sun grows violet through the fine drifting sand, and the fields crack, and drink up the last drops of moisture in the reservoirs, they know the comfort of thick walls, shady porticoes, dark rooms, and wine cooled in vases of porous clay.

We see the same pursuits which distinguished a later Egypt. The finest of cattle are reared and trained, and cared for when sick. Even wild animals are tamed, or kept in inclosures for hunters who wish to take their sport without fatigue. Glass-blowers are plying their trade. Carpenters are imitating rare woods, or making boxes in the forms of trunks of trees and flowers. Shields are covered with hippopotamus hide. Vast granite blocks or statues are dragged by sheer force of the crowds which pull at the ropes. Scribes stand on the stonesledges beating time with their hands. Others, with a spare reed pen over their ear, are taking inventories of estates. Sculptors are rendering in stone, bone and muscle with a skill which surpasses the day of Rameses II. Walls are painted and cut in relief. Men are fishing, fowling, throwing hoops, and

fencing with sticks. Dwarfs attend the grandees, who think since these unfortunates are distinguished by the gods in their infirmities they ought to be special objects of interest to men. The barbers ply their trade in the streets, for even the poorest, who

have no better place than this, can least of all afford to neglect those regulations of society which so widely distinguish them from the barbarians.

There are the same serpents, scorpions, wasps, flies, frogs, and mosquitoes, of our day. Most numerous of all are the fleas, which were the plague of vermin not only in Moses' day, but since history began. We see the husbandman climbing at night into towers, trying to escape the gnats, and the fisherman using his nets for the same purpose, hoping the meshes which keep in the fish by day may keep out these intruders by night. There are the great flocks of cranes flying north, and the swallows twittering in the banks the first promises of spring.

The manner of dress is a still more remarkable indication of the civilization of that day. If Menes was accountable for this the priests well might take alarm, for they were married men, and had only a third of the wealth of Egypt to divide among them. The long single robe of the women taxes the utmost ingenuity of the looms. The double garments of the men, the upper part of which is laid aside when at work, like the clothes of the women are exceedingly delicate in fiber and rich in colors. There are bands and squares, and even sentences of the holy books, woven in the borders, as among the Israelites. Besides these are mantles and scarfs, fringes and ribbons. The children challenge admiration by their aprons, which are decorated with imitations of various animals. Otherwise, the little people dress like their parents. But no list of necessary articles is complete without the mention of ear-rings; finger-rings, at least one for every finger, and three for the third finger of the left hand; golden and bronze necklaces in the form of scorpions, beetles, or serpents; anklets and bracelets set with precious stones; and an immense head-dress of false hair. The sandals must turn up at the toes and be laced with gold thread. The soles of the king's sandals will represent the captives whom he thus treads under foot. No gentleman will appear in the streets without a staff.

Many of the half-religious tales of Egypt, if they did not spring from these days, were heard not much later. Among them is the story of the deity who, at the earnest prayers of her lover, became a woman. It was a goddess of Bubastis, where cats are embalmed in honor of Pasht, and where vast repositories of these animals are still to be seen. Anxious to grant the request of the worshiper, and perhaps still more anxious to come from the formalities of the altar to the ardent realities of a home, this goddess imagined she could forget the habits of her early life. The old saying, "awkward as a cat in a crocus-colored robe," did not apply to her, for she seemed to combine the grace of the deities with the beauty of the human image, the image of God. But on the wedding night a mouse ran through the room. In a moment the instinct of her earlier days overcame even love, and she pursued the mouse to the death. Her husband fled in horror.

At this ancient day women were held in great respect. Unlike the fathers of Israel, and the men in all nations about them, the Egyptians had but one wife. Holy women of the higher ranks, made desolate by the loss of their husbands, or desiring to devote themselves to the gods, often took up the temple service. They were then called "god's wife," or "god's mother," "goddess wife of Amun," "god's hand," "god's star." They also appeared in processions of Athor and Bubastis. At the funeral a man and woman held a pillar by a rope tied in a knot, but for what purpose no one can say.

There was a special law declaring females capable of ascending the throne of Egypt. When women came to the throne they were obliged by their position to belong to the priesthood, and in sacred garments to offer sacrifice. A later epitaph of queen Onknas, sister of the Pharaoh called Hophra, who is mentioned in Jeremiah, reads: "The Osirian—or the departed soul who is now with Osiris—queen Onknas, queen with the good heart, the truth-teller. The royal daughter of the truth-teller. Her mother was the divine queen Nitocris, the truth-teller." In a land in whose earliest day women were thus respected and honored, and where there was no nobler virtue than to love truth, we should expect a completeness of civilization such as many nations have not seen in their golden age.

It was no doubt owing to this wonderful state of society that men came to Egypt not only for corn in famine, but for wisdom when all the nations were vainly hungering after knowledge. Here they learned that there was a great original to whom all names and attributes might be traced. They studied to some purpose the holy symbols when they heard of a great deluge on account of sin, and of future dangers, the greatest of which will be by fire and water. They heard of a great spirit who broods over waters, calling forth trees, and animals, and men, and therefore all gods have arks or boats.

Here again the variance between Menes and the priests may have a meaning. The priests, from shame at the number of gods of later days, may have condemned the first king as the destroyer of worship and the enemy of temples, when in reality there was no idolatry in his reign, and no temples of the gods to be closed.

There was also among the people at this time a respect for good manners. An old man named

Phtah-hotep, of the royal family in the fifth dynasty, teaches young people how to win their way to success by good breeding. The basis of order is honor paid to age. How much Phtah-hotep may be considered making a special plea for himself, he cannot be thought unwise when he says, "The obedience of a son to his father is a joyful thing. . . . He is dear to his father, and his fame shall be known to all men on earth. The son who obeys the word of his father will therefore live to a good old age. The disobedient sees knowledge in ignorance, virtue in vice; every day he without fear commits any kind of wickedness, and thus is dead while he lives. His daily life is what a wise man knows to be death, and curses follow him as he walks in his ways. The obedient son shall be happy in his obedience. He shall have long life and the king's favor. Thus I have become an old man on earth. I have lived an hundred and ten years in favor with the king, and with the approval of the elders."

A second treatise of the same writer contains proverbs which are not unlike the words of king Solomon: "Happiness finds every place alike good, but a little misfortune will abase a very great man." "A good word of a good man shines more than an emerald in a slave's hand, or in the mine." "The wise man is satisfied with his knowledge; good is the place of his heart; sweet are his lips."

We may well linger awhile over this part of the story of Egypt, since it helps us realize what is most difficult to understand, that Egyptian civilization was complete, and its government was fully organized, when it first appeared to the world. This seems the greater wonder when we regard the nations with which they came in contact. The tribes of inner Africa, their neighbors on the south, were mere wild men. The Lybians were easily conquered by the Egyptians long after this, because they were terrified by an eclipse; but we are told the priests of the Nile could foretell these eclipses, and calculate the movements of the heavenly bodies. The hungry Syrians came down, clad in skins, to prostrate themselves before the Egyptians, who were clothed in fine linen, and had full granaries. The Greeks were savages, roaming at will, when the Egyptians were settled in cities. The hills of the promised land were dotted here and there with rough stone huts, when Memphis and Thebes had gathered the wealth of centuries into their noble palaces and temples.

## V.

We see the children of Mizraim, son of Ham, leaving the narrow valley of Eschol, and the scanty plains of Hebron, to cross the desert of Shur. Seven years after Hebron was built, as we are told in Numbers, Zoan was built in Egypt. The broad and green plains about Heliopolis satisfied Mizraim. It may be that the spring at that city, the only spring in Egypt, may have reminded him of the lands he had left behind him. Possibly, in the importance always attached by wandering tribes to wells, those too may have made the place sacred.

Some of the family, hoping for even better fortune, ascended the Nile as far as Tanis. The greater part remained nearer the entrance of the valley. They doubtless wished to secure the way by which they might flee back to Syria if they should be overcome by an enemy.

Menes, "founder," turned aside the Nile to enlarge the walls of his capital, Memphis. His reign came to a sad end. The song Maneros so often used in days of mourning, tells us that Menes went for water to give the reapers and was never seen again. He may have been killed by a crocodile, and out of his fate, possibly, came the story of Typhon, the crocodile-headed god who slew Osiris. The name Typhon is found in the sanctuary of Baal Zophon, when by the Red Sea the people of Egypt had occasion to sing again the Maneros in the days of the Exodus.

Horus, the son of Osiris, stands second in the procession of royal statues in the Ramessium, or college of Thebes. He is also known as Thoth, in whom the learned class find their leader and representative in the group of gods. He has still another name Teta. It is believed that he invented the art of using letters, and wrote on astronomy and medicine. The books of Hermes are all ascribed to him, and from his day, the priests tell us, the principles these books taught, and the characters in which they were recorded, were not changed. It is natural that after the troubled reign of his father there should be a time of peace, when the arts sprang up afresh. Teta met with a violent death, it is said, at the hand of his mother, and was made a god.

There seems to be some association between making statues in those days and the worship of them as idols. Statues of men and gods may have sprung up together. Moses condemned them together, as if the one opened the way for the other. There were never any statues in Jerusalem except those of the idols which were brought from other lands.

## VI.

Fresh tribes begin to follow the earlier waves of the inundation from Asia. There are new princes to divide the land. The city of Abydos is built, and soon becomes the rival of Memphis.

In the confusion which follows, Cheops appears. He takes vigorously in hand the quarries near Heliopolis. In the reaction from anarchy to tyranny the people seem ready to serve his gigantic purposes. With the wedge and inclined plane, ropes and rollers, the limestone blocks of the great pyramid rise, tier upon tier. The door of the pyramid is one cube of granite, sliding in grooves. It measures ten feet either way, and weighs sixty tons. It seemed an easy work to bring the granite five hundred miles, polish it like glass, and inlay the jams with cubes of stone and green enameled earth.

Beside this oldest of monuments, except Babel, a vast temple was built of rose-colored granite and oriental alabaster. Its courts and porticoes are regarded as among the wonders of this land of marvels.

The noble sphinx is not long after quarried from the hill itself, and begins a watch which is not yet ended, though hundreds of kings and conquerors have passed away before it like shadows.

Memphis becomes fifteen miles in circumference, and takes its name in the picture language from the pyramid which overlooked its western lake.

King Scker-nefer-ke ascends the throne. The Lybians are conquered. The rocks of Sinai receive an inscription in which is mentioned the destruction of certain wandering tribes of Arabia who troubled his copper mines. So early had this people begun to value "the riches of the everlasting hills." The more enduring monuments of his day are the buildings in basalt and granite, which are among the most magnificent specimens of art in Lower Egypt.

In the tomb of Amten, the great officer who was buried near the pyramid, we see pictures of the parks and farms, flower gardens and orchards. The very

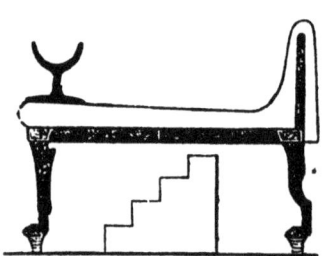

couches appear, with their steps and crescent-shaped pillows. From these pictures we may restore the days long since ended. The elegant summerhouses of Amten, his boats with their colored sails, his musicians and dancers, are all there in unfading colors. The confirmation which each of these tombs gives of the records of the rest affords a satisfaction and confidence in their story, and

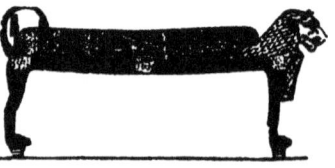

a vividness of impression which is only less satisfactory than seeing the land ourselves. No nation is so fortunate in the record of ways and habits of earlier days, though there is no nation so sadly at loss for exact figures and names. We can live among them, walk with them, enter their houses, and worship in their palaces. They will not hide from us any custom or manner of life. In this they seem like men. But when we inquire of their history and sacred things, which are so very familiar to the Israelite, they are mere children, and, like the child-god Harpocrates, put their fingers upon their mouths in token of silence.

Wars now become the occupation of the empire. There are campaigns in foreign lands, and fierce battles at home. Great encampments spring up on the eastern borders of the land. There are built about these military cities brick walls seventy feet thick and fifty feet high, with battlements in the form of shields, square towers, ramparts, ditches, and often walls across these for annoying the enemy. They are usually a single gate; or if there were two, one opens on the river. To quiet all this confusion, Queen Nitocris comes ruling the land with a strong scepter. A caravan route is opened from the upper Nile to the Red Sea, and frequent wells are dug for the merchants. With Nitocris ends the dynasty of Memphis.

## VII.

This brief quiet is followed by still greater disorder. Strangers break in upon the land about seven hundred years after Menes, following the great highway by which so many have come for good or ill to Egypt. Either invasions have broken the power of government, or rival kings have previously destroyed the land, otherwise it is difficult to account for the fall of arts and order. It is wonderful that during these days Egypt should still have kept the foremost place among the nations.

The country is now divided into Ta-Res (southern region,) and Ta-Meheet (northern region.) As one declines the other comes into notice. The king of Memphis, however, in the end appears under the rule of the king of Thebes. A new empire, with Thebes as its capital, springs forth fully developed, and asserts with a fresh civilization its place in history. How long before the god Amun had been worshiped in this land of Ta-Maheet we do not know. He did not appear in Lower Egypt. There must have been a strong, steady, irresistible force about this dynasty òf Thebes, gathering silently its powers until it was able to rule the land, and then shedding forth the light of Amun, so that nothing could hide from his rays.

This middle age of Egypt is filled with the story of the eleventh dynasty, as it is often called. Two shields are seen on the inscriptions. One is ornamented by the bee and plant of Upper Egypt, reading, "The king of an obedient people," and the name within  is a sun's disk and a symbol of "The guardian of truth, beloved of Amun, light of the world." The second has an egg and a goose, "Son of the sun," and beneath this is the family name. Each king has

## The Story of Egypt.

his own banner for the field, which is like the shield in its design. These are similar with the later reign of Rameses, who is represented by the great bull—beloved of truth, and the image of Thmei, the goddess, carrying the sign of life, the cross with the handle, an arm to represent power, and a hoe.

The country rapidly acquires strength. The names and titles of court officers refer to new kinds of luxury. The boundaries of the kingdom are pushed out in every direction, but especially toward Ethiopia, "the land of Cush, beyond the second cataract."

Under one of these kings, Amenemhe III., the city of Crocodilopolis is built. Near this is the famous labyrinth with its three thousand chambers, large and small, and its innumerable winding passages and splendid porticoes, sacred to the worship of crocodiles. The pyramid on the fourth side of the vast courtyard is three hundred feet square, and is made with bricks which have much straw in them. These bricks are laid with fine gravel, with binding layers of reeds. They are then cased in stone. The large halls, however, the thousands of niches, connecting corridors, roofs, and columns, are built of granite or limestone.

This king has discernment enough to perceive that true strength came less by conquest than by developing the resources of the country. In the Theban oases, ninety miles from the nearest canals, wells are dug four hundred feet deep. These supply a fertile country nearly one hundred miles square. Another oasis, called Siwah, west of Memphis, has a hot fountain of the sun, and a well sixty feet deep hidden among thick palm groves. These works, with the obelisk at Heliopolis, have survived many centuries.

There is still another monument of the same days, the funeral grottoes on the east side of the river. The chambers, thirty feet square, are painted in brilliant colors. One of these bears the name of Nahar, son of Numkept and his wife Rotei. Through his

mother, Nahar became duke and privy counselor Numkept, his father, governed the district. The inscriptions say of this Nahar, "Never bowed servant so before their master."

The walls of these tombs, like those of Memphis, show us how the cattle are fattened, the land ploughed, the grain harvested, and the Nile made to be useful in carrying goods. We see the furniture of the houses, how the servants knead the bread, bake the meats, and draw the wine for feasts.

There were campaigns in Ethiopia during these days, but the age, on the whole, was one of peace, suited to encourage those delicate and harmonious proportions in building of which the exterior of the tomb is itself an illustration.

Nahar seems to have been one of the great personages of the day, since he was sent to guard the gold caravans which came across the desert to Coptos.

But his elegant furniture at home, and the fat cattle he brought in tribute to the king, were of far less importance to him than the record of his life. This he desires us all to praise. "The whole land was sown from north to south. Nothing was stolen from my stores. I myself labored, and all the province was in full activity. No child was ever ill-treated, nor widow oppressed, by me. I have never troubled the fishermen, nor disturbed the shepherd. No scarcity took place in my time, and a bad harvest brought no famine. I gave equally to the widow and married woman, and in my judgments I did not favor the great at the expense of the poor." All this brings us nearer the heart of that day than the most sumptuous temples or grandest treasures of art. We can afford to lose walls and tilled fields, statues delicately cut in hardest stone, and granaries, when we keep such testimonies to true life and honest endeavor.

In an adjoining tomb Ameni Amenemha records his titles. He is "captain of infantry," " seal bearer," "governor of the goat district," " cousin—or acquaintance—of the king," and "superintendent of the priests." His best title to honor is the generosity with which he supplied the poor during a famine from his own treasure city. The royal wardrobe and pleasure grounds are painted on his walls, as if his character gained him constant admittance to the king, even when Amenemha was engaged in his recreations.

## VIII.

Once more we are lost in a confusion of kings, conquests, and dissensions. As in the days of the Judges, every man does what is right in his own eyes. There is, however, some appearance of order in the new route to Kasseir, on the Red Sea, which brings in the trade of southern Arabia.

The Nile, about this time, burst through the sandstone hills of Silsilis. It was probably the work of an earthquake, but might well have seemed in later times a prophecy of that violence which burst through the barriers the king had placed along the eastern frontiers, and suddenly, with a great tide from those inexhaustible fountains of life in central Asia, laid waste the nomes of Lower Egypt.

Not far from this age was painted upon the tombs the clearly marked features of the four great divisions of the human race which were known to the Egyptians. Horus, the good deity of Egypt, conducts them to Osiris. Those strangers which are supposed to be most remote from his care and favor are represented as lofty in stature, with light hair and blue eyes. Their savage garments of skins, and the marks upon their flesh, place them among the rudest of the human race. They are the Tarnhus, the ancestors of that people which gave a Thales and a Plato to the world, and in the changes of years came to represent to the nations the light of that wisdom which had long before faded in the temples of the Nile. Ra was destined to go into eclipse before Baal.

The race which precedes these wild Tarnhus in importance to the Pharaohs are the Nahajes. Their thick lips, woolly hair, and retreating foreheads, are thought worthy only of sport. The Egyptian artist represents them often clad in skins, with the tail left in such a way that it is difficult to say whether it belongs to the skin itself or the man who wears it.

In advance of these, yet in barbaric costumes, with bare feet and arms, and full, curly beards, are the Hebrews, or Assyrians. They have yellow complexions, and beaked noses. Yet how dim appear, even now, the rays of the Asiatic civilization which dwelt afterward in noble houses with lintels of polished stones, columns hung with tapestry, and bases of sculptured alabaster. It gives one a new impression of the fact that these great nations are yet in their infancy when the kingdom of the Nile had been in its glory for so many centuries.

There are besides these, other strange nations.

But in the place of honor, near Horus, is seen the real image and perfection of men, the race of Egypt, the Rut-n-Rom—" germ of men." With their slender figures, noble countenances, straight noses, clear eyes, and white garments, they seem like gods themselves. Indeed, they say the gods were born on the banks of the Nile.

Yet this noble race will presently be broken under the yoke of the rude savages. They are soon to take up the lamentation of Jeremiah: " Behold, a people cometh from the north. They carry the bow and buckler. They break and destroy without pity. The noise of their coming is like the roar of the sea. They come up as a cloud. Their chariots fly as the whirlwind. Woe unto us! I looked upon the earth, it was a desert. The mountains trembled. The birds of the heavens were fled. The cities were broken down. The whole land shall be desolate. It is a mighty nation, whose language thou knowest not. Their quiver is an open sepulcher. They shall eat up thine harvest."

An Egyptian historian tells us: "The anger of the god was aroused against us: I know not why. And there appeared from the east an ignoble race, who suddenly came upon us, and took our country without a struggle. They slew part of the chiefs, and bound the rest with chains. They burned our cities, and threw down the temples. Those who were not slain were reduced, both women and children, to servitude. Their king, Salatis, reigned at Memphis, and made all provinces pay tribute by occupying them with garrisons. They were called Hycsos, or shepherd kings, for *hac* in the sacred tongue means king, and *sos* is the common name for shepherd." The names of chiefs among the Semitic tribes are still called Hac. These tribes no doubt Abram found in Canaan.

260                    *Egypt.*

The occasion of this invasion is very likely to have been the claim the Hycsos had upon the Egyptian throne, through marriage with the family of the Pharaohs. Possibly some fugitive from the Nile gave them an excuse for the invasion by offering them large rewards if they would re-establish him in his rights. But when the shepherds were able to do this they preferred to serve themselves. Possibly a part of the nation welcomed the strangers as a relief from tyranny.

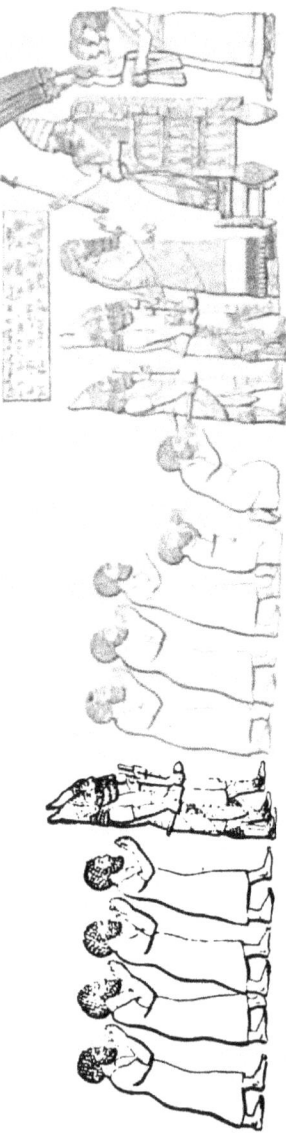

The character of this mysterious people, like their motive in coming, is not easily determined. As the land grew prosperous during their reign, and the kings of Upper Egypt had some treaties with them, it is not unlikely that they had a fitness for civilization which distinguished them from barbarians. In dress and religion they were entirely unlike the Egyptian. We must again return to the Assyrian court for any thing like a shadow of their dress or manners. Moreover, they were shepherds, "an abomination to the Egyptians." Possibly they were an advance guard of the Philistines of Syria and the nomad races of Arabia, to whose later appearance Amos refers.

The difficulty of knowing who these Hycsos were is increased by their leaving no portraits upon the monuments. We know the exact features of most of the Pharaohs, but of these men the ancient walls say nothing. Their successors removed all traces of their conquests and the long years of their rule. In the same way they destroyed all suggestion of the Exodus. Both the Hycsos and the Israelites were regarded as a race of robbers and savage shepherds, a bearded, ignoble people.

Of some such invasion, and downfall of the king, Ezekiel utters his curse: "I am against thee, Pharaoh, king of Egypt, the great dragon that lieth in the midst of his rivers, which saith, 'My river is mine own, and I have made it for myself.' But I will put hooks in thy jaws, and I will cause the fish of thy rivers to stick unto thy scales.... I have given thee for meat to the beasts of the field, and to the fowls of the heaven ... because thou hast been a staff of reed to the house of Israel. When they took hold of thee by the hand, thou didst break and rend all their shoulder." Isaiah might well describe this: "Behold, the Lord shall come into Egypt, the idols shall be moved, the heart shall melt. I will set the Egyptians against Egyptians, city against city, and I will give them over to a cruel lord; and a fiercer king shall rule over them. The river shall be wasted."

An Egyptian explorer, sent into Syria in the

twelfth dynasty, found only wandering tribes there. He does not mention these Canaanites. But they came suddenly and disastrously, and commenced their work by breaking every temple and palace into fragments. The rulers of Egypt fled to Thebes and Philae.

These foreigners were, however, soon conquered by the arts and civilization of their vanquished subjects. The gods of Egypt, the prejudices of Egypt against shepherds, the habits of dress and forms of government, were adopted by the shepherd kings. The temples were restored. Set, however, the national god of the Hittites, was added to the gods of the land. They then build a city around the eastern frontier, to keep off other tribes like themselves.

It was just at this rule that Joseph appeared. Like his mother, and, indeed, like the shepherd race, he was fair of form and face, or as his master, the captain of Pharaoh, said, "goodly and well-favored." The regular price of a slave, as we know by the book of Leviticus, twenty shekels for a lad under twenty, was paid for him. His sagacity prepared him to rule over Egypt. His honesty made him worthy of it. We see represented on the monuments the ring, the herald, and the second chariot, the royal titles of the regents, the exemption of temples from taxes, the wagons with oxen and horses which brought Jacob, and the ownership of the lands by the crown. One of the moral tales most often told to this day in Egypt is the story of the lad Joseph, under another name. His noble life, and the great service he performed for his brethren and Egypt, is still heard through all the land. Such men cannot die, though they pass away from the sight of men, for the world cannot afford to forget them.

A contemporary Theban king stands in the royal list with the title "Sustainer of the World," like Zaphnath, the title of Joseph in Hebrew. The influence of the reforms of this son of humble Jacob seems to have reached Thebes. We see the influence of Egypt on the Hycsos in the style of sarcophagus they used. For them, as for the Pharaohs, the winged arms of the goddess Isis reach over the dead as she is believed to have protected Osiris. The household furniture of their reign shows a desire to revive olden days. Wealth and peace distinguished Memphis. A struggle and discontent under foreign rulers mark the history of Thebes. Here and there the strange beard and long hair of the hated Mizraite is seen, with Egyptian costume  and outstretched hands, before the altars of the gods. The sphinxes have sometimes lions' manes instead of the regular head-dresses which are a peculiarity of the far East, where the favorite way of representing their conquests is the figure of a lion over a prostrate man. The features of the statues are angular and peculiar. The difference in races, and the confusion which naturally follows where the two streams meet, appear every-where.

## IX.

King Tiaaken, the last of the vassals who paid tribute to the hated usurpers, lived at Thebes. He gradually raised the spirit of the nation, until, feeling strong enough to meet the shepherds, he threw off his allegiance to them.

War now followed through several reigns, until the victorious Egyptians had driven the strangers as far as Avaris, the great fenced city. There they made a successful stand against the four hundred and eighty thousand soldiers of Tiaaken.

At length a treaty was made by which the shepherd kings went out with their property. Two hundred and fifty thousand men of the followers of the Hycsos are said to have settled down in Syria. Some of them, however, became herdsmen by Lake Menzaleh, where they still remain.

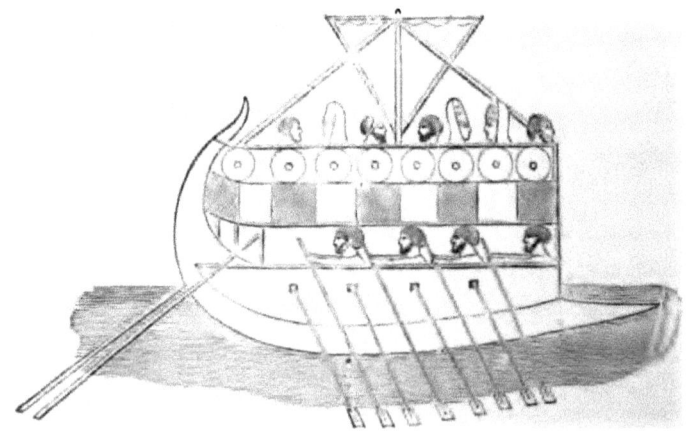

The funeral inscription of Ahmes, chief of seamen records the part he took in this war. The ships of the enemy, with their two banks of oars, their sharp beaks, the shields of the soldiers, the high caps of the women, and the beards of the men, are represented to us in the pictures of the far east.

The exploits of Ahmes are thus narrated: "When I was born, in the fortress of Ilithyia, (in Upper Egypt,) my father was lieutenant of the late Tiaaken. I was lieutenant in turn with him in the ship named 'The Calf,' in the reign of the late king Ahmes. I went to the fleet to the north, to fight. I had the duty of accompanying the king when he mounted his chariot; and when the fortress of Tanis (Avaris) was besieged, I fought on foot before his majesty. A naval battle took place on the Water of Tanis. I was on board the ship called 'Enthronization of Memphis.' The king praised me. I received a golden color for bravery. The battle was south of the fortress. Tanis was taken, and I carried off a man and two women, three in all, whom his Majesty assigned to me as slaves."

Paaken, the king, married an Ethiopian princess, and by her right claimed the throne. The monuments represent this princess as having regular features and a straight nose. Ethiopia and the land of the negro are clearly distinguished.

The national life developed like a garden after a storm. Enormous columns, with capitals carved to represent lotus and papyrus buds, appeared on every side. New cities came into life by the river and the great canals. The Theban jewelers surpassed all former efforts in working gold into chains, daggers, and necklaces.

The troops pushed across the desert into Syria, and

engaged in battle with the fragments of the shepherd race, and stormed their fortified towns. The Amalekites and Edomites fell under the sword. The hill cities, having no bond of union, perished as in the days of Joshua. The Rotennu, who held Nineveh and Babylon, were conquered. The Hittites, in the valley of the Orontes, were subdued. Tribute was gathered, and military service was exacted, from every nation. The names of Ames and Tothmes were inscribed from the Upper Nile to the Euphrates.

It is not a little singular that bears now are seen among the strange objects brought to Thebes.

Bears often appear in Assyrian hunting scenes. They are the singular way-marks of these conquests. Horses also appear for the first time on the monuments, coming from Naharayn or Mesopotamia.

Tothmes I. covers the tops of his obelisks with gold taken from the enemy. These great stones often weigh three hundred and eighty tons, and require seven months in preparation. The wealth of India also is brought into the palaces of Thebes.

The monuments record the name of Queen Hatasou, who made three reigns illustrious by her genius She built the superb temple of Mendinet Aboo, and added to the glory of Karnak an obelisk ninety feet high. An ineffectual attempt was made to erase her name from this stone. The inscription reads, " King Tothmes III. has made this work for *her* father Amun."

The Story of Egypt. 267

The seventeen years' usurpation of Queen Hatasou at last came to its close. It was a brilliant reign, full of warlike exploits and noble buildings. The bas reliefs describe the country of Arabia and the rich harbors full of commerce. In the far east the conquests were made which supplied the treasuries of the queen.

X.

When Hatasou had passed away, Tothmes III. appeared as if from an eclipse. This administration seems to have been distinguished at home for order and progress, and abroad for uninterrupted victories. It was said of Egypt, " She placed her frontier where it pleased herself." From Abyssinia to Armenia she was feared and obeyed. The lists of towns, and the records of booty, cover many stones at Karnak. At first the Rotennu rebel. The Canaanites retake their cities, except a few like Gaza. A year was spent in preparation. Then about the middle of May the army set forth. At Megiddo, in the plain of Esdraelon, where so many battles have been fought, he met the enemy. With one onset he burst through the strong lines which were posted in the ravines. Then he rearranged his forces. The king commanded the center of the army. His right rested on Karnak. His left reached beyond Megiddo. A vast host of men, brought from every tribe of Syria, were drawn up in the ranks of the enemy. But such was the fierceness of the Egyptian attack, and the utter rout of the Asiatics, that the garrison of Megiddo did not dare open its doors as a refuge to the fugitives. The gates were kept shut, and the confederates were drawn up the ramparts by cords.

Eighty-three were killed of the enemy, and three hundred and forty were taken prisoners. The pursuers did not even heed the booty in their haste, but the enemy found refuge in the mountains. The Egyptians captured over two thousand horses and about half as many chariots, beside great plunder in gold, and garments, and armor. Megiddo was soon starved into submission.

Another year Tothmes III. marched to the land of the Assyro-Chaldeans, built a fortress at Carchemish, and received tribute of the king of Nineveh and the king of Ashur, and brought back their standards with bulls and bows upon them.

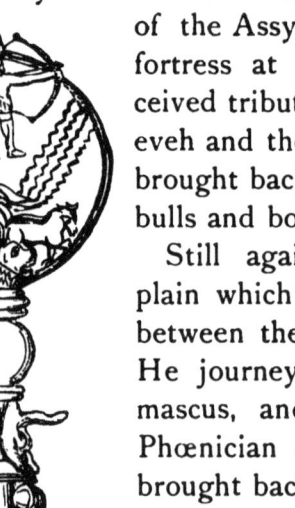

Still again he took the rich plain which lies before Baalbec, between the ranges of Lebanon He journeyed eastward to Damascus, and westward to the Phœnician coast, from which he brought back wheat, cattle, honey, and iron.

Kadesh also was taken. Assyrian princes were now carried to Thebes, as the inscription runs: "Here they are bringing the sons and brothers of the chiefs to put them in the power of the king, and to be led into Egypt. If any one of the chiefs should die, his Majesty will set free his successor to occupy the place." Soldiers also of these countries eagerly enlisted under the banner of Tothmes III.

Thus by tribute, by the education of the rulers, and the familiarity of the foreign soldiers with the Egyptian arts, the influence of the kingdom of the Nile was extending even more rapidly in peace than in war.

From the land of the Africans Tothmes received ivory, gold dust, ebony, lions' and panthers' skins. One hundred and fifty African princes pass in review, each bearing the name of a conquered tribe.

In the Mediterranean, also, Tothmes III. acquired supreme control. No doubt his fleets, as well as the ships of Solomon, were manned by Phœnician sailors. The Egyptians never seem to have had trouble with these tributary maritime cities about Tyre and Sidon, as they had with the Canaanites of the interior. Cyprus and Crete yielded. The southern islands of the Archipelago, a large part of the coast of Greece, and perhaps southern Italy, were numbered among his tribute-paying countries. The northern coast of Africa, as far as Algeria, saw his ships.

The prosperity of this reign is displayed in a vast number of monuments in every city from Heliopolis and Memphis to Philae, but especially at Thebes.

It is at the Theban temple at Karnak that we find a poem to his honor.

Amun, the supreme god of Thebes, is speaking:

"I am come—to thee have I given to strike down Syrian
    princes:
Under thy feet they lie throughout the breadth of their country.
Like to the Lord of Light, I made them see thy glory,
Blinding their eyes with light, the earthly image of Amun.

I am come—to thee have I given to strike down the Asian people;
Captive now thou hast led the proud Assyrian chieftains;
Decked in royal robes, I made them see thy glory;
All in glittering arms and fighting, high in thy war car.

I am come—to thee have I given to strike down western nations;
Cyprus both and the Ases have heard thy name with terror.
Like a strong horned bull, I made them see thy glory;
Strong with piercing horns, so that none can stand before him.

I am come—to thee have I given to strike down men of the seaboard.
All the land of the Maten is trembling now before thee;
Fierce as the huge crocodile. I made them see thy glory;
Terrible Lord of the Waters, none dare even approach him.

I am come—to thee have I given to strike down island races;
Those in the midst of the sea have heard the voice of thy roaring.
Like an avenger of blood, I made them see thy glory,
When by his victim he stands prepared to strike with his falchion.

I am come—to thee have I given to strike down Lybian archers;
All the isles of the Greeks submit to the force of thy spirit.
Like a lion in prey, I made them see thy glory,
Couched by the corpse he has made down in the rocky valley.

I am come—to thee have I given to strike down the ends of the ocean.
In the grasp of thy hand is the circling zone of waters;
Like the soaring eagle, I made them see thy glory,
Whose far-seeing eye there is none can hope to escape from.

The spirit of these lines is carried out upon the wall pictures of the East. We see there the terrible bowmen with heavy shields, the covering under which the forces approach the walls, the battering-ram of wood, the chains by which the men on the walls seek to draw up the ram or those below try to pull it down; falling stones, and the tower of the assailants. The defenders are cast into the ditch full

of water, or are helping one another out. The women plead for mercy upon the walls, or encourage their husbands.

In this reign are first seen cameleopards. Horses are also again brought into Egypt from the east, led by Syrian princes, who wear tight garments and long sleeves.

## XI.

Amen-Hotep II., or Amenophis, follows Tothmes III. There is the same story of insurrection and fresh conquests in the east and south, the same processions with apes and peacocks from India, gold dust and ostrich feathers from Ethiopia. It is not by these, however, he will be ever remembered, but by the colossal statues on the plains of Western Thebes. A great highway extended from the river to the palaces and the tombs in the western hills. It was to adorn this broad avenue that a row of sitting statues was placed with their faces looking calmly for the temple or funeral processions from across the Nile. The hands of these statues rest on their knees. Smaller figures stand by them in front of the thrones. The carved pictures represent the god

Nilus binding up for the king the reeds of the river or the grain of the field. They have not much expression, but are grandly quiet and solemn. The most distant is said, when the sun fell upon its lips, to have saluted the morning with the sound of music, and to have called up the city to its labors.

The king following, Amun-Hoteh, took his daughters into battle. At home he is associated with his family. Indeed, Queen Taia is the ruling spirit of the age. Some revolution takes place by which, for the first time in Egyptian history, a new god is introduced. This god is represented by the sun, and is called Aten. It is possible this may be a similar word with the Hebrew Adoni. There was evidently a persecution of the gods. The temples were closed through the entire land. Images and names were destroyed on the monuments, especially that of Amen, god of Thebes. The king gloried in the name of Chu-en-Aten, "Glory of the solar disk." He even moved the capital from Thebes to Tell-el-Amana.

It has been thought that this change in worship was caused by the king's mother, Queen Taia. Whence she came we have no record. Herodotus says from Nineveh. Her name and that of her parents suggests a foreign family. Her blue eyes, light hair, and features, are certainly not Egyptian. It has been conjectured that she may have been the famous Semiramis of Nineveh, and in proof of this we are reminded of the title, "Uben Ra," which may be seen, in Egyptian sacred writing, on the walls at Nineveh. It is possible that she may have conquered the empire of the Nile.

Another authority suggests a connection with the children of Israel, whose corrupted worship of Jehovah might well have been carried on under the visible form of Chu-en-Aten. The sacred furniture of the desert, especially the table of show-bread, is seen now for the first time in Egyptian temple service; and we read in the book of Chronicles of "Bithiah, the daughter of Pharaoh, which Mered took." The meaning of Bithiah in

Egyptian is Chu-en-Aten. Mered means rebel. The Israelites may, by marriage, have thrust themselves into court influences, and the severe persecution of later days may have been embittered by the remembrance of this temporary influence and possible authority.

The history of Egypt is now like a river which sinks into the desert. For a long time we can discern no trace of life except the prolific growth of dynasties, with frequent insurrections in Egypt and occasional conquests abroad. The Land of Promise seems to be occupied by fragments of Canaanitish tribes, each having separate cities, and paying tribute to Egypt.

Seti I. was evidently a soldier of fortune, who held the throne through his wife. His son reinstates the god of the shepherds, and calls the founder of that dynasty "ancestor." The magnificent palace of Karnak, the most marvelous of all the tombs in the valley of kings, and, above all, the great hall of columns at Karnak, (see page 37,) are mementoes of his work. The Arabs yielded before his arms, and the Assyrians are represented cutting down the trees of their forest, as if to open a passage to him. When we see the proud despots of the far east acknowledging an Egyptian king, we may well respect the power of his reign. There seems to have already begun the recognition of that resemblance of ideas and equality of power which either makes friendships strong or enmities bitter. The Egyptians never despise the men of Nineveh. Both of them now glory in the date-bearing trees, multitudes of fish, and abundant rivers of water. Both delight in

gorgeous trappings, tassels, and plumes. The bow is the weapon each of them carries as a sign of state. Their bracelets, ear-rings, and canopies, are similar. They each ride in two-wheeled chariots, drawn by two horses driven by a charioteer. Their attendants wear daggers, and carry quivers and spears. The officers of each direct the march by staffs. Seti I. is the first who seems to fairly introduce this eastern people to Egypt, though others have conquered them. Yet not even in this reign are the features of the two races confused. Each appears on the monuments with his own peculiar character, and features, and dress.

Seti I. recovered for his race the entire empire won by Tothmes III., except the provinces on the seaboard. The fleets of the rising Grecian power seem to have driven him from the ocean. The commerce of the Red Sea, however, and the canal which led to it, and even the crocodile lake, are represented justly as among the triumphs of his reign.

## XII.

Rameses Mei-Amun, son of Seti I. and Queen Twea, was brought up in a truly royal way. All the boys born near the palace on the same day with the prince were provided with nurses and teachers. When they grew older they became the companions, and at last the faithful officers, of the prince.

Seti I. boasted that he had conquered nearly fifty eastern nations. He was saluted as " Lord of diadems, Favorite of Ptah, the good deity, Sovereign of two worlds, Eternal as the sun." He determined that if possible young Rameses should gain still larger possessions and honors. Therefore he made conquered kings, governors of provinces, and even the priests in the name of the gods, honor him as if he were indeed " Ra, their lord and father." If the prince went abroad, twelve men of noble birth carried him in a shrine resplendent with jewels. His attendants wore splendid robes and almost royal armor, and held above him a silken canopy. If he came into the temple he was at once adored with incense, and praised in hymns. He saw passing before him in review the shrines of the gods, each one of which declared that the prince is on earth the living image of those virtues, graces, and powers, which their gods represented in the heavens. The highest priests, who are presumed to know the will of Osiris, declared, "Thou shalt joyously control the world. The force of thy arm shall triumph every-where. I give thee, O my son, the scythe of battle to restrain foreign nations."

When Rameses was yet young, Seti I. passed away, leaving great riches, the most powerful of armies, a well-trained navy, a well-developed country, an obedient people, and, what is more, a great name to be honored. The inscriptions say: "When yet a little child, wearing plaited hair, no monument was made without you. At the age of ten you commanded armies." His portrait on the walls represents him in a child's garments, with a finger on his lips in sign of infancy, and yet crowned with the double head-dress of Upper and Lower Egypt.

The young king began with the conquest of

Arabia, and the pursuit of wild beasts in the desert. But he was not left long to choose his own ways. A great tide of men showed itself in the East, pressing ever westward from that fountain of life, the center of Asia. The citadels of Lebanon, and cities near the Euphrates, threw off their allegiance to Rameses. This was their custom on the death of each Egyptian king.

But Rameses gave them little time for rest. He had never learned to obey before he began to rule, and the same terrible energy which afterward led him to be an oppressor at home made him now a dreaded leader in foreign lands. Affable, cordial, and liberal to his friends, he raised a great and loyal army, and entered, a mere child, upon his career of conquest.

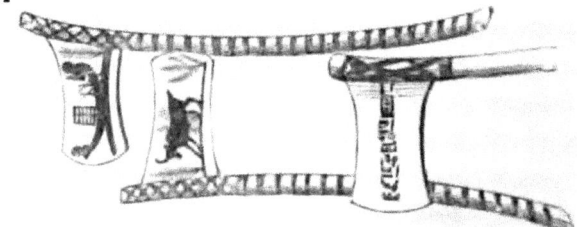

By his great exploits he soon became known as Rameses the Great, or Sesostris. His army passed along the great plain of Philistia, crossed the land of Canaan, and swept on its resistless way across the plains of Mesopotamia in the track of Abram, and still on into the unknown mountain land from which afterward came the kingdoms of the Medes and Persians. He is said to have turned from the extreme east to the west, and, marching through the mountains of Taurus, to have reached the great Euxine Sea.

The first fruit of these victories was great booty. Then military colonies sprang up to overawe the nations. But the most enduring influence of his campaign he did not live to see. Among the tribes which are represented on the walls at Karnak are the Iouni, or Javans, who have blue eyes, and long golden hair. These scattered tribes he welded together by the violence of his arms, and from this union was developed the courage and energy which gave life to Greece. Thus, the finest progress in peaceful arts which the ancient world saw was the result of the wars of Rameses II.

Rameses also met the warlike Khites, or Hittites, of Syria, who had gathered an army from nearly all the tribes round about them. The prince of Atesh

led them into the conflict. The city near which the great battle took place was in the north of Syria, by the left bank of a river called Aranta. No doubt the river was Orontes, since that is the only great river in the land. Near the city the king made himself famous by his bravery. The story is told twice, in the Rameseium on the walls of Luxor, Ipsembak, and Beit-el-Walley, and also in the papyrus of Sallier.

Not far from Kadesh, by the treachery of two of the enemy, he was drawn with his body-guard into an ambuscade. It was high noon. Twenty-five hundred chariots surrounded him. The archers and horsemen of the king fell back before the enemy. A messenger was sent to the rear to urge on the army. Meanwhile, with rash courage, the king, scorning retreat, at once commenced the fight. In the court poem of Pentaour we hear unbounded praises of the majesty and strength of Rameses, then twenty-three years old. Like the god Month, the god of war, all alone he urged on his chariot against thousands. He reminds his guardian deity, Amun, of his piety, and prays, "Did I not march at thy word? Have not thy counsels directed me? Have I not built thee everlasting trees in stone, the obelisks eternal, and offered thee thirty thousand oxen, sweet-bearing herbs, and choicest perfumes, in sacrifice? With booty have I filled thy house. For thee great ships bear booty over the sea. Thee I invoke, O my father, in the midst of strangers. No man is with me. None of my archers and horsemen heard when I called for help. But I prefer Amun to thousands of millions of archers, to millions of horsemen, to myriads of young heroes all assembled together. The designs of man are nothing. Amun overrules them."

Amun hears. From Hermonthis he comes, and

answers, stretching forth his hand: "I am near thee, thy father, the Sun. My hand is with thee. I am the Lord of hosts, who loves courage. I have found thy heart firm, and my heart has rejoiced. I will make them leap into the water, as the crocodile springs in. They shall be thrown one on another, and kill each other before thee." This was like the faith of Moses in the everlasting arms. Israel

was safe when he made the eternal God his refuge, and God always went out with him against the enemy.

The master of horse faltered when he saw the many chariots, and his heart gave way with fear. A mighty terror seized all his limbs. He said to his Majesty, "My good master, generous king, sole protector of Egypt in the day of battle, we are tarrying alone in the midst of the foe; halt in thy course, and let us save the breath of our lives. What can we do, O Rameses Meiamun! my good master?"

Thus did his majesty reply: "Have courage! Strengthen thy heart, O my comrade! I will plunge into their midst like the hawk from on high darting down upon his foe! Hurled to the ground and slain, they shall roll in the dust. Amun would not be a god did he not make glorious my countenance in the presence of these countless legions."

Six times did the king enter the midst of the

enemy. "I pursued them like Baal in the hour of his might. Like Month, in a moment's space, I mowed them down. I slaughtered them. I was alone to shout aloud. Not one of them lifted up his voice. They could no longer hold the bow and spear."

At last the generals and horsemen of his army come, with their many banners, to the rescue. "Your comrades have not satisfied my heart. Is there one of them who has deserved well of my country? If your lord had not risen in his might, all of you had been lost. Each day I transmit honors from father to son, and when some misfortune falls upon Egypt, you abandon your duty. You remained in your tents and fortified camps. Take note of the day and hour, each of you at your posts. One and all of you have done ill. I govern Egypt like my father, the sun. Each day I sit in judgment, hearkening to all the complaints that come to me. When sacrifices shall be offered in Thebais, city of Amun, great shall be seen to be the fault of soldiers and horsemen. But I have made manifest my valor alone. The whole world has made way to my arm, and I was alone, and no other was with me. This I have done in the sight of my army."

At evening, as the soldiers came from the camps, they saw the whole region covered with dead, and red with the blood of the valorous warriors of Khita. At daylight the foot could not find place, so numerous were the dead.

The army glorified the king:

"Good and mighty man of war, with unshaken heart, doing the work of thine archers and mounted men! Son of the god Toum, thou hast wiped out the land of Khita with thy victorious falchion! Thou, good warrior, art lord of armies, doing battle for thy soldiers! Great heart! Foremost in strife, bravest of the brave, before the whole world, which rises up against thee, reign over Egypt, and chastise the barbarians."

On the next day, with the early light, the battle was joined afresh. Rameses rushed into the conflict like a bull that dashes among the geese. The great lion, that walked beside his coursers, fought with him. Rage filled all his members, and whatever appeared against him was overthrown, slain in front of his horses, and a single heap of bleeding bodies extended along the ground.

A bridge was behind the Khitas. It was their only escape. Mei-Amun, the terrible, forced his way to it, fighting desperately. What clouds of spears and arrows! What crash of chariots! What deadly shocks of arms! What cries of terror and madness filled the mountains! The chief of the Khitas falls. His writer of books, his scribe, Khirapsar, his general Rabsuna, chief of archers, and Tarekennas, chief of cavalry, are slain. The battle changes to a rout. Fighting gives place to slaughter. The hooked chariot dashes to and fro like the reapers at the harvest. The river receives the desperate fugitives. Masraim, brother of the king, the chieftain of the land of the Khirabs, and a few others, only escape.

Then Khetasar, watching the battle from the walls, knows the day is lost, and, to save his capital from assault, hurries a messenger with a writing to great Rameses: "It is thou who art the sun, the god of the two horizons! Thou art Soutekh, great conqueror. The sun is in all thy members. Thy feet are in the reins of Khita forever. May this writing satisfy thy heart, strong one, supreme king, loving justice, sword of terror, rampart of thine army in the day of battle, king of Upper and Lower Egypt, of boundless ardor, chosen of Phra, Rameses Mei Amun! Thou canst slaughter thy slaves. They are in thy power. As thou comest to-day do not continue the slaughter. We are prostrate, ready to obey thy orders. Valiant king, honor the race of warriors. Grant us the breath of life."

The council of Rameses prays for them: "They have done well to throw their hearts before the supreme king. They make no conditions, but do homage to appease thy wrath."

The Khitas are pardoned, and the king says to his comrades: "Give yourselves up to rejoicing. Let it ascend to heaven. We have triumphed like lions. The terror of my name has hovered over them. I am for the land of Kemi. I have done battle with all the parts of earth. Amun-Ra has been on my right hand, and at my left. His mind has inspired me, and gone before to prepare the downfall of mine enemies. With the world at my feet, I am on the throne forever."

## The Story of Egypt.

Then Rameses marches southward and homeward with his army. Terror is left behind him, and the fame of his greatness brings princes from every side to do homage. He reaches the city of Rameses, and rests between the royal double gateways, like the sun in his double abode in the heavens. The horses which were alone with him in the battle are stabled in the temple of the sun, and it is commanded that they shall never again suffer the harness. They are sacred to Ra, the preserver. The king himself loves always to be represented carrying two golden horses in one hand, and his bow in the other.

Weapons, ivory, incense, gold, follow the king, as tributes from the subjugated nations. The temples are the treasure-houses of many provinces. The high priest may well bless the king in the name of the god: "May thy return be joyous. Thou hast broken the bows of the barbarians, cast down their leaders, pierced their hearts, and rejoiced those who followed thy sacred banners. The world has stood still before thee! My mouth praises thee!"

With all the rejoicing, the Khitas were not entirely subjugated. It was many years after this that an embassy came from Khetasar to make peace. The terms of this treaty, which was the earliest in history, were engraven on a pillar of stone, and above it the principal god of either nation was placed, as if watchful of the good faith of his people. It is itself significant of the progress of nations outside of Egypt that they who were but lately despised, and counted as savages and barbarians, should be thought strong enough to make terms. It is still more strange to find that both parties promise not to make war directly or indirectly upon each other, not to give asylum to fugitives, and to afford the merchants entire freedom of trade. Long experience in treaties could hardly have made them more just and prudent.

A tribe of this ally of Rameses was afterward settled in Hebron, and one of the princesses of the Hittites became a wife of king Solomon.

At length there seemed no more worlds to conquer. Askalon, Salem, afterward Jerusalem, and many other cities, were captured. A fortress was built by the Egyptians to guard the valley of Lebanon. Rameses receives the daughter of Khetasar as his wife, with an Egyptian name which refers to the treaty with her father, "Gift of the great sun of Justice." At Avaris, away from his own gods, he built her a temple to Sutekh, as Solomon long after built a temple at Jerusalem for his Egyptian wife.

Then the king was able to reduce his army. He made his soldiers noble gifts before he dismissed them to their lands. There they turned farmers, and

leaned on their staffs, or drove the oxen that tread out the grain.

On the north, barriers were raised to defend the mouth of the Nile. A great wall was built from Pelusium to On. Every city commenced a magnificent temple to its principal god. Canals and causeways rose on every side. Great obelisks were quarried, to bear the record of his conquests. Immense statues were made of single stones, and their inscription shows that the work was done by captives brought in from the subject nations.

A writing of this day records the travels of an Egyptian officer along the Syrian plain. The familiar names are seen of Sidon, Sarepta, and Tyre, and they are described as rude collections of fishermen's huts. Another paper speaks of the preparations, full of forethought, for the march of troops. Here we recognize the name of Zoar, the last of the cities left by the Dead Sea from the days of Lot.

With whatever interest we meet these tokens of peace at home and abroad, and delight in the destruction of tribes who had ever a spear or bow in hand; however much we recognize the real progress of the race in treaties of peace and settled cities, we cannot overlook the cruelty of this great sovereign of the world.

No glory of imperishable granite will atone for the inscriptions which they preserve, many of which speak of the trophies of battle in this manner: "There were living captives more than two hundred head ... negroes three hundred and fifty head ... living heads in all one thousand and fifty-two." The campaigns of this great warrior had then become only expeditions for hunting slaves! Another inscription may show the fate of those who would not willingly serve the proud king. It is found upon a carved pillar of a later reign: "After having vanquished his enemies, and enlarged the frontiers, he came back from the country of the Upper Ruteni, and filled the heart of his father, Amun-Ra, with joy, for he had with his own war-club killed seven kings, captured in the city of Tashis, and led in chains on board his vessel. Six of these, after having their heads cut off, were hung opposite the pylons of Thebes. The other enemy was conveyed by water to Nubia, and hung to the wall of the city of Napata, to display to the evil races of Cush the victories won over the nations, and the manner in which he chastises them."

The kindness of the Egyptians as a race was no barrier to the cruelty of their great kings. Generations of slaves built the monuments of Amunoph and Rameses. Mud hovels sheltered the workmen who lifted proud palaces. Famished slaves carved the massive forms which look out from the highways with placid and even sad countenances. Hopeless captives lifted the great ceiling-stones, and painted them blue, and covered them with stars. Ignorant savages reared the statues of kings and gods, who stand with their backs against the wall, sustaining shady porticoes of philosophers, historians, scribes, and priests. The great men of the world came to Egypt to consult the famous physicians and wizards, and feast with her nobles, but the poorer people came to toil and die.

The king Rameses, in his old age, was known no longer for his conquests, but for his building. His name is preserved on a vast number of bricks, which form the walls of palaces, temples, canals, houses, and tombs. Every one of them might tell its story of suffering and wrong.

The Lybians were trodden under the sandals of this "life-bestowing god." The Wentnowr and the Akars were exterminated. Then he thought the dangerous Hebrews, kinsmen of the terrible Asian people, might rise in revolt, and break away from their tasks, and he sought to weaken them also. "And the Egyptians made the children of Israel to serve with rigor." A papyrus, of a date not remote from Rameses' day, carries still the sentence of some unfortunate captives: "That for twelve years these men intrusted with the making of bricks be kept and closely watched in the workshops, so as to see that they deliver exactly the number of bricks that they are ordered to make, without rest or cessation."

Moses was reared, perhaps, in this day, and the death of Rameses recalled him from banishment. What art, and splendor, and wisdom, combined to dazzle his boyish eyes! The writing of his desert days bore the trace of expressions, and words, and terms, which the priests taught him under their temple roofs. The poets and statesmen of this day were his teachers. What faith was his, to go out from these porticoes and halls, where the capitals of the columns were twenty yards in circumference, and the roofs were lifted a hundred feet! The walls were full of scenes fitted to stir the ambition of his noble soul. Thrones and powers held undisputed sway, and were not lightly to be despised. The gathered riches of a long reign, brought from every nation, were waiting his command. Pleasures of every kind, fitted to his, as well as to every other disposition, abounded. Yet all this he forsook, that he might exchange the honors of Pharaoh for the reproach of his people, and the comforts of a present season for the hope of a coming Messiah.

The stones of Thebes are silent concerning the cruelty of their maker, but from a letter of the same Pentaour who so lavishly praised the conquests of the king, we read: "Have you, my teacher, Ameneman, chief librarian of Rameses, conceived the life of a peasant? Insects destroy a part of his harvest. Multitudes of rats are in the field. Next come troops of locusts. Cattle break in. Sparrows alight in flocks on his sheaves. If he delays, robbers steal it. His horse dies of fatigue at the plough. The tax-collector appears with negroes, and with palm-sticks. He must give them his corn. Then he is carried off by force, bound, to work in the canals. His wife is bound. His children are stripped."

At last the Egyptians began to suffer. As in the closing days of great Solomon, the land wearied in its effort to maintain the splendor of the court. Bitterness of spirit, riots, conspiracy, are always the lusty thorns and thistles which spring up in the rich soil of luxury.

The king's brother envied the throne, and suffered death. The soldiers became enervated and unable to endure arms. The Tahennu, "men of the mist," or Northmen, came down with the Lybians and broke through the barriers of the Nile. The old king, who could not drive them away from the rich fields they have taken, gave them land. Clouds of war came up with threatening fronts along the east. Still the oppression went on with increasing severity.

Misfortunes only infuriated the proud king. The massive sculptures became coarse, and remain as signs of the general decay of the nation. Nothing which is refined, and which has its life in the sunshine of happiness, can blossom in the shadow of a tyrant's throne.

Rameses will be remembered as the first to transport large bodies of men from one country to another. The Asiatics, he thought, would be less likely to give him trouble in Nubia. The negroes were carried into the far East. Every-where he ruled by violence. He imagined that this was his best claim for a great reputation. When he had driven inoffensive tribes into slavery, and exterminated the helpless cities of those who were uneasy under his rule, he hurried with thank-offerings to the temple, to praise the gods and write his deeds on their walls. He did not imagine that a true man would ever seem greater in ruling his own spirit than in taking a city. Nor did he imagine that he would reap from the troubles he had sown.

A large body of Assyrian and Chaldean prisoners, working in the quarries near Memphis, put their taskmasters to death. They took possession of a strong place in that neighborhood. Proud Sesostris vainly attempted to drive them out. He could only stop their incursions into the country by leaving to them the fortress they had seized.

It is not a little singular that this fortress, which they called Babylon in memory of the city whence they had come, should be the capital of later Egypt, as Memphis, the city across the Nile, was the capital of the earlier empire. The power of the Egypt of to-day is well represented by the lightness and the transient glory of this gateway, which is such a

wonderful contrast to the solidity and grandeur of the ancient towers of the Pharaohs. The last days of the king were not, however, unrelieved by brighter fortunes.

He was the builder of a great bridge at Memphis. He raised still stronger barriers than before, to keep away the nations from breaking in on the north, as well as to prevent his own slaves from escaping. A great army was encamped at the Red Sea, the gate of India. The copper mines of Tor, on the Arabian

# The Story of Egypt. 293

shore, the ship-yards of Adulis, the long vessels on the Red Sea, which subdued the nations and brought tribute, are all counted among his great works.

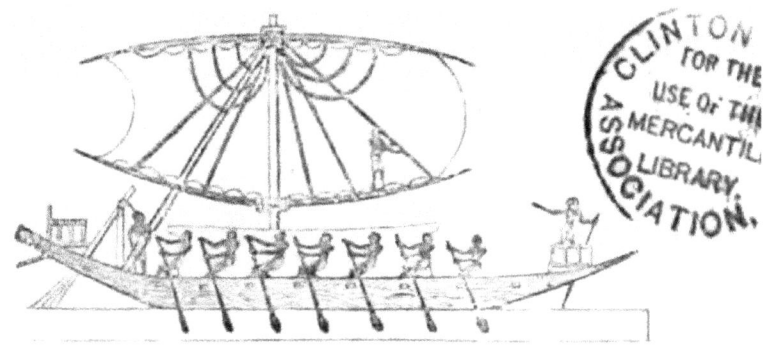

Upon one of the stones of his temples is the record of the king's audience with the people of Okau. The route to their gold mines was in danger of being deserted through want of water: "The beloved of Amun, Rameses, the eternal life-giver, descends to Memphis to accomplish to the divine triad ceremonies of thanksgiving. On the twenty-fourth day of the month Paoni, seated on his throne of purest gold, his head adorned with the two ostrich plumes of justice, he is informed of many who have perished of thirst with the asses they drove thither."

At this moment the officer of the palace who leads visitors to the foot of the throne announces the humble princes of the Okau country: "Behold them, O king, their arms uplifted toward thy throne, drawing nigh with reverence to look upon thy sacred features, and beseech thy limitless power to aid."

Then the chiefs of Okau: "Thy power has no bounds. If thou shouldst give orders to the night, light would appear. We come in haste to implore aid of thee who dost shine on the throne of the world. Say to the mountain spring, Come forth, and the abyss of waters hears thy voice in the heavens. Thou art the sun made flesh."

Then the second dignitary in the empire, the viceroy of Ethiopia, pleads for them: "Since the reign of the gods, the grass has been burned in their country. During the times of Seti, of glorious memory, search was made to the depth of one hundred and twenty cubits for water to refresh the soil. It did not reach the surface. But if thou saidst to Hapi Mou, thy father and the father of the gods, Cause the water to cover the face of the desert, like all thy orders it would be fulfilled in thy presence. Is not this because thou art dearer to the gods than all thy ancestors?"

Rameses replied: "It is my will that a well shall be made to yield unceasing water, as if it sprang from the Nile. The gods, who have flooded my heart with joy, will help. Let the order be copied by the scribes, and published in my double dwelling of light, and sent to the royal son of my land of Cush, and be obeyed!"

It was done. The woven mats kept the soil from the workmen in the opening. At length the water came leaping up, first four cubits above the soil, then twelve. "The king of the waters has hearkened to the king of the earth. The abundant stream overflows to make rich the desert, and quench the thirst of the weary traveler."

And there, according to decree, on the right bank of the Nile, opposite the city of Pselkis, stands this writing, within the temple raised to Thoth

Trismegistus. The long reign of this king, through sixty-eight years, gave abundant time for Moses to gather that wisdom in the desert of Sinai which completed the studies of the palace. It is even said that he was a successful general before he went into Arabia, which is not unlikely, since this is the common discipline of Egyptian princes. His Ethiopian wife may have been gained in one of these campaigns. In all his writings is found language similar in style to that which we see on the Egyptian monuments. The triumphal chant of Miriam has its echo in the songs of Egypt.

Before Rameses died, eighty thousand "lepers and unclean persons," whom he had forced to work in the quarries, rose in insurrection. They gathered hosts of shepherds, twice their own number, from Kadesh, the holy city of the Orontes, with fleets of Northmen, and troops which had been enlisted from foreign nations. These overran all Egypt. The king fled before them to Thebes, and sent his son Sethos, but five years old, to Ethiopia.

At Ipsamboul, on the borders of Ethiopia, is a temple whose outlines open this story of Egypt. On its walls respectful homage is paid to Rameses. Beside the king stands his queen, an equality of honor no other nation of that day would have dreamed of. On the noble front of the temple is a chapel with the inscription to "Nofre-Ari, the royal spouse, whom he loved." Within is a line which shows the husband to have been nobler than the king: "His royal spouse, who loves him, Nofre-Ari, the great mother, has constructed this resting-place in her purity." And the sweet face which looks down from the walls of this place of exile is ever praying for charity in behalf of her lord. It seems to plead for him, saying that the great things of his reign were due to himself and the god Ra, who dwelt in him; but the cruelty was due to the age in which he lived, and to his unworthy advisers.

The sixteen halls of Rameses magnify the exploits of their builder, as warrior, priest, and king. His statues have their arms folded across the breast. He himself stands between Amun, the supreme, and Phrah. How proud is he here, even in exile. He dreams still of war and conquest over the Khitas. Here are the figures of his twenty-three sons and thirteen daughters, the youngest of which is Baunt-Ant. Most of them have already passed away, among them the lamented prince whom he marked as his successor, who had led the processions on the days when all Egypt celebrated the glory of the king and the nation. A great number of monuments of this son remain at Memphis, where he was governor. There he was probably buried among the sacred bulls.

In this city of Memphis, and before a statue of Rameses in the temple of Phtah, Darius, the conqueror, gave orders that his own statue should be placed before that of Rameses. The prophet of the temple, inspired by the remembrance of the greatest of Egyptian kings, replied: " Thou hast not done, O king, all that Rameses did, since the latter not only subdued as many nations as thou, but he also conquered the Scythians, whom thy Persians could not overcome. It is not just, therefore, that thine image should be placed above that of Rameses, since thou hast not surpassed him by thy deeds." Then Darius bowed his head, and Rameses was left alone in his proud pre-eminence.

Such a legend as this, coming from one extremity of Egypt, may well take up the story which was completed at the other boundary, at Ipsamboul. No king so fills the annals of the Nile empire as Rameses II., who in the weakness of old age, and in exile, yielded to the universal conqueror, the god of Amenti, without abating one word of his lofty hopes and kingly pride.

## XIII.

Rameses the Great was succeeded by his son Merenphtah, "beloved of Phtah." His name indicates that his capital was Memphis, where the god Phtah was worshiped. There his great monuments are found. From that city he sent out his armies against the Lybians and the people of the isles of the Ægean, and the ancestors of the Etruscans. But he had work also to do at home. The Tyrrhenians brought, in their ships, their wives and children with them. The unfortunate king records his trials: "These barbarians are plundering the frontiers. Every day these evil men are violating them. They are robbing. They plunder the ports. They invade the fields of Egypt coming by the river. They are establishing themselves. The days and months pass away, and still they remain."

The inscriptions speak of the condition of Egypt as even worse than in the days of the shepherds. Memphis is taken. Heliopolis had fallen. Central

Egypt gives way before them. Merenphtah is driven to Thebes. There is something in these men of the terrible ships, whose castles were in their vessels, whose spears and shields were with them, which is

prophetic of a later day, when their descendants returned with crocodiles upon the prow of their galleys. This was the more sad, since it was the very image the Egyptians worshiped as a representation of the beneficence of the Nile. The river they loved became a highway for their enemies, and their gods seemed to have gone over to the enemy.

Merenphtah, however, stemmed the tide of invasion. Two armies were raised in Upper Egypt. One was sent under the lead of the generals who had fought in the wars of his father, and the other move on the enemies' rearguard by way of the desert. A great battle, lasting six hours, turned at length in favor of the Egyptians. The prisoners they took

## The Story of Egypt. 299

numbered nearly ten thousand, and twice that number were slain. Bronze plates on the coats of mail and armor, and cattle, were the trophies of the conqueror.

The Tyrrhenians were not, however, driven quite away. They dwelt with the foreign tribes already in the Delta, as a continual menace to the Egyptians. The king in his weakness was obliged to give them lands.

Scarcely were the ruins of the palaces restored, scarcely were the lands reclaimed, and before the slaves of the crown rebuilt with brick the walls of temples and dykes, three million souls demanded their freedom. They were dangerously near Memphis, and close by the Tyrrhenians, yet the king would gladly keep them, for their labor was needed. It was not strange that Merenphtah feared the Israelites, yet determined not to let them go. Here at Memphis, where he alone lived of all the sovereigns of his dynasty, the miracles of Moses' staff were performed. It was a severe blow to the pride and prosperity of the land. The scrupulous and cleanly priests suffered with vermin. The bountiful fields and rich herds were smitten. Ra became darkness. Nilus ran blood. No wonder at last that they hurried off the terrible strangers. Nor should we wonder that the army, after its first surprise, should go after the fugitives. The soldiers of Rameses had often trodden that way. The king could not afford the example of weakness this might give to his enemies. Then the flower of the Egyptian army perished in the Red Sea.

Thirty years of disaster followed. At one time

foreigners, invited by oppressed slaves, broke in upon Egypt, and slaughtered the priests, and used the sacred animals for food, and pillaged the temples. The king had no opportunity during these trials to disturb the Israelites in their wanderings. His life was full of bitterness and fruitless struggle against enemies on every side.

During the reign of Seti II., Joshua crossed the Jordan. The conquest of western Palestine must have given the Egyptian king great satisfaction. It  still further weakened the power of his enemies. Nor is it unlikely that the people of Israel paid tribute to Egypt. The master of the great kingdoms of the East would not ask less. It was now his policy to ask no more. The movements of the Hebrew leader would thus be free, and so long as he did not block up the way by the seashore the armies of Seti II. could well afford to let him alone. We do not read that Joshua ever thought of troubling the corn-fields of Philistia. Least of all did 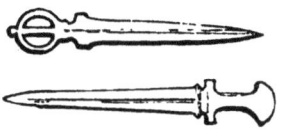 he wish to meet the spears and swords of Egypt.

A transient flush of glory lights up the long centuries of accumulating evil which now gather about the land of the Nile. Among the kings which come and go like shadows of clouds after the early rain in Syria, is Rameses III. He is young when he comes to the throne at Thebes. This city henceforth becomes the great capital of Egypt. There are, however, new names, new titles, and even new forms, in the sacred writing. It is, in part, a new civilization.

The familiar campaigns are repeated, but their triumphs shed a false glow of security over the nation, since they were fought to preserve the empire, not to extend it. The king proudly says, after some great Eastern victories: "I have made these people and their country as if they had never existed at all." But immediately after, there are new battles with the same people. At this time the enemy have wives and children with them in rough carts drawn by oxen. It is easy to slay twelve thousand, but not so easy to dispose of the remainder. They were like flights of locusts. They had no thought of turning back, even if they could. But the pressure of other tribes behind prevented retreat. Death did not seem to frighten them.

Here, too, the ships took part in the campaign. They "looked like a strong wall on the waters."

In one of these expeditions, at a frontier city called the Tower of Rameses, we see a naval fight between the Takkaro ships and the fleet of the Nile. Along the shore are drawn up the chariots and warriors, "roaring like young lions for their part in the battle." The very horses are defiant, and anxious to take part in the fray. But the Philistines had not yet come down the plains from Gaza and Ashdod, and the army could only look on while the fleet joined battle with the Cretans.

The boats with rams' heads run down the strange ships. The slingers on the mast-head, and the sharp-sighted archers on the prow, aim at the oarsmen. Multitudes of the enemy are gathered

in the ships, and their hands are fastened together with braces of wood and iron. The rest of the boats are destroyed.

Then follows the battle with the tardy land force, which came too late to save the fleet. Very bravely they fight, and Rameses, who says, "I was brave as the god Month," and who always honored courage, rears, as his custom is, a pillar in their honor. In this he praises himself, the conqueror, while he praises them, for the braver they were made to appear, the greater is the strength which overcame them. The Egyptians are politic and wise enough never to despise an army. After the victory, embarrassed by the magnitude of his fortune, he is obliged to assign the captive nation the very lands of Philistia for which they contended.

These battles are especially interesting, since they show us how the Philistines were weakened, and kept from destroying the young commonwealth of Israel. It was at this time the journey of the ark of Chons took place, just after the ark of God had been returned from the temple of Dagon to Israel.

Many kings reign at Thebes with the name of Rameses, but the glory of the old empire is departing. It can no more support one in every hundred as a soldier. Foreign gods and their priests rule in Egypt. Asia refuses to pay tribute. Israel is ready to revolt. The Philistines take the Egyptian citadels which are in their land. The priest of Amun rules the king, commands the troops, directs the public works, and claims royal honors. He even makes alliance with Nineveh, and gives his children Assyrian names. Among the presents which he sends to the Euphrates is a sacred crocodile.

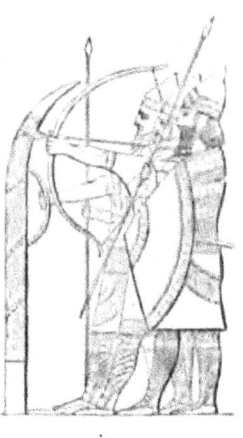

It is just at this fortunate time, before Assyria has risen into importance, and when Egypt is at civil war between a Tanis dynasty and the Theban priest Her-Hor, that David subdues the Canaanites, and widens his borders southward and eastward.

When Solomon ascends the throne, a new line of Egyptian kings from Tanis is reviving the spirit of the Nile kingdom. There is no more hope of subduing the Israelites. It is thought prudent to make them friends. Pharaoh's daughter is sent to Jerusalem, and becomes the wife of the Jewish king. The port of Ezion-geber is founded by the once hated race. The Amalekites between Gaza and Pelusium are subdued. The boundary of Israel is pushed to the river of Egypt. The king of Thebes is obliged to be silent. Two treaties are recorded. The result is that a great trade springs up between Egypt and Jerusalem in horses, and chariots, and linen, which are sent from the Nile in exchange for timber and gold. The book of Kings reminds us that the Hittites and Syrians, bought, through Solomon, chariots costing six hundred skekels of silver, and horses worth one hundred and fifty shekels. A wonderful change has taken place since the days of the proud Rameses. Egypt no longer dictates terms to the nations, but seeks trade from them.

The young prince Hadad, and Jeroboam, find refuge in Egypt. The priests flee from Thebes, and found a new kingdom in Ethiopia.

## XIV.

A new dynasty next appears, with Asiatic names, as if they sprang from hired soldiers, who compose the body-guard of the native kings. Thebes falls. Memphis rises again. But the influence of Egypt on Israel is still seen. Jeroboam is sent back, and establishes at Dan the worship of the Egyptian calf. This is the reign of Shishak, or Sheshonk. His mother is the daughter of the once-despised Tanitic dynasty. His father is an officer of the same race with the Israelites. Urged by Jeroboam, who may in some sense be called a kinsman, he takes up to

## The Story of Egypt.

Jerusalem, as an ally of Israel against Judah, a vast army of a thousand or more chariots, and sixty times as many horsemen. One of the walls of Karnak is filled with the shields of one hundred and thirty-three prisoners, bound with a rope during this war "by the god Amun." The name of Shunem, Adoraim, Gibeon, Beth-horon, Aijalon, Megiddo, are among them. But Jerusalem is found under the title Jehudah-Malek, "Royalty of Judah." The golden shields of Solomon are brought to Egypt, and decorate the altars of the cat-headed goddess of Bubastis, forty-two years after the building of the temple. The king assumes the usual title of former days, "Lord of the Upper and the Lower Regions." The lotus and papyrus are carried on shields before him.

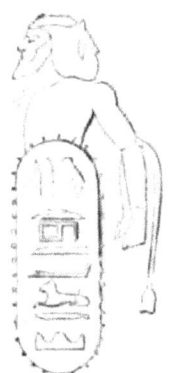

Under Abijah, the successor of Rehoboam, an Egyptian idol was reared in a grove at Jerusalem, and there, according to the records, the worship of Osiris was held, and his priests took possession of the great altar.

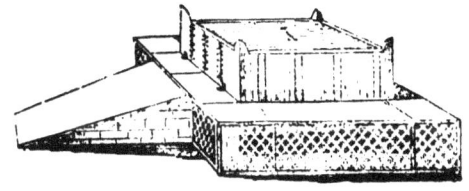

When Asa destroyed the idols, and renewed the altar of the Lord, he broke away from the yoke of Egypt. An immense army, with black troops from

Ethiopia under Zerah, went up to Judah. The prayer of Asa is recorded in Chronicles: "Help us, O Lord, our God! for we rest on thee, and in thy name we go against this multitude." In the valley of Zephathah the Egyptians were discomfited, and the name of Jehovah was honored.

Somewhat later, the despised children of Cush were found on the Egyptian throne. One of these, Shabaka, was called upon by Hosea, king of Israel, for help against the Assyrians. But Sargon of Assyria defeated the united armies of Egypt and Israel. The eagle-headed god of the Euphrates overcame the hawk-headed Horus, and the horses of Assyria were driven by bearded men in the streets of Memphis.

Tahraka, the next king, marched against Sennacherib; but before the Egyptians could relieve Jerusalem, God interposed to save his people. The priests of Phtah ascribed the ruin of Sennacherib in this campaign to mice, who gnawed the shields and bowstrings of the Assyrian host. They reared a statue of Sethos, the king, and in recognition of the favor of the gods made this image hold a mouse in his hand. But the Israelites say a plague desolated the camp of the conqueror. The tide of Assyrian invasion was, by this providence, only deferred. A wave of conquest soon swept in from the Euphrates under the reign of Esarhaddon. Israel was overwhelmed, and Egypt was reduced to a province. Its cities received foreign names.

Two years later the land became free. But the

Assyrians again returned, and drove Tahraka, the Egyptian, into Ethiopia. Assyrian head-dresses and vases were seen on the image of Typhon. Again the Assyrians were driven out, and again they returned. The son of Tahraka once more regained the land, and soon after lost it. The Assyrian staff, and short head-dress, the beard and bracelets of the foreign king, were now seen in the palace of the Pharaohs.

Chaos ensues until Psammetichus appears. The new king opens Egypt to all nations, and revives Egyptian art. He keeps a band of roving Greeks as a body-guard at the port of Sais, and with their aid gains the entire kingdom. Below Bubastis is a settlement of these foreigners called "the camp." The children of the king are educated by Greeks, and he makes a treaty with Athens. Many splendid temples rise through Egypt, especially the hall of Apis at Memphis, with its famous colossal figures of the king, dressed in the garments and titles of Osiris. Ashdod is besieged for twenty-nine years, and taken at last. But the length of the siege shows the weakness of the Egyptian armies.

It is the son of Psammetichus, Necho, who so unwillingly joined battle with Joash, the noble prince of the house of David. The death of the Jewish king, and the wild lamentation of Israel, has made the mention of that day at Megiddo among the saddest things in history.

The fate of Necho was hardly less sad. Just beyond Megiddo, at Carchemish, he met the terrible horses of Assyria, was utterly broken, and fled homeward, having lost all the conquests of his father. The Assyrian had put his foot on the Egyptian in sign of conquest.

The people rest contented and satisfied with their flesh-pots by the Nile. The sacred heifer of Isis still hears the sacred systrum, still receives noble gifts from the people, and abundance of money, hires for her soldiers. Jeremiah, however, foresees her doom: "O thou daughter dwelling in Egypt, furnish thyself to go into captivity: 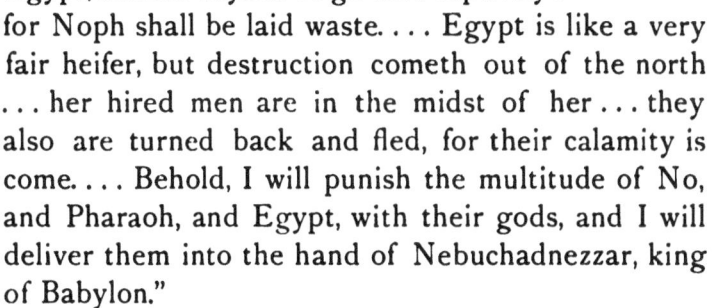 for Noph shall be laid waste.... Egypt is like a very fair heifer, but destruction cometh out of the north ... her hired men are in the midst of her ... they also are turned back and fled, for their calamity is come.... Behold, I will punish the multitude of No, and Pharaoh, and Egypt, with their gods, and I will deliver them into the hand of Nebuchadnezzar, king of Babylon."

Berosus, the historian, tells us that when the Assyrian returned home he left Egypt, Syria, and the adjacent countries in charge of his trusted generals. Judah had not yet submitted to the Chaldean monarchy. Necho still exercised some authority at home, devoting himself to the extension of commerce. A body of interpreters were organized to increase the facilities of trade with distant nations. The great canal of Seti I., from the Red Sea to the Nile, was partly re-opened, but the king left the work suddenly, warned by the priests that he was working for the barbarian.

A long and dreary record of frequent defeats and transient successes follow. Israel, the kingdom of the hills, stands midway between the great rivals which come forth to try their strength from the valleys of the Euphrates and the Nile. It becomes, therefore, unwillingly, the battle-ground of the nations. So long as peace prevails, the city of Jerusalem is at rest as the prey of the stronger power.

But whenever, through unholy ambition or want of faith, the house of David breaks loose from its oppressors and seeks alliance with the heathen, either the feeble reed of Egypt breaks, and wounds the hand that grasps it, or the Assyrian carries the Hebrew away to the willows of Babylon. The latter days of Psammetichus are distinguished by the loss of one hundred and twenty thousand men in an unsuccessful effort to open a canal to the Red Sea.

The history of Egypt now becomes closely connected with the fate of the Jewish Jehoahaz and

Zedekiah. The temple is destroyed, and the throne of David passes away from the sight of the nations. A desperate body of men, raising the standard of rebellion at Jerusalem, call down the vengeance of Assyria, and are compelled to flee to Egypt. They take Jeremiah with them, and settle at Tephanes, near Memphis. The pathetic appeal of the prophet to those who here by the Nile burn incense to the queen of heaven, and pour out drink-offering, and make her cakes, is most touching and earnest. Migdol, Tephanes, and Noph, give the exiles room. There the " Lamentations" are heard.

The prophet Ezekiel takes up the figure of rising waters of the Nile, and pronounces a curse upon the dragon of Egypt; but writing under the shadow of the throne of Nebuchadnezzar, when he would comfort his people with the hope that some of them would be preserved, he speaks of these as *marked* on the forehead by an angel. The word marked is Egyptian, and refers to the Tau symbol of life to the people who dwell by the Nile. In Egypt we notice new goddesses, and even more strange rites than ever before in the temple of Osiris. These are the sure signs of impending ruin.

The dying light flashes up once more in the reign of Amasis. The tribute cities are reckoned by thousands. The famous temple of Isis at Memphis, and Neith at Sais, revive the glory of the ancient days. But public spirit is gone. Cunning and deceit has taken the place of wisdom. Foreign conquests and defeats have alike ruined Egypt. Greek music is heard in the temples of Osiris. Greek soldiers fight the battles of the Pharaohs. The seemingly prosperous reign has no real foundation. Masses of granite, twenty-two feet long and thirteen broad, are quarried at Syene. But many of

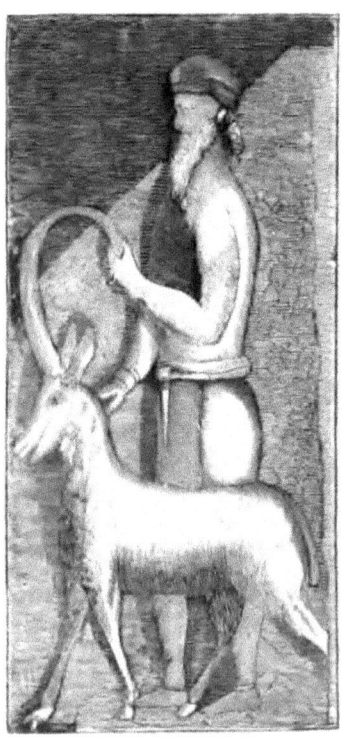

these are dedicated to Jupiter, Juno, and Apollo. Cyprus is gained, but at the cost of a new flood of deities. The inundation of strange gods cannot bring any fertility to Egypt. How much nobler the attitude of the kingdom of the Euphrates, where the Greeks came with power to break, not to direct, the interests of the nation. The Persian proudly pointed to the image of Greece, under the symbol of a ram with one horn, on the pilasters of Persepolis. The same image appears in the visions of Daniel at Shushan. But there, too, it was met with warlike strife. In Egypt the followers of the ram-

## The Story of Egypt. 313

headed Amun quietly yielded up to its influence, and paid it reverence.

The mad career of Cambyses now lights with lurid glare the evening of Egypt. His standards of oxen mock the old glory of the calf Apis. The gods seem again to have turned against Egypt. He comes in the dress of an Egyptian, but breaks the images at the gates of the temples, destroys the walls, and puts the princes to death. Instead of offering incense to Apis, he stabs him with his dagger. "How doth the city sit solitary that was full of people!" "Egypt shall be a desolation," says God,

"for the violence against the children of Judah." "The Egyptians will I give over into the hand of a cruel lord; and a fierce king shall rule over them ... the wise counselors of Pharaoh is become brutish." The ruin is complete.

Egypt revolted, but in the reign of Artaxerxes was retaken. Then came Cyrus, the conqueror of Babylon, who was an ally of Amaris, and wore an Egyptian head-dress. A long list of kings succeeded. At last the Persians appeared under Ochus, who, led by a Greek officer, crossed the desert. He is said to have taken Pelusium by putting the sacred animals of Egypt before his army. This vanguard of cats, dogs, sheep, and calves, the army of the Nile dared not to injure. If this be true, how fitting that the gods who had corrupted them should be the means of their fall. The name of Egypt now became a by-word, and the land a prey of the last comer. The scepter of Menes is utterly broken. The people look upon new symbols. The good deity

with wings gives way to the sign of that spirit which, from its swift-moving wheel, guards the strangers, and shoots his arrows among the discomfited nations. The Egyptians once pitied the Greeks because they had to depend upon the gods for rain. They might now well weep for themselves, since the very stars in their courses seemed raining upon them ruin and confusion of face.

# THE EXODUS.

## THE EXODUS.

Israel in Egypt—A Personal God—Love to God—Unity of God—The Present Life—Israel must leave Egypt—Moses—The Departure.

### I.

FOR four hundred years "Israel abode in Egypt, and Jacob was a stranger in the land of Ham." The strong government of the Pharaohs was their shield of defense from the Philistines on one side and the Lybians on the other. They grew in numbers until they had six hundred thousand men who could bear arms. These were not half Hebrews and half Egyptians, but all of them true descendants of Abraham and Sarah. In no other nation has such purity of race been maintained. All the tribes that came in early days to Egypt insensibly melted away into the population about them. The delicate fancies and fine uses

of all civilized arts won them over to take the names and share the work of Egyptians. But from the very first, no Hebrew forgot his family. Even Joseph, when he bound princes at will, and taught senators wisdom, when he took the Egyptian name of Zaphnath-paaneah, and wore the white robe of state and royal ring, remembered his father's house

His two sons received Hebrew names, which reminded them of his longing for the home of his boyhood. When Jacob came down with his sons, Joseph separated them from the Egyptians, and they remained alone as a family during all their sojourn in the house of bondage. Many of them were absent, employed in trades, and some were living in the houses of their oppressors, but the greater part of the people were in Goshen to the very last. Even in the Exodus, those who least of all would be expected to share the fortunes of their people are seen leaving their trades and stations in which they had found comfort and wealth. There were Ophrah and Joab, craftsmen; Lecah and Laadah, workers in linen; Jokim and Goash and Sacaph, who were potters, and dwelt among the king's plants and hedges. They were, like the poorest, true Hebrews. In fact, when the departure took place, not one Israelite was left behind, though, as Moses tells us, they were scattered broadcast over the land of Egypt.

The Hebrews were, as a nation, disposed to love a settled life, though their fathers were wandering continually. Once settled in the land of Rameses, they began to cultivate the soil, as Isaac did before them, and built not only royal treasure-houses, but cities, for themselves. Two and a half tribes still fed cattle on the rich lands along the edge of the desert, and so completely were they devoted to this pursuit that they kept their love of grazing to the end of their history. Long after this, when they came to the rich lowlands of Jordan, these did not tempt them, nor did the dangers of their neighbors, the Assyrians, terrify them from choosing the green

## The Exodus.  319

rolling hills and rich pastures of Bashan. But the nine tribes and a half were, during their stay in

Egypt, farmers, and dwelt contentedly in houses. It is a singular confirmation of this quiet spirit that, while the patriarchs had camels in abundance, no mention is made of these animals as part of the herds of Israel, either in Egypt or the desert. They were not given to traveling at any time in their history. This spirit made the desert journeys more trying, and kept the later kingdom away from foreign nations.

In government Israel remained patriarchal through the four hundred years of their stay in Egypt. The oldest sons, or elders, were at the head of the tribes. Others were chiefs of families. The princes were chosen for merit, or wisdom, or prudence. They represented the people when summoned by Moses. They also formed his council in the desert, and with the family elders composed the two branches of rulers. A third order of scribes was recognized among those in authority. They preserved the records of the people. This class gained great influence in Egypt, where so much is done by the pen and the chisel. In the cruel edicts of Rameses I., the brick-makers—perhaps, as Josephus says, at work on the pyramids—rendered account to these same "officers of Israel," the scribes. They were punished with the workmen, as if they were accountable for the unfinished tales of bricks which they recorded. The severe trials of the respected keepers of records must have impressed upon the people the wretchedness of their condition.

In religious matters Israel had not entirely departed from the faith of the fathers. The noble case of sycamore-wood which contained the mummy of Joseph reminded them of the great promise of a land in which were the plains of Dothan, where the flocks of Jacob had wandered at will; with the fair corn-fields and the deep well of Shechem, which in every age is a rich inheritance. Many of the children were called by the titles of the great God. The name Jochebed came from the precious name of Jehovah, as yet unrevealed save to a few. No general sacrifice had been made by them as a people, but they were familiar with the offering of lambs in the family. The vivid narratives of God's mercies to the patriarchs, preserved from generation to generation, show how familiar they were with the story of the covenant made at the threshold of Eden, and renewed under the bow of Noah, and again to Abram at Ur of the Chaldees. The meeting of Isaac and Rebecca in the glow of the evening, and of the two

## The Exodus. 321

brothers Jacob and Esau in the dawn at Jabbok, as well as the grief of Jacob for Rachel, and the tears of Joseph's brethren, show us that the leadings of God were not forgotten. In Ezekiel we learn that only part of the people clung to the abominations of the Egyptians. But most of all are we glad to see the people crying to God, and not to the idols of Egypt, for deliverance. The prophecy concerning the four hundred years of captivity may have given them courage, but their cruel wrongs were the immediate occasion of their faith in God. Nor was that faith to be lightly thought of, since four hundred years had passed without a token of God's interest in his people. There were not even signs of promise at the birth of Moses. God seemed to have forgotten his people.

On the other hand, a refining process was needed. Much of the nation had given up the simple patriarchal sacrifice for the gorgeous and elaborate ritual of Egypt. The various symbols of spiritual things which were in harmony with God's purpose, and were used without explanation by Moses afterward, were overshadowed by other distinctively heathen usages which could not be legalized. These led Israel, by the almost irresistible attraction of nature, far beyond simple inquiry concerning the origin of things, into the worship of calves and goats, and even insects and " devils."

The spirit of the nation was not entirely servile. The occupation of so many in trades, and in watching cattle among the dangerous pasture lands near the desert, kept fresh the high courage of the people. We do not know that any served in the

Egyptian army, but in Chronicles we learn that once the children of Ephraim left the king's herds, and, dashing across the desert, made a foray on the cattle of Gath. The Israelites suffered great loss, but they certainly would not have risked the encounter without some experience in arms. Others went to Mount Seir, and smote the Amalekites. There were probably many other excursions, when the hands which were familiar with the hoe learned to use the battle-ax and sword, training themselves to meet their enemies in the desert.

In what way, then, was Egypt so harmful in its influence that a new land must be given and a new life quickened in Israel?

## II.

The religion of Egypt discourages all access of the mind to its Maker. There is no way for the people to gain knowledge of the gods. The individual life is lost sight of. The tone of the Egyptian is not, in spiritual things, thoughtful. Discipline of mind is to a favored few the great aim of life, but the rest do not presume to go beyond simple reverence.

If one enters the temple he sees on every side attentive worshipers. He feels not more impressed with the massive portals than the mysteries which they hide from his eyes. He does not imagine how the priests know of the death and life of Osiris any more than he understands how the priests can calculate the shadow which will creep over the face of the moon or sun a hundred years hence. He is astonished to be told that the milky way is resplendent with the light of stars, and looks up to the ceiling where constellations are named and placed in their proper relations, as if it were the work of gods, not men. If new roads are to be laid out, or new canals dug, the priests come forth to take the direction of the work. If the hardest granite or finest sandstone is to be quarried, a priest issues the command. If he writes, he cannot use the sacred text. He drives his pen from right to left, because he can see more easily the pen when it is coming than when it is going. The priests alone write in the opposite way, and in columns. Beside this, the learned class have very mysterious arts. Many, like Athyrtis, daughter of Sesostris, are versed in divination.

In a word, the Egyptian leaves his temple impressed with the wisdom which is too high for him to attain unto. The amusements of life open themselves with new charms. He can understand the sweetness of delicious perfumes, which find their way through the alabaster cases. He loves his carved boxes. He can enjoy at home the thickly woven carpets with rich colors of palms, and the richer carpets of his gardens, where nature twines the stems of myrtle and box together, and trails over the lattice-work the jessamine and blooming henna. He scarcely inquires who sends the water to his ponds, who ripens the grapes in his arbors, and who gives

the songs to his birds within their nets. He can appreciate the fine linen called Tanitic, and Pelusiac, and Tentyritic. He can throw open his window of gypsum in the evening, when the golden splendor of day has softened into the solemn brightness of the heavens, and listen to the cretola and flute, and clapping of hands of the musicians in the street. He can look at the many tints upon the fields, and watch the lamps lighted in the caves of the hills, where the overcrowded valley sends its people to seek for homes. To care for the king's interests and serve

the priests; to walk in fragrant gardens, and recline on soft couches, and sit on fine chairs; to drink sweet wine and indulge in rich food, is the highest aim of man. It is well to bring offerings to the temples, but its inner doors never unlocked for him. It was well to build an altar at home, or worship the statue of Athor, to have bronze and gilded statues of gods, and beyond that, all forms of learning must lie undisturbed in the hands of the

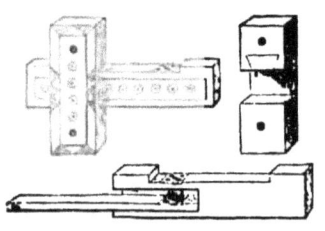

priests who guard the two doors of the unseen world. To the priests the wise men of foreign nations came, to learn a wisdom the first principle of which is that only the rulers must have knowledge. To others it is dangerous. No doubt this want of national training was the occasion of the calamities of Egypt. The few who were willing to serve were helpless without this great body of the people, and they had not intelligence sufficient to know their danger. If the prosperous men of leisure had no key to the temple truths, how entirely beyond the reach of the enslaved Israelites must these things have been. It would have seemed an impossibility to have trained the Israelites in Egypt, each for himself, to meditate upon such themes as sin, his individual relation to God, and how to serve the best interests of the wide world by obeying Jehovah. Yet such themes were to be the light of the high altar from which every Israelite gained the fire for his own dwelling, and the light with which in the fullness of time he should enlighten the Gentiles.

## III.

It was necessary to win the Israelites to love the law of God. But the fascination of Egyptian worship had taken entire possession of their hearts. "Your fathers served false gods on the other side of the flood." At the very moment of departing many of them carried their idols. "In the day I lifted up my hand unto them to bring them forth of the land of Egypt," says Ezekiel, "I said unto them, cast away, every man ... the idols of Egypt ... but they would not hearken unto me." Again and again would they return to Egypt. Once in fear, as they said, lest they should be destroyed by the Egyptian chariots;

then because they longed in their thirst for the sweet Nile. Again, they remembered the flesh-pots of old, or the abundant fishes. But every time when the danger was over, and the want supplied, it was evident that they were still longing for Egypt, because they were fascinated by its idolatry. Does Moses remain longer than they desire? The Egyptian calf, made of Egyptian gold, is set up under Sinai, and with that before them as a sign of mercy and reconciliation, after accepting Jehovah, they propose to return to Osiris Apis. When Solomon set up the idols of Egypt, and when Jeroboam made two calves, and still later, when a timid flock, scared from Jerusalem by the armies of Nebuchadnezzar, careless of the warnings of Jeremiah, took refuge in Egypt, and the women offered incense to Neith, the people of Israel were yielding to an influence they never quite overcame. They were trained in this idolatry in the land of their birth. It was wrought into all that could please the eye or delight the heart. They had seen it as they served in the gates of the envied better classes. They had been warmed by it in every ray of sunshine. They had blessed it with every draught of water. They had gathered it in with every harvest. They could not separate the remembrance of luxuries and superstitions, nor forget that these were blended in a career of almost uninterrupted prosperity through centuries of history. The goddesses kept even

kings at their service, and made princes respect the laws of feast and fast. Why should not such a religion bless them? It meant to them herds standing knee-deep in broad canals, under the shade of trees that were ever green, or wandering in sweet grass over broad pastures. It meant strings of fish, bulti, and kishr, árabrab, and byad. It meant floats of skins heaped high with grain. It meant gardens of onions, and leeks, and all manner of vegetables, given in three crops a year. It meant wrestling, throwing knives, the acting of buffoons, singing, and playing on instruments. It meant splendid spectacles, when the priestesses went, as they scattered flowers, singing the hymn, "If ye have not pure hearts, look on the ground;" when the image of the moon was carried in processions by priests with white robes, who have borders of palms as emblems of consecration, and wreaths of lilies over their foreheads as emblems of purity. It meant feasts, where colored robes were put on Isis and white on Osiris, and the sacred wand of the leaders waved a blessing to pilgrims from Sais and Bubastis. Then floors were strewn with garlands, fans were brilliant with gems of Meroe and gold of Abyssinia. The silken banners, and the children clad in fine garments, made a noble display. The herds sacrificed at the altars were distributed, with wine in abundance, to the hungry multitude. It meant great spectacles at night, when the mysterious fires of the priests of Phra flashed a brilliant red or deep purple over cornice, and band, and capital, and, fading away, left chains of lamps to shine over the great portico, and along the screens of stone. It meant the solemn rites of death, where the asphodel and mystic plantain set forth the shadow and sweetness of the tomb, and in the litany the gods said that the silver chord of friendship which binds good men is not broken, but only loosed.

How could a people without an exodus escape such a superstition? The silence and severity of the desert and the mountains could alone restore that quietness of mind without which no man can see God. They must break away from streets full of the confusion of business, and chanting of processions, before they could learn quietly to think of Him who must be loved and desired before he will reveal himself. The peculiarity of the new faith is to be personal contact with God through love for him and his word. Every man is to journey alone with God, like Enoch or Abram. The exodus is most necessary to the Israelite, or the desire of the eye, and the pride of life, will overcome his love of God.

## IV.

The nation needed to learn the true nature of God. The Hebrew could hardly believe that there is a jealous God when a hundred gods shared his honor unrebuked, when the wealth and glory of the land lay at the doors of rival deities, when armies conquered in the name of these enemies, and those who cherished the hope of his glory were but degraded, unprotected slaves. Lying vanities were trumpeted by substantial gifts, great honors, and an easy life. But truth shared wretched hovels with overtasked

## The Exodus. 329

servants. The Egyptian was a strange illustration of God's anger, the Hebrew of his mercy. The

Egyptian was seen in gardens and temples. The children of the covenant were waist-deep in muddy water, spattered with clay, swinging the heavy hoe, shaping the bricks, bending under the yoke, and beaten by taskmasters.

The impression was natural that there might be a God of Abram, and Isaac, and Jacob; that possibly he might be a god of the Syrian hills. But these were far off. Here Ra extended his beams, each of which had a hand of blessing for the queen, her children, and subjects. Here Un-nufre, revealer of good, in the form of a man, kindly taught the wisdom of the gods. He was Lord of the universe, born in the abodes of Amun-Ra, like Jubal making music for the people. From him came fruitful seasons, to fill all hearts with gladness and all lips with song, and to win roughest men to peaceful industry. Here Athor kept her feast in the month Athyr, when the Pleiades reveal themselves, and the people sow seed. Then the sacred boat of the goddess, covered with flowers, moved over the waters. The king and queen recognized her goodness. She was Lady of Het. By her the peach was made, with leaves like the tongue, and stone like the heart of those who love her. Here was Harewakhu, "the sun on the horizon," with his mystic name, and powers to keep the departed safe in all the faculties of his mind and body. When protected by him Horus would not strike off his life on the block of Hades, or bring him to Set, the monster with the hippopotamus' head, devourer of the unprotected. Here they prayed to the goddess, "Living forever! engendered of heaven! child of Netpe! offspring of time! our mother who is over us—save us."

When the desert surrounded them, and the great reach of plains widened, they could realize the unity of God. The only voice they heard was that which he had given the winds or the tempest. They no longer saw one class of wise men studying the habits of the gods in the movement of the sacred ibis, another class of priests spending days in devising honors for sacred cats, a third prostrate before a hawk, or turning aside in the way to let a sacred beetle pass. Still more were they set free from the bewildering question, "Who, then, is God?" by seeing no temples built with hands to rival deities, but only Sinai, appointed at creation as God's temple, or the single tent of the tabernacle.

Moreover, it was of the utmost importance that no man, however great, should interfere between these men and God. The demands of Pharaoh could not always be obeyed with the laws of Jehovah. Two masters could not be served. Even Moses ruled by the authority of God. He claimed nothing by his own right or power. Israel had no king or law but Jehovah. The tabernacle could not be made a prison, as the Egyptian temple often was, for those who offended the ruler.

They needed to be taught the wide distance between man and his Maker, as there is between man and the creation below him. So Israel sacrificed the spirit of inquiry, and gained a simple trust. They watched with awe the high priest when he went into the holy of holies, knowing that God was not like man, and only mercy could keep the fires of Sinai from destroying the wicked. But they rejoiced when the high priest came back, with the gentle fires of his incense sending up a cloud of sweet savor, the pomegranates and bells on his skirts giving forth a peaceful sound, and the stones in the breastplate shining with the light of reconciliation. Honored as the priest was, he seemed after all only a man like themselves. Whatever authority great Aaron had was derived from God, and to be used

for the service of his people. The Egyptian king worshiped his ancestors, and considered himself to be a god, but the high priest of the Hebrews was only a servant. The proverb is every-where heard, When the tale of brick is doubled, then comes Moses. But it is not Moses who delivers them, but God, the King in the heavens. He whose ways are as much above men's ways as the heavens are above the earth,

## V.

The health of Israel demanded a change. The crowded and wretched quarters of the nation had no doubt threatened the life of the people. The tradition among the Egyptians that the people were driven out because of leprosy seems to have arisen from some such sickness among them. The hand of Moses, the face of Miriam, and the strict laws concerning lepers, seem to point to the same troubles. There was room enough in the desert. The cool, fresh, dry air of the wilderness brought healing with it. The nation grew strong. The vine Israel, the

favorite figure of the Holy Scriptures, grew too rank in the rich, dark soil of Egypt. But when it was transplanted into the loose desert soil it grew exceeding strong, and was thus prepared to bear fruit in the Land of Promise.

A sound body was necessary to a sound mind and a light heart. Acacias, dense tamarisk bushes, white thorns, mulberry-trees, and spice plants, took their place with the words of the Commandments in training God's people. The dry table-lands gave inspiration to the worship of the nation.

## VI.

But one other great change was especially needed. The thoughts of the nation were to be withdrawn from those rites and beliefs which made the future world exercise too much influence over the present. The afflictions which overtake all the living prepare the heart to receive any light which may cheer the valley of shadows. No religion has carried its faith so far as the Egyptian. Their funeral ritual, and their story of the future existence of the soul, answered every question of the anxious heart.

Moses well understood this. He was to beguile them from living in the future by magnifying the interests of the present time. The civilization of the new land was to be founded on active duties, personal sacrifices, present sins. They were to be taught to observe that punishments and blessings were, for the greater part, immediate and evident. Or, if not immediate, these would be the experience of coming generations in this life, and not in the unseen world. They needed to learn that as a man lived he should be prospered in flocks and herds, and that extraordinary providences of God were always about them, in turning red granite rocks into streams of water, and white deserts into tables of manna. Even Solomon, in the long, solemn petitions of the temple, when he restored at Jerusalem the integrity of this religion of the old covenant, did not refer to any thing beyond the present world. Certainly Moses knew at the bush that God was God of the living, and David was sure that he should go to his much-loved son, and that no soul perished with the body. But such doctrines found no place in the teaching of the old masters of Israel. Nor did the prophets dwell on the unseen world. Moses, and all who follow him, seem carefully to avoid referring to this doctrine of the future condition of departed souls.

When we recall the tenacity with which colonies cling to the beliefs of the mother country, and what peculiar love of Egypt was shown by Israel in other things, it becomes a wonder how Moses could accomplish this great change. Yet he did gather into present service the thoughts which in Egypt are wasted in conjectures concerning the future.

## VII.

The people had grown into a nation. Greater numbers were not needed to take possession of the Promised Land. They had learned all that was necessary beyond what God might teach them by Moses. It was time they should be separated. God did not rudely break the bands which held the nations. Whatever was harmless in the old, he continued in the new order of life. He did not mean that four hundred years of influence should prove only an offense to the new faith. Both nations engraved holy words over their doors and posts, rejected swine, and believed the world was created in Autumn. The scapegoat of the old Egyptian temple, which seemed to carry away into the wilderness the sin of the people, was still to be seen let

loose from the tabernacle. The dress, girdle, and breast-plate of the priests, the sacred ark, the

arrangement of the tabernacle, the altar without steps, the laver for washing, the anointing oil, belonged to both services. The habit of covering the head, and of baring the feet, before the altar, the feasts of tabernacles, lighting lamps, and carrying green boughs, of first-fruits and trumpets, were preserved to win the affections of Israel from the old habits. The people learned not merely to suffer restraint, but, what is far better, to exercise wisdom.

The pattern of the tabernacle, which was given on the mount with so much detail, no doubt was interpreted in its symbols by the knowledge Moses had gained in Egypt. In the perfect cube of the holiest place, and the other apartments, which were multiples of this, he doubtless saw the symbol of stability and perfection. How much nobler was this than the triad which was represented in a right-angled triangle in Egypt, the symbol of creating force, receptive matter, and the universe. The ark of Israel no one thought of worshiping, but the gods of Egypt degraded the spiritual symbol into forms of living things. The "cunning work" of the vail probably refers to the use in embroidery of metals, the weaving of golden tissue into the linen. If the vision of Ezekiel's cherubim may be presumed to have been taken from this cherubim of the tabernacle, we know that the forms on the curtain before the holiest place were very similar with Egyptian symbols. This same vail had also bands of blue, purple, crimson, and white, a suggestion of the rainbow, and a blending of the thoughts of the heavens, royalty, life, and purity. This, too, was taken from the temples of the Nile.

At the same time God vindicated the originality of his law, and consulted the peculiar genius of his chosen people. He made new distinctions between clean and unclean animals. So long as these were observed, the Israelite sacrificed what the Egyptian worshiped. Moses, for this reason, told Pharaoh that the sacred customs of his people would cause them to be stoned in Egypt. The exclusiveness of race was secured by the distinctions of clean and unclean animals, as well as the minuteness of their ritual. God, by these regulations, at the same time provided a diet suited to their peaceful life in the narrow country prepared for them.

Against idolatry there was pronounced the severest judgment. Witchcraft and magic was punished with death. Graven images of any likeness or figure of man or beast, altars of cut stone, food carried in the solemn processions of the dead, marking the flesh with names of idols, sacred groves, or " termenos," were all forbidden. Shaving the head for the dead, undue mourning, those thoroughly Egyptian customs, were also condemned. And, above all, the widest difference was seen between the animals who lived in the Egyptian Adytrum and the si-

lence and sacred presence of the Shekinah in the holiest of holies, where the pure light dwelt between the cherubim.

*The Exodus.*

## VIII.

Besides all this, God had promised that Israel should go out of Egypt with great substance, and enter a land flowing with milk and honey. The description of the country, and of its inhabitants, left no question concerning the place whither they were going. A vague presentiment came over the people that their deliverance was at hand. The story of the man Moses was familiar to them. They heard of the marvelous glory of his person, his mental gifts, his training in all the wisdom of Egypt, his frequent visits to his true mother and his own people, his bold defiance of Egyptian law, where he not only dared slay a follower of Osiris, but even buried his unembalmed body in the sand. Then, when he was yet considered a prince of the royal house, he fled into the desert. Perhaps they may have heard from Aaron how this courtly man, with Egyptian chivalry, defended the daughters of the Midianitish priest, and was then waiting with the same high spirit to answer their call. Aaron was sent for him. They thought the shepherd's rod might guide Israel. They did not dream of him as even greater than the patriarchs, the first of prophets and workers of miracles.

Moses returned. The strife went on between him and the priests of Nilus, and of Isis, goddess of the all-sustaining earth, and of the entire host of deities. From October to April the people waited. What the heart is to the body, the Nile is to Egypt, yet the river rose and turned into blood. The frogs came up from the retreating waters. The wind swept from drying fields the lice in clouds like dust. From the cisterns and reservoirs came up the terrible gnats. The cattle sickened. The priests themselves were seized with afflictive eruptions. A grievous pestilence of hail swept down the flax and barley, upon which all men, especially the poor, depended. The locusts came in, as Joel describes them, upon the unusual east wind, as if the God of Israel kept even distant lands in his power. Then "the eye of earth," the plants which answer the face of man, were swept away. Darkness came between the Egyptians and their sun god, and the nation was in affliction. From all parts of the earth, and then from heaven itself, death seemed waiting for them. Pharaoh's proud heart only grew more determined. Moses and Aaron are driven from the presence of the angry king. Yet the man who came down from Sinai in such miserable fashion, with a single ass, is greater with God than all armies and learning could be without him.

## IX.

At last the night of deliverance comes. Every family of Israel is standing by the table upon which lie the fragments of the passover supper. A light flickers over their anxious faces. Nothing is to be left behind which can be carried in the folds of their outer garments. At the city of Rameses, under the pyramids, by Lake Menzaleh in the north, in Bsatin by the Nile, at Pithon in the lowland pastures, and far on to the eastern end of the valley at Heroopolis, in every Hebrew household, the people are waiting

## The Exodus. 341

the signal for the march. The tools for working silver fabric and the rough moulds for the bricks, the cup-bearers' jars and the fishermen's nets, are alike forgotten as they stand there, shoes upon their feet, staff in hand, and their kneading troughs, full of

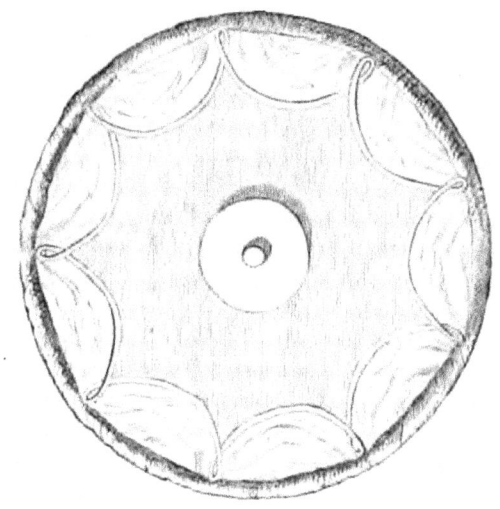

unleavened bread, on their shoulders. It is midnight. A sharp cry of terror and agony goes up from the king's palace. Every ear is familiar with the shrill tidings of death. Another answers it. A third cry is heard. The households are all wakened, to find death has come to the first-born. The whole land is terrified with the sudden vengeance of the God of Israel. The priests mourn for the dead gods as if the greatest of calamities has come upon them. All the animals they worship lie breathless before them. The herdsman mourns for his flock. Who can care for the dead? The embalmers are not exempted. All are to-night real mourners. One thing they can do and must do. They must get rid of the Hebrews. So they press on them the jewels of gold and of silver, precious stones, choice vessels, garments of linen, and beg them to go. Go, says proud Pharaoh, and bless me. Get you gone, say the Shoterim, the taskmasters. Take all, but leave us, say the people.

From the houses whose lintels are sprinkled with blood pour forth the astonished Israelites, like those that dream. The full paschal moon shines among the stars in the deep clear skies of an Egyptian spring-time. From every street, from distant cities, from field, and farm, and camp, come in the Hebrews. Joyful are the salutations between those who have been a long time separated. Hurried are the inquiries concerning absent friends, the way they are to go, and the end of these marvelous signs. What surprises them most is that none need to be carried for sickness. Every man, and woman, and child is in marching order. Some are full of anxiety. Some are light of heart. The old are glad that they lived to see the hour of departure, and the young already imagine they are in the Land of Promise.

But all this confusion must not be suffered. They are too much exposed to the enemy. They have work to do.

With a grand light about his countenance, and the manner of a conqueror in every gesture, Moses stands beside Aaron. About them are gathered the leaders of the nation, the elders and princes. They are to march eastward to the edge of the wilderness. The command is sent forth.

The "Hak," or chiefs of tribes, and "Zahen," the leaders of families, gather the people in companies.

## The Exodus. 343

The great flocks of sheep and herds of cattle are hurried from the stalls and the pastures. Arms are hastily snatched from the distracted guards in the streets. Slings they will all carry, for every ground will furnish them missiles, outside the rich lowlands of Egypt. The great procession now begins to move.

"The Promised Land" is the word that passes from rank to rank. Then many a lingering look is given the huts so familiar, and so loved, even in misery. There are the grain heaps. There lie the hoe, and basket, and chisel, they shall use no more. There stand the walls of the brick treasure-houses, and the massive fronts of palaces with their deep shadow. Every stone seems to cry out to them. Here rise the majestic gates of the temple, their battlements reaching up to heaven, as if they lifted the stars. Upon them is Horus in vast outline, balancing his thunderbolts ready to strike. Will he thunder upon these fugitives? Typhon leers with wicked look, and open mouth, and terrible horns. Mendes, with the head and legs of a goat, threatens to perform his office of avenger of fields.

Isis mildly, sadly, in pity looks upon them with long pensive eyes, low, retiring forehead, spare cheeks, and mouth almost breaking into a smile. Within that "sekos," or holy place, is the mysterious Apis, their god. Will he forgive them their flight? Still farther on are the vast colossi, with folded arms; kingly statues, in immense mass, full of physical power, as if Pharaoh had come out to frown upon their departure. Here are the guard-houses. Will the way be closed with chariots and soldiers? 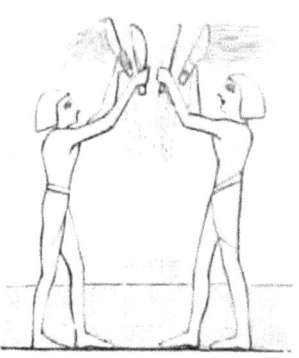 There is no buckling on of armor, for the universal mourning has not spared the soldier. A greater enemy than Syrian or Canaanite has broken in upon his household. No weapon can reach that last great enemy.

 Through the long avenues of sphinxes they come, a stream of life. They have reached the wide gardens, and the royal parks, full of antelopes, the lakes with villas and shade trees, and now they pass the brick-fields, with a profound silence which is full of the expression of fear. Will they not be brought back to these places for yet greater suffering?

Still beyond, the canals grow more frequent, and the narrow bridges delay the multitude, who anxiously fear the coming of day, and listen for the rattle of the chariots behind them.

Then they reach the hills full of their dead. Every path is familiar. Every shadow has its story. Must they leave these behind them? Can only one of all the dead of the multitude go up with them? And Joseph's body is solemnly borne past the crowd, guarded by the half-armed soldiers.

Backward look the Israelites. Far off rise the pyramids on the horizon. Under them the lights are hurrying to and fro in the temples, for none can sleep to-night. Nearer, the moon shows the countless roofs of the houses of Memphis, Pithona, and Rameses. The colonnades seem to reach out their arms to invite the fugitives back again. The hanging gardens and terraced hillsides, the obelisks, like petrified moonbeams, and the stone stairs of the quays, the monuments which cover the burial-place of Apis, and the flowing banks of the Nile, recall the splendor of the days which are past. Here they had dragged the vast stones, thirty feet long, twenty-two feet broad, and twelve feet high, costing the labor of two thousand laborers three years. Here they had sung at their labor as they drove the oxen about the grain. Here the priests had watched them from the temple towers. Here the vines had grown for them, and the doves had nestled in their cotes. Here they had rested in the evening, and heard the dreary chant of the fisherman bringing the fish into his net. Here Abram found his Egyptian wife. Here Jacob came, an old man, owning only a tomb in the Land of Promise, to meet his son, ruler of ten million acres of rich land of Egypt. Here he longed to hear again the voice of Rachel, and, dying, thought of the oaks of Mamre and the caves of Machpelah. Here Joseph had driven to meet Asenath, under the lofty obelisk of On, and his love sanctifies the plain, and the pavilions of the lake, and the Babylonian willows above it. Shall we leave all these houses of clay to crumble to the dust, or be homes for cormorant and bittern? Shall we not hear again the merry ziczac scream, and the lark spring up from the meadow grass in the morning, and the brown pigeons call to their mates, and the ducks cry to their timid brood in the reeds of Goshen?

Five hundred years of grief and captivity have not made the Israelites hate the land, but only the taskmasters. They know the danger of being brought back again. The prospect lies in the return, not of the sunny fields, but the mines of Sinai. "The shepherds, disgraceful men," they have often heard, "are like dogs on the Nile banks, who drink and run away before the crocodile of the law can seize them." But what if the law should now overtake them? What can hide them in the desert? What joy can there be in the desolation where centuries of sunshine have gathered as if in a furnace, where millions have died in hunger, and the memories of man have often turned in grief, but never in gratitude?

There before them is the plain, doubtless dotted soon after the deluge by the tents of Ham. There they yearly remembered, in the inundation, the waters of Noah. This hill was an Ararat after their wanderings. No country is so well and safely watered as Egypt. Is it not good enough now for

## The Exodus. 347

Israel, full of shops and warehouses, murmuring acacias and grain-fields, cities and tombs? Many a man here has seen the land whither Moses would lead us, and it is full of hills difficult to climb, and

dreary pastures, where trees never grow. There were twelve days of desert to Berenice, and thirty beyond this to Arabia, where only they could flee, if the armed men of Philistia opposed them an entrance to the Promised Land. India, with its frankincense and gold, should we flee thither, is a land of slaves, as well as Egypt, and India is a hundred days off, even with ships; we know not how far off without them. Straight before us are the awful defiles of Edom, where Esau lies in wait for Jacob. We hear that the phœnix-bird of Osiris goes only to the desert to die, and then, in new life, brings the old body, embalmed, back to the temples of the sun at Heliopolis. Shall we do better if we go? Who will live to see the returning?

348  *Egypt.*

Yet the Israelite is a stranger in the land of Egypt. God has for him another country. That is enough. With bravery and faith he presses onward.

And as the moon goes down, and the sun comes up, a marvelous change, though they know it not, has overtaken the people. The fetters of bondage have fallen. Israel has become a nation, for Israel has come out of Egypt.

Every step onward in desert, and battle, and want, is a step toward rest, and peace, and plenty The land of palms, and springs, and vineyards lies before them, just beyond the sea of death, and over the Jordan.

# INDEX.

## ALPHABETICAL INDEX OF SUBJECTS.

Abijah introduces Egyptian idols, 305.
Afternoon on the Nile, 102.
Amenophis, king, 271.
Amenti, land of the dead, 187.
Amun, the god, 146.
Amusement, love of, 71.
Animals worshiped, 157, 161; reasons for, 167.
Aoura, valley of, 193.
Apis, 159.
Arks of gods, 45, 175.
Ark of Konsou and Israel, 156.
Ark of Israel, 44.
Army, 171.
Arts, 125.
Assault of city, 271.
Assyrians, ancestors of, 257.
Assyrian houses, 236.
Avaris, city of refuge, 17, 264.

Baal, 257.
Balances, soul weighed in, 194.
Banners, 173.
Barbers, 242.
Bears, 266.
Books of Egypt, 116.
Brick-laying, 253.
Brick-making, 134, 135, 328.
Bulls of Assyria, 236.

Calf, sacred, 158.
Cambyses, 313.

Canals, 89.
Carpenters, 28, 127.
Carpets, 58, 59.
Casts, 111.
Cat goddess, story of, 243.
Cave-dwellers, Egyptians not, 239.
Chairs, 53.
Chapel of temple, 42, 43.
Chapel memorial, 44.
Chariots, 173.
Chariots, construction of, 176.
Cheops, 249.
Children and parents, 73.
Children, dress of, 68.
Children in the temple, 121, 161.
Chons, journey of, 152.
Cities of the Nile, 102.
Climate of Egypt, 85.
Colossi of Thebes, 272.
Conflicts of the dead, 190.
Courts of temple, 34.
Court-yards of house, 55.
Couches, 250.
Crocodiles, 103.
Crops, 88.

Darius and Rameses, 297.
David, 303.
Dead, embalmed, 198.
Dead, divine honors, 196.
Desert, 16.

Dining-rooms, 58.
Divining cup, 166.
Dolls, 56.
Doll in tombs, 213.
Dove in tomb, 20.
Dress, ancient Egyptian, 243.
Dress of poor, 24.
Dress of rich, 54, 64.

Edom, enemy of Israel, 347.
Egypt, celestial, 193.
Egypt, land of, 77.
Egypt, under Rameses, suffers, 290.
Egyptian rites and Moses' law, 336.
Egyptians, whence they came, 235.
Embalming, necessary, 199.
Embalming, process of, 201.
Exodus expected, 339.

Farmers, 123.
Farmers, ancient, 241.
Fields enriched by river, 82.
Fish, 91.
Fishing, 93, 99.
Flies of Egypt, 18.
Flowers, 101.
Fowl, 20, 94.
Fruit, 66.
Funeral boat, 208.
Funeral procession, 207.
Furniture of table, 64.
Future life to Egyptian and Israelite, 334.

## Alphabetical List. 351.

Garden, 55.
Garden at tomb, 214.
Gateway, 33.
God, unity of, 330.
Gods, chief of, Ra, 143.
Gods first acknowledged, 245.
Gods, innumerable, 152, 156.
Gods, kings associated with, 40.
Gods in procession, 175.
Gods, reign of, 234.
Gods turn against Egypt, 314.
Goshen, 19; re'ation to Egypt, 21; to Israel, 21.
Grandeur in monuments, 40.
Granaries, 104.
Greece, Egypt influences, 230.
Greeks, ancestors of, 256; coming into Egypt, 308; influence on Egypt, 312.
Grottoes of Beni Hassan, 254.
Guest-room, 58.

Hatasau, queen, 266.
Head-dress of prince, 26.
Hebrews, condition in Egypt, 318; form of their government, 319; by what means the race was kept pure, 317.
Hermes, books of, 116, 248.
Highway into Egypt, 22.
History, Egyptian ignorant of, 233, 251.
Hittites, 262, 279.
House, 25, 51.
Holy day at Thebes, 168.
Horus, the god, 248.
Hosea, 306.
Hunting, 133.
Hycsos, 259,

Idols, fascination in, 325.
Idolatry, 338; not seen at first, 142.

Industries in early days, 241.
Inundation, 241.
Isis, 147, 151.
Israel, condition of, 320; elders and princes, 319; health of, 333; race preserved, 317; under Rameses, 288; under Meremptah, 298.

Jeroboam, 304.
Jerusalem falls, 305; relation to valley empires, 310.
Joseph, 263.
Joshua, 300.
Judges of Egypt, 118.

Karnak, 105.
Kar-Neter, journey in, 189.
King first appears, 235; figure of, 170; and god, 40; mourned for, 114; place of, 112; priest, 180.
Kitchen, 61.
Kneph, ram-headed god, 146.
Knowledge serves the dead, 190.

Lakes, artificial, 90.
Lamps, festival of, 165; in Egyptian tombs, 220; in Greek tombs, 230.
Learning, 41.
Light, management of, in building, 37.
Light, office to dead, 191.
Looms, 128.

Maneros, 248.
Manifestation to light, 188.
Manners of ancient Egyptians, 245.
Megiddo, battle of, 267.
Memphis, 248; size of, 250.
Menes, 234.
Metal-working, 129.

Mines, suffering in, 130.
Mirror, 60.
Mizraim, 247.
Moses, in ark, 43; and Rameses, 295; waited for, 339.
Mourners hired, 200.
Mummy, 202; worshiped, 205.
Music, 69.
Music, military, 171.
Musicians, place of, 63.

Nebuchadnezzar, 309, 311.
Necho, the king, and Israel, 308.
Neith, 147.
Nile, abundance of the, 78; festival, 79; overflow, 79; runs blood, 85; source of, 81; strength of, 93; symbol of Osiris, 81; worshiped, 83, 84.
Nineveh, 274.
Nisroch, Assyrian god, 236.
Num, the creator, 145.

Oases, 253.
Obelisk, use of, 33.
Ornaments, of temple, 39; of women, 65.
Osiris, 67; legend of, 149, 150; offerings to, 162; relation to the dead, 214; relation to the soul, 186.

Painting on walls, 57, 59, 63.
Painting, unchanged in style, 119,
Papyrus, 101.
Philae, 82.
Philistines, 302.
Phtah, the god, 147.
Phtah-hotep, 246.
Plagues, 299.
Poem Tothmes III, 269.
Priests, discipline of, 120; office of, 114, 118, 120; orders of, 178.
Priestesses, 174.

## Alphabetical List.

Princes, training of, 113.
Prisoners, treatment of, 174, 287.
Proverbs, 246.
Pyramids, 221; compared with Belus, 223; of Mycerinus, 225.

Quails, 18.
Queens, office in temple, 40.

Ra, sun god, 112; emblem of soul, 219.
Rafts, 98.
Rameses the Great, childhood, 277; bravery, 280; tyranny, 281; wars of, 278.
Religion, man and his Maker, 322; similar to the Assyrian, 141; sincerity in, 139; unchanged, 140; unsatisfactory, 323.
Rites of Israel compared with the Egyptians, 337.
River, 98; a highway, 96; of Egypt, 15.

Sacrifices, 162; human, 181.
Sandals, 57.
Sarcophagus, 203.
Screen of temple, 35, 36.
Scribe, 55, 132.
Sculpture, 38.
Sea dreaded, 93.
Seasons, 85.
Sennacherib campaign, 306.
Serpent, brazen, 165.
Seti I., the king, 274.
Shadoof, 86.

Shepherds despised, 134.
Show-bread, 164, 273.
Ships, 97; combats of, 264, 301; great voyage of, 124.
Shipbuilders, 128.
Shops, 125.
Silsilis, 84, 256.
Sled for stone, 84.
Soldiers of Egypt, 122, 171.
Sphinx, dromos of, 31, 32; great, at Memphis, 226, 249.
Solomon, 304.
Sports at table, 69, 70; in the field, 70.
Staff, 243.
Statues and idols, 248.
Sun and soul, 195; worshiped, 143.
Superstitions have germs of truth, 168.
Symbols, fondness for, 157.
Syrian cities come into notice, 287.

Tabernacle, 44; and temple, same plan, 45.
Table of the sun, 187.
Taia, the queen, 272.
Temple, a college, 41; door to Amenti, 121; plan of, 31; position, 31; litany of, 179; luxury in, 36; sculptures relate to future world, 185; services of, 162.
Thebes, 104, 252.
Thoth, 248; a god, 155; name and work, 156.

Thummim of Hebrews, 156.
Toilet, 60.
Tombs, decorations of, 220; described, 213; extent of, 228; for kings, 217; for the poor, 215; longed for by Israel, 229; resold, 215; testimony to ancient Egypt, 239; true house of man, 186.
Tothmes III., 267.
Transmigration of soul, 192.
Treasures, 58.
Trees, sacred to Assyrian and Egyptian, 237.
Trials of the dead, 210.
Tyrrhenians, incursion of, 297.

Valley of Nile, 77.
Vegetables, 65.

Warlike, Jews were not, 182.
Watering the land by foot, 87.
Weapons, 171, 172.
Wearing, 129.
Welcome in house, 27.
Wells in day of Rameses, 293.
Wicked judged, 197; punished, 97.
Wine-jars, 57; kinds of, 62.
Women, in temple, 244; respect paid to, 72.
Wood-workers, 126.
Workmen, various, 132.
Worship of heroes, 143.

www.ingramcontent.com/pod-product-compliance
Lightning Source LLC
Chambersburg PA
CBHW050924240426
43668CB00020B/2426